Applied Econometric Analysis:

Emerging Research and Opportunities

Brian W. Sloboda
University of Phoenix, USA

Yaya Sissoko
Indiana University of Pennsylvania, USA

A volume in the Advances in Finance, Accounting, and Economics (AFAE) Book Series

IGI Global
PUBLISHER of TIMELY KNOWLEDGE

Published in the United States of America by
IGI Global
Business Science Reference (an imprint of IGI Global)
701 E. Chocolate Avenue
Hershey PA, USA 17033
Tel: 717-533-8845
Fax: 717-533-8661
E-mail: cust@igi-global.com
Web site: http://www.igi-global.com

Library of Congress Cataloging-in-Publication Data

Names: Sloboda, Brian W., 1968- editor. | Sissoko, Yaya, 1961- editor.
Title: Applied econometric analysis : emerging research and opportunities / Brian W. Sloboda and Yaya Sissoko, editors.
Description: Hershey PA : Business Science Reference (an imprint of IGI Global), [2020] | Includes bibliographical references and index. | Summary: "This book examines the application of econometric methods as used by researchers in academia, public policy, and areas in social science and business"-- Provided by publisher.
Identifiers: LCCN 2019024176 (print) | LCCN 2019024177 (ebook) | ISBN 9781799810933 (hardcover) | ISBN 9781799810940 (paperback) | ISBN 9781799810957 (ebook)
Subjects: LCSH: Econometric models. | Econometrics. | Economics--Mathematical models.
Classification: LCC HB141 .R418 2020 (print) | LCC HB141 (ebook) | DDC 330.01/5195--dc23
LC record available at https://lccn.loc.gov/2019024176
LC ebook record available at https://lccn.loc.gov/2019024177

This book is published in the IGI Global book series Advances in Finance, Accounting, and Economics (AFAE) (ISSN: 2327-5677; eISSN: 2327-5685)

British Cataloguing in Publication Data
A Cataloguing in Publication record for this book is available from the British Library.

Advances in Finance, Accounting, and Economics (AFAE) Book Series

ISSN:2327-5677
EISSN:2327-5685

MISSION

In our changing economic and business environment, it is important to consider the financial changes occurring internationally as well as within individual organizations and business environments. Understanding these changes as well as the factors that influence them is crucial in preparing for our financial future and ensuring economic sustainability and growth.

The **Advances in Finance, Accounting, and Economics (AFAE)** book series aims to publish comprehensive and informative titles in all areas of economics and economic theory, finance, and accounting to assist in advancing the available knowledge and providing for further research development in these dynamic fields.

COVERAGE

- Investments and Derivatives
- Economic Indices and Quantitative Economic Methods
- Economics Geography
- Economic Downturn
- Comparative Accounting Systems
- Risk Analysis and Management
- Theoretical Issues in Economics, Finance, and Accounting
- Accounting information systems
- Stock Market
- Economics of Innovation and Knowledge

The Advances in Finance, Accounting, and Economics (AFAE) Book Series (ISSN 2327-5677) is published by IGI Global, 701 E. Chocolate Avenue, Hershey, PA 17033-1240, USA, www.igi-global.com. This series is composed of titles available for purchase individually; each title is edited to be contextually exclusive from any other title within the series. For pricing and ordering information please visit http://www.igi-global.com/book-series/advances-finance-accounting-economics/73685. Postmaster: Send all address changes to above address.

Titles in this Series

For a list of additional titles in this series, please visit:
https://www.igi-global.com/book-series/advances-finance-accounting-economics/73685

Mapping, Managing, and Crafting Sustainable Business Strategies for the Circular Economy
Susana Serrano Rodrigues (Polytechnic Institute of Leiria, Portugal) Paulo Jorge Almeida (Polytechnic Institute of Leiria, Portugal) and Nuno Miguel Castaheira Almeida (Polytechnic Institute of Leiria, Portugal)
Business Science Reference • © 2020 • 280pp • H/C (ISBN: 9781522598855) • US $195.00

Handbook of Research on Accounting and Financial Studies
Luís Farinha (University of Beira Interior, Portugal) Ana Baltazar Cruz (School of Management, Polytechnic Institute of Castelo Branco, Portugal) and João Renato Sebastião (Polytechnic Institute of Castelo Branco, Portugal)
Business Science Reference • © 2020 • 487pp • H/C (ISBN: 9781799821366) • US $295.00

Emerging Tools and Strategies for Financial Management
Begoña Álvarez-García (Universidade da Coruña, Spain) and José-Pablo Abeal-Vázquez (Universidade da Coruña, Spain)
Business Science Reference • © 2020 • 357pp • H/C (ISBN: 9781799824404) • US $225.00

Recent Advances and Applications in Alternative Investments
Constantin Zopounidis (Technical University of Crete, Greece & Audencia Business School, France) Dimitris Kenourgios (National and Kapodistrian University of Athens, Greece) and George Dotsis (National and Kapodistrian University of Athens, Greece)
Business Science Reference • © 2020 • 385pp • H/C (ISBN: 9781799824367) • US $205.00

Growth and Emerging Prospects of International Islamic Banking
Abdul Rafay (University of Management and Technology, Pakistan)
Business Science Reference • © 2020 • 341pp • H/C (ISBN: 9781799816119) • US $215.00

Economics, Business, and Islamic Finance in ASEAN Economics Community
Patricia Ordoñez de Pablos (The University of Oviedo, Spain) Mohammad Nabil Almunawar (Universiti Brunei Darussalam, Brunei) and Muhamad Abduh (Universiti Brunei Darussalam, Brunei)
Business Science Reference • © 2020 • 374pp • H/C (ISBN: 9781799822578) • US $215.00

IGI Global
PUBLISHER of TIMELY KNOWLEDGE

701 East Chocolate Avenue, Hershey, PA 17033, USA
Tel: 717-533-8845 x100 • Fax: 717-533-8661
E-Mail: cust@igi-global.com • www.igi-global.com

Table of Contents

Foreword

I firmly believe that our colleges and universities serve a unique role in our society; they are the only institutions that are responsible both for the creation of knowledge and for its dissemination.

By providing this edited collection, Yaya Sissoko and Brian W. Sloboda highlight a variety of applied econometric techniques and, in turn, promote the rigorous testing of economic theory. This is quite an important contribution since it is only through careful analysis that we can evaluate the predictions of models that are intended to depict economic relationships and interactions. The results of such analyses provide vital feedback that informs theory and contributes to improvements in theoretical modeling. Acknowledging that student research is a transformative, high-impact educational practice, this book also offers the detail and direction necessary to facilitate student research and, thus, furthers the creation and dissemination of knowledge. Similarly, while generally external to institutions of higher learning, non-academic practitioners, such as business analysts and public policy researchers, will find useful guidance in this book.

Sissoko and Sloboda have assembled an excellent set of studies that collectively demonstrate an impressive breadth of empirical techniques. This is a reflection of the editors' knowledge and their enlightened insight. I will leave it to the editors and the contributing authors to provide more complete depictions of their efforts. Here, I wish to take the broader perspective and note that each chapter provides a separate example and the methodologies presented range from relatively common econometric techniques to more advanced and sophisticated procedures. Moreover, the ordering of chapters is such that there is a general heightening of complexity as one moves through the book, from initial chapters that focus on OLS, panel regression, and times series analysis to later chapters that employ logistic regression techniques, the vector error correction model, the autoregressive distributed lag model, and frequency domain causality analysis. Yes, this is an impressive array of studies both in scale and scope.

As an empirical academic economist, I see the significance of this book. It is a useful guide that will benefit researchers, practitioners, teachers, and students as they work to expand their skillsets and, in turn, produce high-quality research that broadens our collective understanding of the world.

Roger White
Whittier College, USA

Preface

Most researchers have mostly likely heard during their education experiences, "Econometric analysis can be fun!" We learned quickly that econometrics is more than compiling data and running an ordinary least squares (OLS) regression to answer a research question. Specifically, econometrics helps us to identify good ideas from the bad ones and provides an assessment to research questions. Econometrics is applied economics that enables us to see the complicated world in order to assess the relationships in which policymakers, analysts, and businesses use to base their decisions or prescribe policy. *Applied Econometric Analysis: Emerging Research and Opportunities* is an interdisciplinary book using applied econometric methods to investigate interesting research questions. It consists of ten chapters authored by individuals from disciplines of economics, business administration, and finance. The book addresses the applications of econometric methods to various fields in economics and business. To that extent, it should be interesting to academicians, researchers, practitioners in the general field of economics as well as allied fields.

This monograph represents a collection of articles by various authors working in the general area of economics and allied fields. To that extent, this is an interdisciplinary study. All chapters that are included in this monograph are invited articles that are subjected to two levels of review before publication. This speaks to the high quality of each chapter and its contributions to the applications of econometrics. As seen from the list of wide-ranging articles of both macroeconometrics and microeconometrics, the monograph is a conglomeration of basic and applied research that has resulted in these interesting articles. All chapters are applied; consequently, there are no theoretical discussions presented. In empirical research, the acquisition of the appropriate data is paramount. These chapters not only present applications of econometric methods, but some authors may also provide unique datasets that could be used in empirical research and answer specific research questions. To that end, some chapters may be more interesting to academicians, while some may be more appealing to researchers in economics or public policy. This book would be essential reading for academicians, researchers, and students who are involved in applied economics, business or social science research, and are destined to know the latest research. The aim of these chapters is more expository and provides current empirical applications that may be related to microeconomics, macroeconomics, political science, public policy, business administration, or finance use of time series and cross-sectional data.

The target audience of this book is professionals and researchers working in the field of economics and public policy as well as other areas of social science and business. This edited volume will be suitable as a standalone book to understand the latest research questions in economics and other social sciences. That is, this volume will be applicable to academicians, practitioners, and graduate students in economics, public policy, business, and the social sciences.

ORGANIZATION OF THE BOOK

The book is organized into 10 chapters. The first four chapters present methods using macroeconometric methods, while the remaining chapters cover microeconometrics methods. A brief description of each of the chapters follows.

In the first chapter, "Oil Prices and Economic Growth in Major Emerging Economies: Evidence From Asymmetric Frequency Domain Causality," by Cecik, Dibooglu, Kantarci, and Caliskan, the authors show that there is a strong correlation between energy prices and economic activity. The relationship particularly holds true for crude oil as changes in oil prices are associated with changes in production costs, and economic activity also generates significant demand for energy and crude oil. This paper examines the relationship between economic activity and crude oil prices using causality tests in the frequency domain and considering the difference between positive and negative changes in both oil prices and economic activity as the relationship can be asymmetric. We present empirical results for major emerging economies to include Brazil, Russia, India, China, South Africa, and Turkey. Empirical results indicate that for most countries, there is bidirectional causality between crude oil prices and economic activity, whereas only negative oil price shocks seem to negatively affect economic activity.

In Ceylan's chapter, "Dynamics of the Relation Between Producer and Consumer Price Indexes," the relationship between the Producer Prices Index (PPI) and the Consumer Price Index (CPI) in the U.S. is analyzed for two sub-periods: one spanning from 1947 to 1982, the post-war period marked by demand-side economic policies, and the other starting in 1983 when supply-side economic policies were introduced by the Reagan Administration. As the series in question are found to be cointegrated, a Vector Error Correction Model is employed for the analysis. Regarding the long-run equilibrium relationships, it is found that the loading for the PPI series is statistically significant for both periods, while the loading for the CPI is barely significant for the first period, and it is insignificant at any acceptable level for the second. Thus, the CPI represents the common trend in the system in both periods, but it does so more clearly in the second period.

In the chapter entitled "Autoregressive Distributed Lag Approach to External Credit and Economic Growth in Nigeria," Adediran and Alege examine if increasing external credit flows to boost economic activity has exposed Nigeria to the negative effects of external structural changes. Therefore, how does the Nigerian economy grow when there is a decline in external credit? This study attempted to answer this question by comparing the flow of external credit to economic activities. This is a distinction from previous studies that had compared stock of external credit to economic activities. Using annual data covering 36 years for the period of 1980 to 2016, the study adopted the neoclassical growth model and estimated the model using the Autoregressive Distributed Lag (ARDL) approach. The study argued that to the extent that expenditure is credit financed, GDP should be a function of credit flow, which represents new borrowing.

In the chapter "Macroeconomic Surprises and Turkish Financial Market," İşcanoğlu-Çekiç and Gültekin investigate the impacts of macroeconomic news originating from Turkey, the United States, Euro Zone, and China on Turkish financial markets. We consider Purchasing Managers Indices and Gross Domestic Products growth rates as macroeconomic news. The study covers the period from May 4, 2015 to January 1, 2019, and six sectoral indices are included in the analysis. Our findings show that impacts of macroeconomic surprises on abnormal returns are significant for all the sectors except Holdings & Investments and Insurance sectors. We also provide evidence that impacts of macroeconomic surprises on volatilities are significant for only Holdings & Investments, Technology. The findings of the study support the view that foreign country surprises may have an impact on the Turkish financial market, and these effects may vary among sectors. This study has also provided evidence that the Turkish financial market is more responsive to GDP surprises than PMI surprises. These results are consistent with the results of Fedorova et al. (2014) and Gok and Topuz (2016) which show the response of the Turkish stock market to GDP news. In general, this study supports the low response of the Turkish financial market to macroeconomic news at the sectoral level. The Insurance sector especially shows low sensitivity to both the market conditions and the macroeconomic surprises. As an outcome of this study, it can be concluded that the Turkish financial market offers opportunities to develop various investment strategies.

In the chapter entitled "The Convergence Behind the Curtain: An Examination of Crime Rates in Pennsylvania Counties," Habacivch, Redilla, and Jozefowicz extend the applications of unconditional and conditional β-convergence and unconditional σ-convergence analysis to Part I crime rates in a panel data sample of Pennsylvania counties during the period from 990 to 2015. This chapter is a nice blend of econometric methods that investigates sociological issues of crime. Temporal structural breaks at specific points in the business cycle during the time frame as well as spatial breakpoints between rural and urban counties in Pennsylvania are acknowledged in the analysis in order to avoid spurious inferences regarding convergence behavior. Unit-root testing is performed on measures of dispersion as well as directly on the underlying crime-rate series via panel-data tests for non-stationarity. Their findings support the existence of both unconditional and conditional β-convergence in the pooled, urban, and rural samples during 1990-2015. Visual and statistical evidence reveal the presence of σ-convergence in the three samples across the time span as well. The comprehensive convergence analysis of appropriately disaggregated data performed in this study offers strong support for the predictions of modernization theory.

Hannah and Mercer provide an interesting application of the gender wage gap in professional sport. The chapter, which is entitled "Gender Inequality in Professional Tennis," examines the gender wage gap in professional sports using a pooled cross-section of professional tennis players across the years of 2011 to 2015. The dependent variable is the prize money earned by the top fifty male and top fifty female ranked tennis players in the world. This prize money is measured in 2015 real dollar value. The independent variables include number of tournaments played, age, rank differentiation, gender, and WTA/ATP score. Gender inequality is measured by determining the wage gap shown through the mean prize money earned by the professional tennis players from 2011 to 2015. While prize money for men and women has recently become equal in the Grand Slam tournaments, there is evidence to show that women's prize money is considerably lower in the less-publicized tournaments. Results of the ordinary least squares (OLS) regressions suggest that there is evidence for a gender-related pay disparity in professional tennis due to a number of statistically significant variables to include WTA/ATP score (+), age (+), and the gender (-) and year (+) dummies.

The chapter entitled "Socioeconomic Influences on Fertility Rate Fluctuations in Developed and Developing Economies," written by Good and Maticic, investigates the socioeconomic factors that determine the varying fertility rates among developed and developing nations as well as the implications of this information. Social and economic variables are analyzed using a panel of 20 nations with annual data from 1991 to 2015 in order to determine the most sizable and significant variables that impact fertility rates. A one-way fixed effects model is utilized. This study includes an aggregate model as well as two models isolating the fertility rates of developed nations and of developing nations in accordance with Chow-Test results. The results find that there is a divergence between the determinants of fertility rates based upon the development level. It is clear from these results that fertility and population control issues are specific to the state of a nation's development; thus, blanket policies will not fully address the issue of excessive population growth.

Abdul-Wakeel Karakara and Osabuohien examine the microeconomic datasets that are usually large, mainly survey data, in their chapter entitled "Categorical Dependent Variables Estimations With Some Empirical Applications." These data are samples of hundreds of respondents or groups of respondents (e.g., households). The distributions of such data are mostly not normal because some responses/ variables are discrete. Handling such datasets poses some problems of summarizing/ reporting the important features of the data in estimations. This study concentrates on how to handle categorical variables in estimation/reporting based on theoretical and empirical knacks. This study used Ghana Demographic and Health Survey data for 2014 for illustration and elaborates on how to interpret results of binary and multinomial outcome regressions. A comparison is made on the different binary models, and binary logit is found to be weighted over the other binary models. A multinomial logistic model is best handled when the odds of one outcome versus the other outcome are independent of other outcomes alternatives as verified by the Independent of Irrelevant Alternatives (IIA). They also provide conclusions and suggestions for handling categorical models in this study and future studies.

Kiracı's chapter, "Financial Determinants Affecting Leasing Policies: Empirical Evidence From the Airline Industry Airline," examines how companies have started to develop strategies to increase their market share and expand their network structures with the effect of globalization. In this process, one of the most important sources of airline companies to achieve competitive advantage is aircraft. Airline companies must increase the number of aircraft in the fleet to expand their network structure. On the other hand, the high price of aircraft has led airline companies to adopt new financing strategies. Recently, leasing is one of the financing methods used frequently by airline companies. Therefore, this study focuses on the leasing policies of airline companies. This study aimed to reveal the factors affecting the leasing policies of airline companies. In this context, 26 airlines operating in the period from 2000 to 2017 were analyzed empirically. Panel data analysis was used as the method in the study. The empirical findings of the study indicate that return on assets, asset structure, tangibility, leverage ratio, and liquidity affect the leasing policies of airline companies.

In the chapter entitled "Does Regional Variation in Startup Concentration Predict Employment Growth in Rural Areas of Ohio, Pennsylvania, and West Virginia?" Sissoko and Sloboda investigate measures of entrepreneurship, such as average establishment size and the prevalence of start-ups, to determine the correlation with employment growth within rural areas using generalized linear models (GLM). GLM is not widely used in empirical econometrics. Is it possible for entrepreneurship to occur outside of urban areas and be active in rural areas such as Ohio, Pennsylvania, and West Virginia? There are causal links of entrepreneurial finance to industry or city growth (e.g., Samila and Sorenson (2011)), but there is little link of the evidence of entrepreneurship outside of urban areas overall. This chapter examines the regional variation in startup concentration used to predict employment in the rural areas of Pennsylvania, Ohio, and West Virginia by metropolitan statistical area (MSA)/micropolitan areas for the year 2017. More specifically, we use data from the Quarterly Workforce Indicators (QWI) and the Longitudinal Employer Household Data (LEHD) from the Census Bureau that tracks all employers in the U.S. private sector economy. They examine the impact of these externalities as measured by entrepreneurial activity on employment growth. Moreover, they find significant differences in new firm formation rates from industrial regions to technologically progressive regions using the generalized linear models (GLM). GLM allows for this effect to vary along the range of the explanatory variables. Variations in employment are explained by population growth, the number of startups, human capital variables, and share of proprietorships.

CONCLUDING REMARKS

While *Applied Econometric Analysis: Emerging Research and Opportunities* covers a myriad of econometric methods, it is by no means an exhaustive presentation of these methods. Also, while each chapter clearly outlines the content for presenting empirical work, each chapter does not attempt to show how research should be performed. Specifically, each of the chapters clearly outlines the development of the research starting with its research questions, providing specific sources of data that can be used, and clearly outlining the econometric method used. All authors ably explain their empirical results and the meaning of these results in the formulation of the appropriate policy. More importantly, the careful explanation of the empirical results is important and will be a good education for any reader either as beginning researchers or more advanced researchers refreshing themselves on methods and research. It is considered a prerequisite that the readers of *Applied Econometric Analysis: Emerging Research and Opportunities* are educated and informed on the research design as well as econometric methods (e.g., Stock and Watson (2019) and Wooldridge (2019)), in order to appropriately apply these methods herein.

Brian W. Sloboda
University of Phoenix, USA

Yaya Sissoko
Indiana University of Pennsylvania, USA

REFERENCES

Stock, J. H., & Watson, M. W. (2019). *Introduction to econometrics* (4th ed.). Pearson/Addison Wesley.

Wooldridge, J. M. (2019). *Introductory econometrics: a modern approach* (7th ed.). South-Western Cengage Learning.

Chapter 1
Oil Prices and Economic Growth in Major Emerging Economies:
Evidence From Asymmetric Frequency Domain Causality Tests

Emrah I Cevik
Namik Kemal University, Turkey

Sel Dibooglu
University of Sharjah, UAE

Tugba Kantarci
Namik Kemal University, Turkey

Hande Caliskan
Namik Kemal University, Turkey

ABSTRACT

There is a strong correlation between energy prices and economic activity. The relationship particularly holds true for crude oil as changes in oil prices are associated with changes in production costs, and economic activity also generates significant demand for energy and crude oil. This chapter examines the relationship between economic activity and crude oil prices using causality tests in the frequency domain and taking into account the difference between positive and negative changes in both oil prices and economic activity as the relationship can be asymmetric. The authors present empirical results for major emerging economies including Brazil, Russia, India, China, South Africa, and Turkey. Empirical results indicate that for most countries there is bidirectional causality between crude oil prices and

DOI: 10.4018/978-1-7998-1093-3.ch001

economic activity whereas only negative oil price shocks seem to negatively affect economic activity.

INTRODUCTION

Energy sources such as crude oil, natural gas, and coal are important inputs for many sectors and have an important role in economic activity. Even though the use and production of energy sources varies among sectors, crude oil still occupies a central role in the global economy in comparison to other energy sources. Hence, oil prices affect several macroeconomic indicators (such as output, trade balance, inflation, stock markets, and exchange rates).

The share of primary energy sources in total energy consumption in Figure 1 shows crude oil is still an important energy source today. Crude oil is not only the highest primary energy source in the world, but the share of crude oil as the primary energy source increased from 34% to 49% between 1965 and 2017. However, it is evident that crude oil consumption started to decline in the new millennium. Coal is the second highest consumed energy source after oil while natural gas is third as shown in Figure 1.

Figure 1. The share of primary energy resources in total energy consumption
Source: BP Statistical Review of World Energy

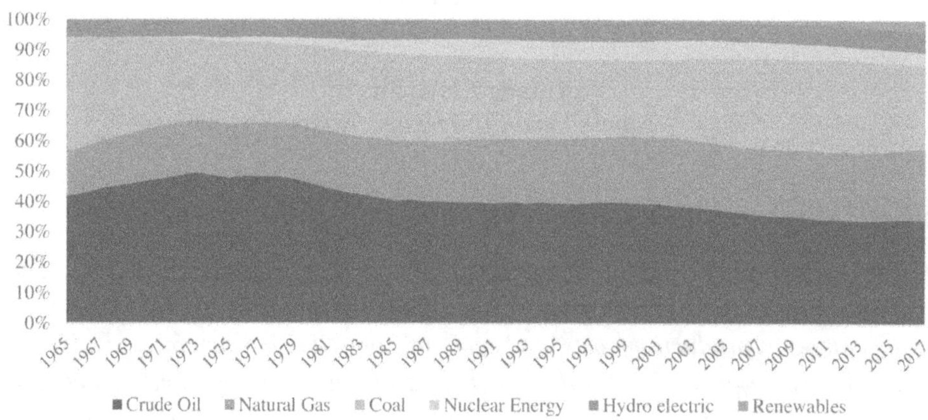

Crude oil use around the world is shown in Figure 2. It is evident that oil consumption has increased year after year, and while total oil consumption was 1,523 million tons in 1965, it reached 4,470 million tons in 2017. North America has the highest oil consumption in the new millennium, while Africa has the lowest within the sample. The use of crude oil in the Asia Pacific region has been on the rise significantly, and since the 2000s, it has become the region with the highest petroleum consumption as two of the largest economies in the world, China and India, are located in this region.

Figure 2. Crude oil consumption by geographical region
Source: BP Statistical Review of World Energy

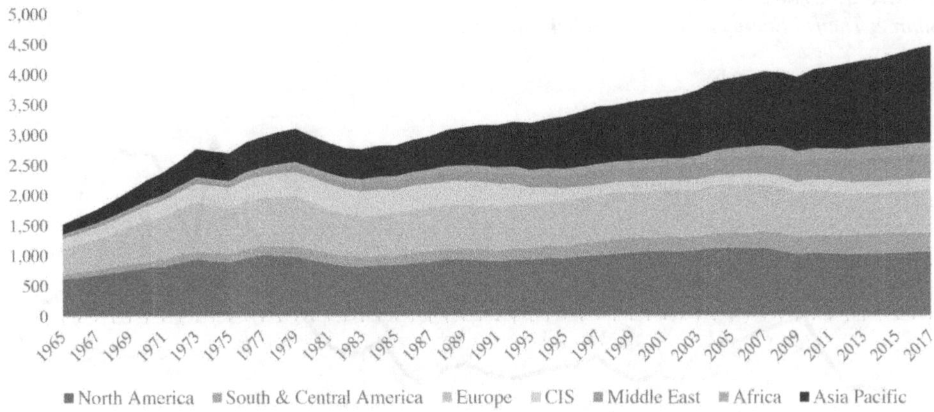

A closer look at oil consumption in 2017 shows that the highest oil consumption was observed in the USA (19.5%) and China (13.3%). These countries are followed by India, Japan, Saudi Arabia, Russia, Brazil, South Korea, Germany, and Canada, respectively, and these countries account for 60% of total oil consumption in the world. Moreover, these results show that crude oil has an important place not only for developed countries but also for developing countries. Therefore, changes in oil prices will have a significant effect on economies of developed and developing countries alike.

Global oil prices in the international market are influenced by various factors. These include microeconomic activities as well as political and geographic reasons. Demand and supply side effects are prominent in the determination of oil prices as well. For example, oil prices are vulnerable to demand shocks such as taxes or speculation and supply shocks such as oil production costs or the decrease in oil stocks. The increase in oil prices increases input costs for an oil importing country, causing increases in budget deficits and decreases in investments while reducing production and possibly labor productivity.

Crude oil prices (White Texas Intermediate-WTI) are presented for 1973-2017 in Figure 3. Until 1978, crude oil prices were lower than $20 per barrel, and prices exhibit an upward trend thereafter. After the Iranian revolution in 1978, oil supply decreased, and in 1980, the price of oil reached $40 per barrel. In 1980, oil prices showed a downtrend again, and they were below $30 until the end of the 1990s. At the beginning of the 2000s, a significant uptrend in oil prices emerged; in 2008 the price of crude oil exceeded $ 100 and reached a historical peak. Since then, oil price volatility has increased. While prices were $61 in 2009, they increased to $95 thereafter. After 2013, prices started to decrease. and in 2017, prices were down to $50 per barrel.

Figure 3. Crude oil prices
Source: The US Energy Information Administration

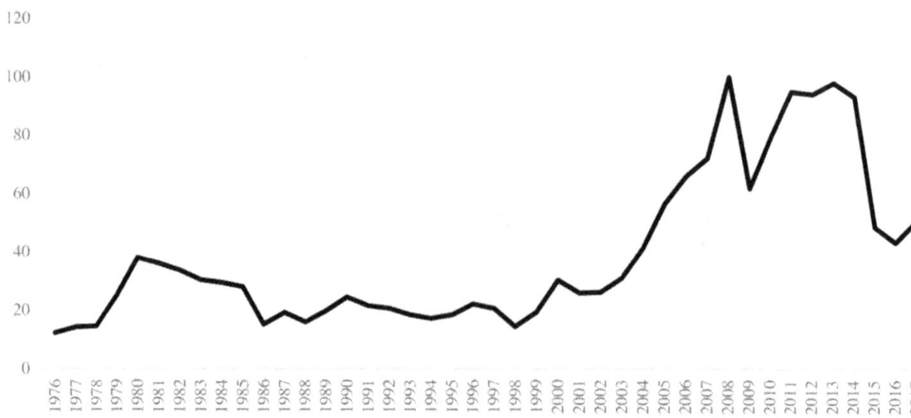

The impact of oil prices on countries can be overly broad and directly affect the economic as well as political developments. There is evidence that oil prices are a significant factor influencing economic growth rate (Syzdykova, 2018, p. 2). Shocks in oil prices lead to efficient use of oil or development of alternative energy sources. However, increases in economic activity lead to increases in oil consumption (Wong et al., 2013, p. 1581; Sarwar et al., 2017, p. 10).

The effects of oil prices on the business cycle and on economic growth have been studied extensively in the literature. The main conclusion is that unexpected oil price shocks negatively affect economic growth in oil importing countries, whereas it has a positive effect in oil exporting countries. Hamilton (1983) provided evidence that all but one of US recessions in the aftermath of World War II can be attributed to unexpected oil price increases. However, subsequent work has challenged this result, and further work is warranted since there have been many global developments in the last few decades. While increases in oil prices benefit oil-exporting countries in the short-run, such increases have negative effects on the macroeconomic environment elsewhere in the world. As a result, both oil exporting and importing countries have suffered from higher oil prices in the long run. Moreover, empirical studies show that the effects of oil prices on the growth rates are asymmetric, and one would need to distinguish between the effects of positive and negative oil price shocks separately.

The principle objective of this chapter is to investigate the effect of oil prices on the growth rates in both oil exporting and oil importing countries. As far as countries, we consider Brazil, Russia, India, China, South Africa, and Turkey as these are major emerging economies, and the sample includes net oil exporting and importing countries. Since 2001, some of these countries have been known as BRIC countries in the literature and include Brazil, Russia, India, and China. We also include South Africa and Turkey as these two countries have similar characteristics both in population density and economic development, and sometimes, the group is collectively referred to as BRICS-T. Since BRICS-T countries have high oil production and consumption potential, they play a significant role in the world oil market. For example, Russia has an important position in oil exports and energy consumption. While Brazil and Russia are the most important oil exporters in the world, China and India are significant oil importers. While a quarter of the world's oil is produced in Brazil, Russia, China, and India, a quarter of total oil consumption occurs in these countries. Based on such figures, these countries can be expected to exert a significant influence on international oil prices, and these countries will also be affected by changes in oil prices.

Countries with energy reserves such as Brazil need high investments to explore and produce oil. In Brazil, oil plays a significant role directly or indirectly in all sectors and oil prices are an important factor in economic expectations (de Salles & Almeida, 2017, p. 402). Increasing oil production in Brazil has been a long-term goal of the government. Today, Brazil is the ninth largest oil producer in the world and the third largest in the continents of North and South America following the US and Canada (EIA, 2019). Russia is the world's third largest crude oil producer and the second largest natural gas producer. In addition, most of the oil (70%) in some European countries, particularly in the Netherlands, Germany, Poland, and Belarus, is provided by Russia. On the other hand, approximately 36% of Russia's budget revenue is from oil and natural gas activities (EIA, 2017a). The fact that Russia is an important energy exporter makes it vulnerable to fluctuations in world energy and fuel prices. Therefore, a downward trend in oil prices may be harmful to economic activity. For example, the Russian economy has been one of the countries most affected by the 2008 global economic crisis due to the decline in oil prices (Ghalayani, 2011, p. 135).

India imports approximately 100 million tons of crude oil and other petroleum products annually. This necessitates a large sum of foreign exchange depletion. A rise in the world crude oil price may lead to a significant increase in trade deficit and affect economic activity in India (Wani et al., 2015, p. 20-21). Moreover, oil prices may be influenced by demand factors and developments in oil importing countries. For example, with its 1.3 billion inhabitants, China is the most populous country in the world and has experienced rapid economic growth in recent decades. Energy demand has increased proportionally to meet the needs of the growing manufacturing sector. While China was the world's largest energy exporter at the beginning of 1990s, it has become the world's largest energy consumer and the second largest oil importer since 2013 (Khan et al., 2017, p. 39-40). Turkey is an oil importer country due to its limited domestic oil reserves. In addition, Turkey is on the crossroads from Central Asia, Russia, and the Middle East to the Europe and Atlantic markets, thus becoming more important in supplying oil and natural gas as a transit center (EIA, 2017b).

In this chapter, we use state-of-the-art time series analysis methods and combine an asymmetric causality test suggested by Hatemi-J (2012) with frequency domain Granger causality test proposed by Breitung and Candelon (2006). This new econometric methodology allows us to examine the relationship between oil prices and economic growth in terms of asymmetric effects of positive and negative oil prices shocks on economic growth as well as distinguish between short-run and long-run effects.

LITERATURE REVIEW

The relationship between oil prices and economic growth has been the subject of many studies in the literature. Empirical results addressing the relationship between oil prices and economic growth has varied in terms of the direction of causality direction, countries, or country groups. Some of these studies are summarized below.

Rodriguez and Sanchez (2005) examined the impact of oil price shocks on real economic activity in OECD countries using a VAR model and found evidence favoring a non-linear relationship between oil prices and real GDP. Their results show that oil-importing countries are negatively affected by the increase in oil prices. On the other hand, there was no uniform relationship for oil exporters: increases in oil prices affected growth positively in Norway, while England was negatively affected.

Lardic and Mignon (2008) examined the long-term relationship between oil prices and economic growth with conventional and asymmetric cointegration tests for developed countries. While the conventional cointegration test results indicate lack of cointegration between the variables, the asymmetric cointegration tests suggest cointegration between oil prices and economic growth. Hanabusa (2009) analyzed the relationship between oil prices and economic growth by using causality-in-mean and variance tests for Japan. Empirical results show bidirectional causality between economic growth and oil prices in mean and in variance.

Berument et al. (2010) examined the impact of volatility in oil prices on economic growth in 16 countries in the MENA region using a SVAR model. Empirical results suggest shocks in oil prices have a positive and statistically significant effect on growth in most oil-exporting economies (Algeria, Iran, Iraq, Kuwait, Libya, Oman, Qatar, Syria, and UAE). On the other hand, shocks to oil prices are not significant on economic growth in Bahrain, Djibouti, Egypt, Israel, Jordan, Morocco, and Tunisia.

Ghalayani (2011) examined the relationship between oil prices and economic growth via Granger causality test for G-7, OPEC countries, China, India, and Russia with no relationship between the oil price and economic growth in most of the countries. While economic growth in G7 countries is affected from oil price shocks, an increase in oil price was not a Granger cause of economic growth in oil exporting countries. Moshiri (2015) investigated the non-linear effects of oil price shocks on the macroeconomic variables by using a VAR model. Accordingly, the effects of positive and negative oil price shocks on economic growth are asymmetric and heterogeneous in oil exporting countries.

Gülay and Pazarlıoğlu (2016) examined the relationship between economic growth, real exchange rate, and crude oil prices for Turkey using Gregory and Hansen co-integration test for 1984-2010. According to the results, there is a negative relationship among economic growth, oil prices, and the real exchange rate. Gadea et al. (2016) analyzed the relationship between oil prices and economic growth for the US using a long span of data from 1875-2016. They found no long run relationship between oil price and economic growth. Moreover, they found no persistence in the response of economic growth to a shock in oil prices.

Shahbaz et al. (2017) estimated the relationship between oil prices, labor force, capital, economic growth, and electricity consumption through panel data analysis using data from 157 countries between 1960 and 2014. The results indicate that there is a relationship between oil prices, electricity consumption, and economic growth. Yıldırım et al. (2018) analyzed the regime-dependent relation between oil prices and the stock market by means of Markov-Switching VAR model for BRICS countries. Empirical analysis results showed that the responses of the stock market to an oil price shock vary over the regimes for all countries. In addition, it was found that the stock market responded to oil price shocks as positive and statistically significant in the high-volatility regime. Finally, Van Eyden et al. (2019) examined the effects of volatility of oil prices on economic growth using panel data from 17 OECD countries between 1870 and 2013. They showed that an increase in the volatility of oil prices negatively affects economic growth. Moreover, net oil exporters such as Norway and Canada were negatively affected by the uncertainty of oil prices compared to other countries.

ECONOMETRIC FRAMEWORK

After the seminal paper of Granger (1969), many studies have empirically analyzed the causal relationships between various economic and financial time series. Several improvements in testing methodology have occurred over the years in the literature. For example, Granger (1988) proposed a cointegration test for nonstationary time series in which causal relationships can be examined by using an error correction model (ECM). Toda and Yamamoto (1995) suggested a test procedure based on an augmented-VAR model to examine the causal relationships between variables. Hatemi-J (2012) proposed a test procedure that is based on positive and negative shocks for each series. A further recent development on the Granger-causality test has been its extension by Breitung and Candelon (2006) in the frequency domain. The frequency-based decomposition of spectral density is based on Geweke (1982) and Hosoya (1991) and employs a Wald-type testing procedure for detecting causality at given frequencies. Breitung and Candelon (2006) developed this test procedure based on frequency-domain causality measures by using a bivariate vector autoregressive (VAR) model and showed that the test procedure is superior to other frequency-domain tests. In order to illustrate the test, we first outline the testing procedure by Geweke (1982), Yao and Hosoya (2000), and Hosoya (2001).

Suppose we have two integrated variables such as y_t (economic growth) and x_t (oil price). In order to describe the asymmetric frequency domain causality test between the variables, we need to first define the positive and negative shocks for each series. If the variables follow the random walk processes:

$$y_t = y_{t-1} + \varepsilon_{1t} = y_0 + \sum_{i=1}^{t} \varepsilon_{1i} \tag{1}$$

$$x_t = x_{t-1} + \varepsilon_{2t} = x_0 + \sum_{i=1}^{t} \varepsilon_{2i} \tag{2}$$

where $t = 1, 2, \ldots, T$, the constants y_0 and x_0 are the initial values and the variables ε_{1i} and ε_{2i} imply white noise residuals, we can define the positive and negative shocks as the following:

$$\varepsilon_{1i}^{+} = \max\left(\varepsilon_{1i}, 0\right),\ \varepsilon_{2i}^{+} = \max\left(\varepsilon_{2i}, 0\right),\ \varepsilon_{1i}^{-} = \min\left(\varepsilon_{1i}, 0\right),\ \text{and}\ \varepsilon_{2i}^{-} = \min\left(\varepsilon_{2i}, 0\right).$$

Therefore, residuals can be defined sum of positive and negative shocks as $\varepsilon_{1i} = \varepsilon_{1i}^{+} + \varepsilon_{1i}^{-}$ and $\varepsilon_{2i} = \varepsilon_{2i}^{+} + \varepsilon_{2i}^{-}$. Due to this definition, y_{1t} and y_{2t} can be defined as:

$$y_t = y_{t-1} + \varepsilon_{1t} = y_0 + \sum_{i=1}^{t} \varepsilon_{1i}^{+} + \sum_{i=1}^{t} \varepsilon_{1i}^{-} \tag{3}$$

$$x_t = x_{t-1} + \varepsilon_{2t} = x_0 + \sum_{i=1}^{t} \varepsilon_{2i}^{+} + \sum_{i=1}^{t} \varepsilon_{2i}^{-} \tag{4}$$

Finally, the positive and negative shocks of each variable can be defined in a cumulative form as

$$y_t^{+} = \sum_{i=1}^{t} \varepsilon_{1i}^{+},\ y_t^{-} = \sum_{i=1}^{t} \varepsilon_{1i}^{-},\ x_t^{+} = \sum_{i=1}^{t} \varepsilon_{2t}^{+},\ \text{and } x_t^{-} = \sum_{i=1}^{t} \varepsilon_{2t}^{-}.$$

Note that, by construction, each positive as well as negative shock has a permanent impact on the underlying variable. The next step is to test the causal relationship between these components. Here, we describe testing for a causal relationship between positive cumulative shocks. The vector $z_t^{-} = \left(y_t^{-}, x_t^{-}\right)$ can be used for testing causality between negative cumulative shocks.

After defining the positive and negative shock for each series, in order to describe the frequency domain causality test, $z_t^{+} = \left[x_t^{+}, y_t^{+}\right]'$ can be defined as a two-dimensional vector of time series observed at $t = 1, \ldots, T$. It is assumed that z_t has a finite-order VAR representation of the form:

$$\Theta\left(L\right) z_t = \varepsilon_t \tag{5}$$

where

$$\Theta\left(L\right) = I - \Theta_1 L - \cdots - \Theta_p L^p$$

is a 2 x 2 lag polynomial with $L^k z_t = z_{t-k}$. It is assumed that the error vector ε_t is white noise with $E(\varepsilon t_j{=}0$ and $E\left(\varepsilon_t \varepsilon_t'\right) = \Sigma$, where Σ is positive definite. Let G be the lower triangular matrix of the Cholesky decomposition $G'G = \Sigma^{-1}$ such that $E\left(\eta_t \eta_t'\right) = I$ and $\eta_t = G\varepsilon_t$. If the system is assumed to be stationary, the MA representation of the system can be formulated as the following:

$$z_t = \Phi(L)\varepsilon_t = \begin{bmatrix} \Phi_{11}(L) & \Phi_{12}(L) \\ \Phi_{21}(L) & \Phi_{22}(L) \end{bmatrix} \begin{bmatrix} \varepsilon_{1t} \\ \varepsilon_{2t} \end{bmatrix} = \Psi(L)\eta_t = \begin{bmatrix} \Psi_{11}(L) & \Psi_{12}(L) \\ \Psi_{21}(L) & \Psi_{22}(L) \end{bmatrix} \begin{bmatrix} \eta_{1t} \\ \eta_{2t} \end{bmatrix} \tag{6}$$

where $\Phi(L)=\Theta(L)^{-1}$ and $\Psi(L)=\Phi(L)G^{-1}$. Using this representation, the spectral density of x^+ can be expressed as:

$$f_{x^+}(\omega) = \frac{1}{2\pi}\left\{ \left|\Psi_{11}\left(e^{-i\omega}\right)\right|^2 + \left|\Psi_{12}\left(e^{-i\omega}\right)\right|^2 \right\} \tag{7}$$

Geweke (1982) and Hosoya (2001) define the measure of causality as the following:

$$M_{y^+ \to x^+}(\omega) = \log\left[\frac{2\pi f_{x^+}(\omega)}{\left|\Psi_{11}\left(e^{-i\omega}\right)\right|^2} \right] = \log\left[1 + \frac{\left|\Psi_{12}\left(e^{-i\omega}\right)\right|^2}{\left|\Psi_{11}\left(e^{-i\omega}\right)\right|^2} \right] \tag{8}$$

If $\left|\Psi_{12}\left(e^{-i\omega}\right)\right| = 0$, it can be said that y^+ does not Granger cause x^+ at frequency ω. In follow up work, Yao and Hosoya (2000) suggested estimating $M_{y^+ \to x^+}(\omega)$ by replacing $\left|\Psi_{11}\left(e^{-i\omega}\right)\right|$ and $\left|\Psi_{12}\left(e^{-i\omega}\right)\right|$ with estimates obtained from the fitted VAR model, the delta method can then be applied for testing the null hypothesis. However, this method is based on complicated nonlinear restrictions on the VAR parameters, and hence, this procedure is overly difficult to implement.

Breitung and Candelon (2006), on the other hand, proposed a much simpler approach to test the null hypothesis that y^+ does not Granger-cause x^+ at frequency ω:

$$M_{y^+ \to x^+}(\omega) = 0 \tag{9}$$

Using

$$\Psi\left(L\right) = \Theta\left(L\right)^{-1} G^{-1} \text{ and } \Psi_{12}\left(L\right) = -\frac{g^{22}\Theta_{12}\left(L\right)}{\left|\Theta\left(L\right)\right|}$$

where g^{22} is the lower diagonal element of G^{-1} and $|\Theta(L)|$ is the determinant of $\Theta(L)$. It follows that y^+ does not Granger-cause x^+ at frequency ω if

$$\left|\Theta_{12}\left(e^{-i\omega}\right)\right| = \left|\sum_{k=1}^{p}\theta_{12,k}\cos\left(k\omega\right) - \sum_{k=1}^{p}\theta_{12,k}\sin\left(k\omega\right)i\right| = 0 \tag{10}$$

where $\theta_{12,k}$ is the (1, 2)-element of Θ_k. Thus, a necessary and sufficient set of conditions can be written as follows:

$$\left|\Theta_{12}\left(e^{-i\omega}\right)\right| = 0$$

$$\sum_{k=1}^{p}\theta_{12,k}\cos\left(k\omega\right) = 0 \tag{11}$$

$$\sum_{k=1}^{p}\theta_{12,k}\sin\left(k\omega\right) = 0 \tag{12}$$

The approach is based on the linear restrictions in the equations above. To simplify the notation, we let $\alpha_j=\theta_{11,j}$ and $\beta_j=\theta_{12,j}$ so that the VAR equation for x_t^+ can be written as:

$$x_t^+ = \alpha_1 x_{t-1}^+ + \cdots + \alpha_p x_{t-p}^+ + \beta_1 y_{t-1}^+ + \cdots + \beta_p y_{t-p}^+ + \varepsilon_{1t} \tag{13}$$

The hypothesis $M_{y^+\to x^+}\left(\omega\right) = 0$ is equivalent to the linear restriction

$$H_0 = R\left(\omega\right)\beta = 0 \tag{14}$$

where $\beta = \left[\beta_1, \ldots, \beta_p\right]'$ and

$$R(\omega) = \begin{bmatrix} \cos(\omega)\cos(2\omega)\cdots\cos(p\omega) \\ \sin(\omega)\sin(2\omega)\cdots\sin(p\omega) \end{bmatrix} \tag{15}$$

In order to the test the null of no causality, the ordinary F statistic that is approximately distributed as F (2, T-2p) for $\omega \in (0,\pi)$ can be calculated.

This study will implement these steps in order to examine the relationship between oil prices and economic growth in major emerging economies where we distinguish between the effects of positive and negative oil price shocks.

Table 1. Unit root test results

Variables	Levels		First Differences	
	ADF	PP	ADF	PP
Oil -WTI	-1.86	-1.663	-12.37***	-12.36***
Output				
Brazil	-1.75	-1.93	-10.14***	-21.12***
China	-1.82	-2.03	-6.20***	-15.01***
India	-1.27	-1.60	-3.64***	-26.79***
Russia	-1.57	-1.59	-18.63***	-18.63***
Turkey	-0.42	-0.50	-18.76***	-18.74***
S. Africa	-1.96	-2.05	-15.92***	-24.72***

Note: *** indicates stationarity at 1% significance level.

DATA AND EMPIRICAL RESULTS

We examine the relationship between crude oil price and economic growth by using monthly data from 1997:1 to 2019:2. We consider West Texas Intermediate (WTI) crude oil price as global oil price and industrial production for economic growth. The crude oil price series are collected from the EIA website, and industrial production data are obtained from the World Bank Global Economic Monitor. The natural logarithms of the variables are used in the empirical analysis.

We first examine the time series properties of crude oil prices and industrial production by means of Augmented Dickey-Fuller (ADF) and Phillips-Perron (PP) unit root tests. The unit root test results are presented in Table 1. These results indicate that the null hypothesis of the unit root cannot be rejected for data in levels. On the other hand, when the first difference of the series is considered, the null hypothesis can be rejected at the 1% significance level. Unit root test results indicate that the maximum integration order of the variables is 1.

Bretiung and Candelon (2006) showed that frequency-domain causality tests can be employed with nonstationary variables, and the test procedure is robust for the lag-augmented Granger-causality tests suggested by Toda and Yamamoto (1995). Therefore, we estimate the VAR model with $p + d_{max}$ lags, where p is the optimal lag length, and d_{max} is the maximum order of integration.

In order to examine the causal link between economic growth and global crude oil price in Brazil, we estimate bivariate VAR model. The Akaike Information Criterion (AIC) suggests three lags are sufficient to render the residuals white noise. Then, we use a frequency domain causality test procedure suggested by Breitung and Candelon (2006), and the results are presented in Figure 4. Notice that frequency-based causality test is employed for all frequencies in the $(0, \pi)$ interval.

Figure 4. Causality test results for Brazil
Note: The dashed line is the critical value at the 5% significance level.

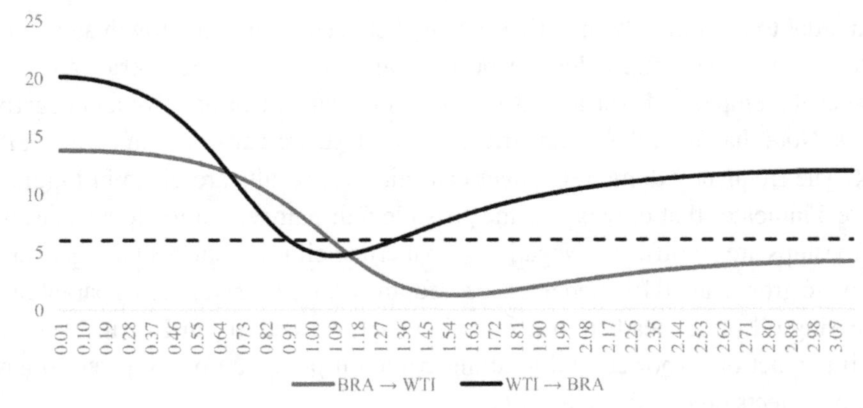

The results in Figure 4 show bidirectional causality between oil prices and economic growth in Brazil. On the other hand, although WTI is the Granger cause of economic growth both in the short and long runs, the causal link running from economic growth to global crude oil price is statistically significant only in the long run. In other words, the null hypothesis of no causality from economic growth to global oil price can be rejected in the frequency range [0.01, 1.1]. Note that $\omega = 1.1$ corresponds to 6 months as such developments in the Brazilian economy affect global crude oil prices after 6 months. However, causality going from the global crude oil price to economic growth cannot be rejected within $\omega \in [0.9, 1.3]$ which corresponds to a cycle length between 5 and 7 months.

Figure 5. Asymmetric causality test results for Brazil
Notes: The dashed line is the critical value at the 5% significance level. The subscripts "p" and "n" indicate positive and negative shocks, respectively.

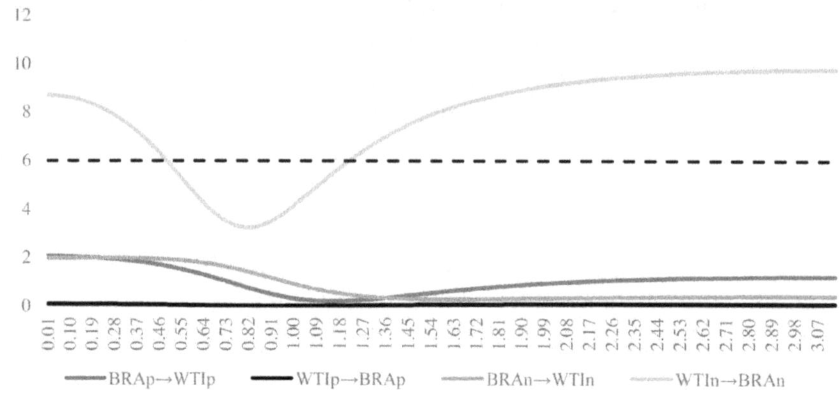

In order to examine asymmetric causality between economic growth and global crude oil price, we first calculate positive and negative shock series for each variable and employ a bivariate VAR model for each pair of positive and negative shocks. Note that as in the symmetric causality test, we consider three lags in the VAR. The frequency domain Granger causality test results are given in Figure 5. Figure 5 indicates that only one of the possible four pair-wise directional causality relationships are significant. Negative global crude oil price shocks Granger cause economic growth at all frequencies except for the [0.51, 1.22] range. To paraphrase, decreasing oil prices leads to a decline in economic activity in Brazil. Note that Brazil is a net oil exporter, and a falling crude oil price can be expected to have negative effects on economic activity.

Frequency domain Granger causality test results for Russia are presented in Figure 6.[1] The results in Figure 6 show bidirectional causality between economic growth and global crude oil prices. These results are consistent with expectations because Russia is one of the largest oil exporters in the world, and hence, developments in economic activity potentially can affect crude oil prices and vice versa. Note that the null hypothesis of no causality running from crude oil price to economic growth is strongly rejected in the long run. On the other hand, the causal link from economic growth to crude oil prices is borderline in the [0.01, 0.42] frequency range.

Figure 6. Causality test results for Russia
Note: The dashed line is the critical value at the 5% significance level.

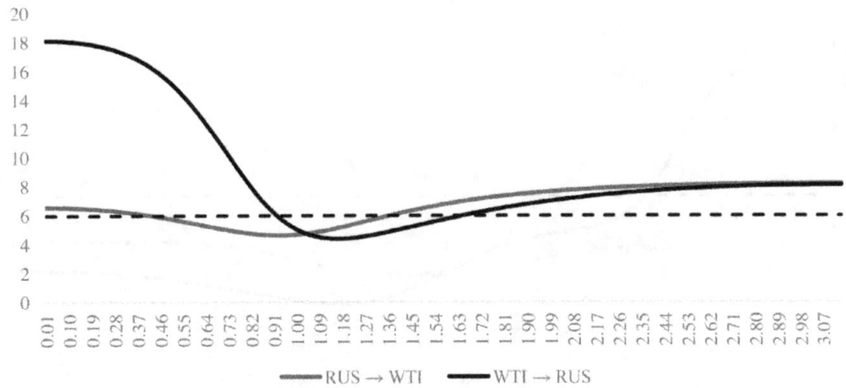

The frequency domain Granger causality test results for positive and negative shocks are presented in Figure 7. The results in Figure 7 indicate that decreasing crude oil prices Granger cause a decrease in economic activity in Russia in all frequencies except for in [0.82, 1.08] the range, which corresponds to a cycle length between 5 and 7 months. Also, we find that positive economic growth Granger causes increases in crude oil prices in the short run (between 1 and 5 months) as the null hypothesis of no causality can be rejected in the [1.12, 3.14] frequency range. Similarly, a decline in economic activity causes a decrease in crude oil prices in the short run. We cannot validate a causal link between positive crude oil price and economic growth. This suggests that decreases in oil prices lead to a decrease in economic activity in Russia, and the global crude oil price is affected from economic growth only in the short run.

Figure 7. Asymmetric causality test results for Russia
Notes: The dashed line is the critical value at the 5% significance level. The subscripts "p" and "n" indicate positive and negative shocks, respectively.

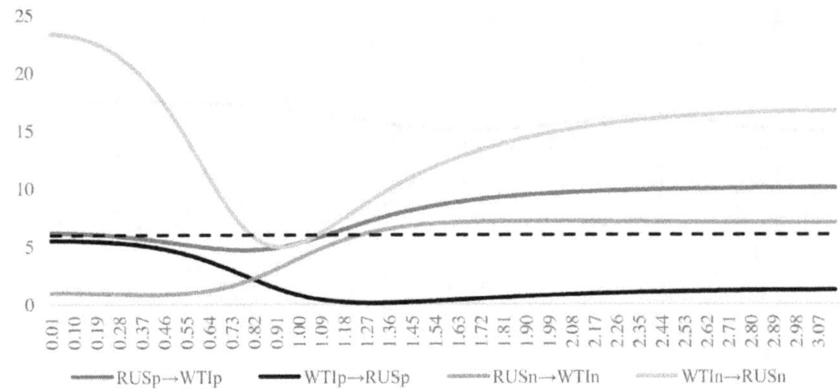

Figure 8. Causality test results for India
Notes: Dashed line is critical value at 5% significance level.

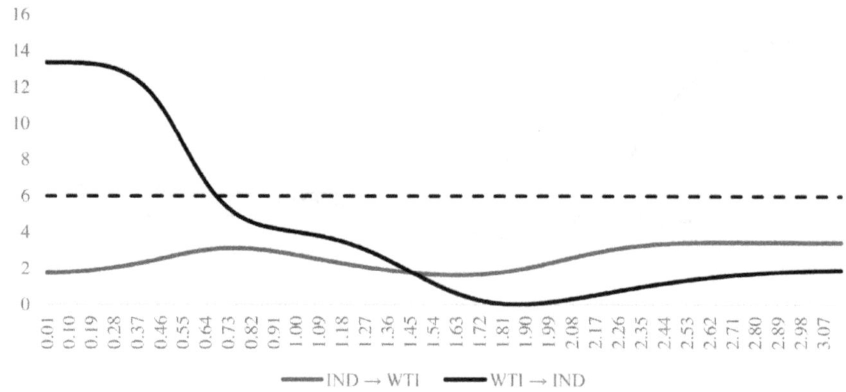

We estimate VAR model with four lags and calculate the frequency domain Granger causality test to examine the dynamic relationship between economic growth and crude oil prices in India. The results in Figure 8 suggest a unidirectional causality running from crude oil price to economic growth. Note that causality from crude oil price to economic growth is statistically significant only in the [0.01, 0.69] range, indicating developments in the crude oil price affect economic growth in India after 9 months. This finding is consistent with a priori expectations because India is the third largest country in terms of oil consumption.

Figure 9. Asymmetric causality test results for India
Notes: The dashed line is the critical value at the 5% significance level. The subscripts "p" and "n" indicate positive and negative shocks, respectively.

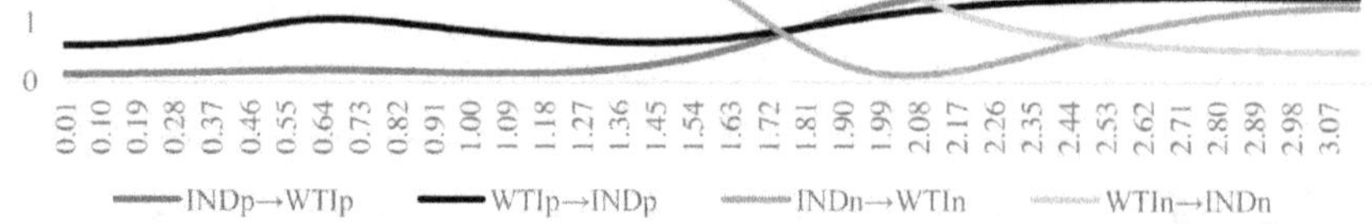

The asymmetric Granger causality test results that are presented in Figure 9 indicate causality running from negative crude oil price shocks to economic growth. Note that the null hypothesis is rejected only in the [0.87, 1.48] frequency range, which corresponds to a cycle length between 4 and 7 months. Therefore, decreasing oil prices cause a decrease in economic activity in India. This finding is at odds with reality because crude oil is an important input in economic activity in India and elsewhere. Since increases in crude oil prices lead to increased production costs in oil importing countries, the decline in crude oil prices can be expected to increase economic activity. On the other hand, if the decline in crude oil prices is demand-driven, it can point to economic stagnation, and hence, negative shocks in the oil price may lead to decreased economic activity in some countries.

Figure 10. Causality test results for China

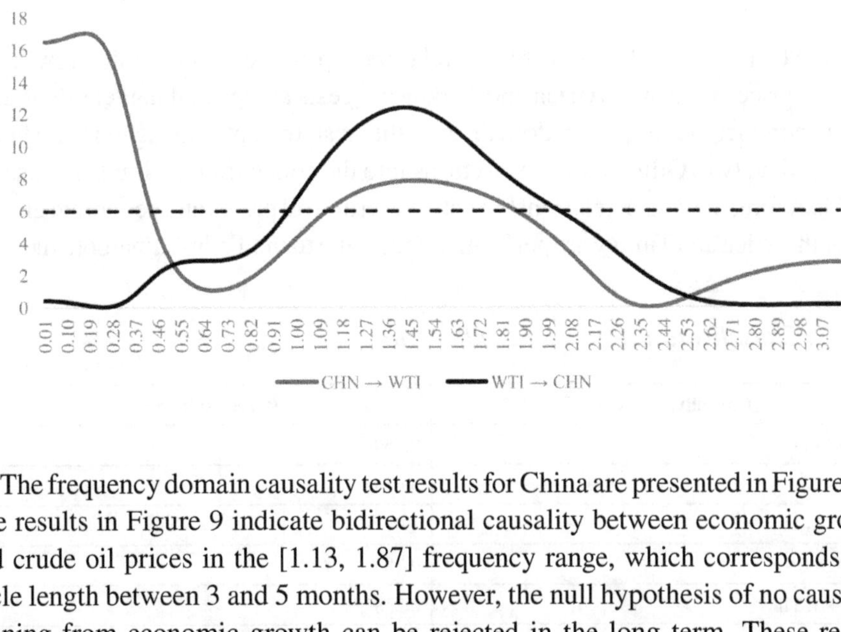

The frequency domain causality test results for China are presented in Figure 10.[2] The results in Figure 9 indicate bidirectional causality between economic growth and crude oil prices in the [1.13, 1.87] frequency range, which corresponds to a cycle length between 3 and 5 months. However, the null hypothesis of no causality running from economic growth can be rejected in the long term. These results suggest that developments in the global crude oil price and economic activity in China affect one another. This result is not unexpected as China is the second largest oil consumer in the world.

According to asymmetric frequency domain causality test results in Figure 11, a decline in the crude oil price Granger causes a decline in economic activity in China both in the short and long runs. In addition, a decrease in economic activity in China leads to a decrease in crude oil prices. As seen in Figure 10, the effects of negative shocks in both economic activity and crude oil prices are more pronounced than the effects of positive shocks.

Figure 11. Asymmetric causality test results for China (6+1)
Notes: The dashed line is the critical value at the 5% significance level. The subscripts "p" and "n" indicate positive and negative shocks, respectively.

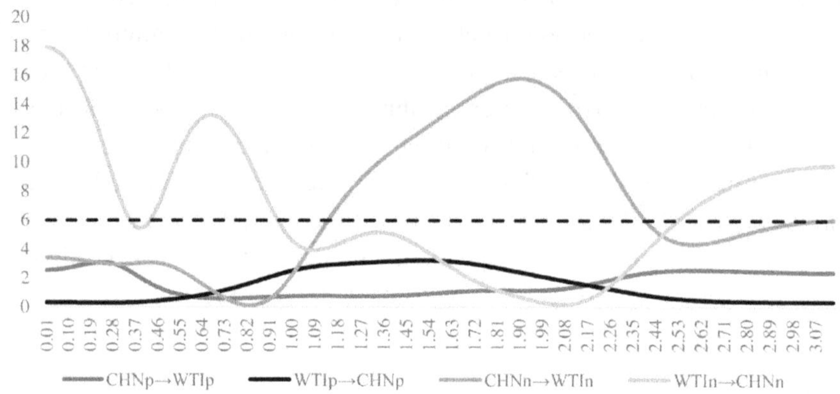

The AIC in the VAR models for the relationship between economic growth and crude oil prices for South Africa and Turkey suggests an optimal lag length of 2. In order to conduct the frequency domain causality test, the optimal lag lengths should be larger than two. Otherwise, the test turns into the conventional Granger causality test. Therefore, the causal relationship between crude oil prices and economic growth for South Africa and Turkey are performed according to the Toda-Yamamoto method.

Table 2. Causality test results for South Africa

Causality Direction	Test Statistics
SA → WTI	2.459
WTI → SA	4.619*
SAp → WTIp	1.071
WTIp → SAp	0.783
SAn → WTIn	6.238**
WTIn → SAn	2.834

Notes: ** and * indicates statistically significant causality relation at 5% and 10% level.

The causality test results for South Africa are presented in Table 2. The results in Table 2 indicate a causality relationship from crude oil price to economic growth. On the other hand, we cannot ascertain a causal link running from economic growth to crude oil price. According to the asymmetric causality test results in Table 2, we only find a causality relationship between economic growth and crude oil price in terms of negative shocks where a decline in economic activity in South Africa causes a decrease in crude oil price.

Table 3. Causality test results for Turkey

Causality Direction	Test Statistics
TUR → WTI	7.129**
WTI → TUR	4.776*
TURp → WTIp	9.082**
WTIp → TURp	0.187
TURn → WTIn	4.353
WTIn → TURn	8.947**

Notes: ** and * indicates statistically significant causality relation at 5% and 10% level.

Finally, the causality test results for Turkey are presented in Table 3. The results in Table 3 suggest a bidirectional causality relationship between economic growth and crude oil prices in Turkey. The asymmetric causality test results indicate an increase in economic activity in Turkey Granger causes an increase in the crude oil price. Also, negative shocks in the crude oil price Granger lead to a decline in economic activity.

Note that in Turkey and South Africa, economic activity Granger causes a decrease in world crude oil price. This does not necessarily suggest that these countries are large enough to wreak havoc in world oil markets. If the economies in South Africa Turkey are sufficiently synchronized with major economies, there will be a causality running from economic activity to crude oil prices in these countries.

CONCLUSION

Fossil fuels still constitute a major component in world energy supply; as such, they play an important role in economic activity. Even though energy sources show variety among sectors, crude oil still occupies a central role in the global economy compared to other energy sources. Hence, oil prices affect several macroeconomic indicators, and the literature has documented a strong correlation between energy prices and economic activity. The relationship particularly holds true for crude oil as changes in oil prices are associated with changes in production costs, and economic activity also generates significant demand for energy and crude oil. This paper examines the relationship between economic activity and crude oil prices using causality tests in the frequency domain and considers the difference between positive and negative changes in both oil prices and economic activity as the relationship can be asymmetric. We present empirical results for major Emerging Economies to include Brazil, Russia, India, China, South Africa, and Turkey. Empirical results indicate that for most countries there is a bidirectional causality between crude oil prices and economic activity, whereas only negative oil price shocks seem to negatively affect economic activity.

These findings have several policy implications, particularly for countries where oil prices have negative effects on economic growth: governments can rely on alternative renewable energy sources such as solar, wind, and other alternative renewable energy sources. Stable oil prices help stabilize production costs and improve investment, production, and employment as well as generate subsequent improvements in economic growth. Governments can also reduce regulatory and tax uncertainties pertaining to the energy sector and seek alternative renewable energy sources where there are potential sources of alternative energy as well as design domestic policies that restrict exchange rate volatility which can amplify domestic energy price volatility. Finally, our results suggest that oil exporters should focus on diversifying their production base and not rely extensively on the oil sector as a major source of revenue.

REFERENCES

Berument, M. H., Ceylan, N. B., & Dogan, N. (2010). The impact of oil price shocks on the economic growth of selected MENA countries. *Energy Journal*, 149–176.

Breitung, J., & Candelon, B. (2006). Testing for short and long-run causality: A frequency domain approach. *Journal of Econometrics*, *132*(2), 363–378. doi:10.1016/j.jeconom.2005.02.004

de Salles, A. A., & Almeida, P. H. A. (2017). The crude oil price influence on the Brazilian industrial production. *Open Journal of Business and Management*, *5*(02), 401–414. doi:10.4236/ojbm.2017.52034

EIA. (2017a). *U.S. Energy Information Administration*. Retrieved from https://www.eia.gov/beta/international/analysis_includes/countries_long/Russia/russia.pdf

EIA. (2017b). *U.S. Energy Information Administration*. Retrieved from https://www.eia.gov/beta/international/analysis_includes/countries_long/Turkey/turkey.pdf

EIA. (2019). *U.S. Energy Information Administration*. Retrieved from https://www.eia.gov/beta/international/analysis_includes/countries_long/Brazil/Brazil_2019.pdf

Gadea, M. D., Gómez-Loscos, A., & Montañés, A. (2016). Oil price and economic growth: A long story? *Econometrics*, *4*(4), 41. doi:10.3390/econometrics4040041

Geweke, J. (1982). Measurement of linear dependence and feedback between multiple time series. *Journal of the American Statistical Association*, *77*(378), 304–324. doi:10.1080/01621459.1982.10477803

Ghalayani, L. (2011). The interaction between oil price and economic growth. *Middle Eastern Finance and Economics*, *13*, 127–141.

Granger, C. W. J. (1969). Investigating causal relations by econometric models and cross-spectral methods. *Econometrica*, *37*(3), 424–438. doi:10.2307/1912791

Granger, C. W. J. (1988). Recent developments in the concept of causality. *Journal of Econometrics*, *37*(1-2), 199–211. doi:10.1016/0304-4076(88)90045-0

Gülay, E., & Pazarlıoğlu, M. V. (2016). The empirical role of real crude oil price and real exchange rate on economic growth: The case of Turkey. *Ege Academic Review*, *16*(4), 627–639.

Hamilton, J. D. (1983). Oil and the macroeconomy since World War II. *Journal of Political Economy*, *91*(2), 228–248. doi:10.1086/261140

Hanabusa, K. (2009). Causality relationship between the price of oil and economic growth in Japan. *Energy Policy*, *37*(5), 1953–1957. doi:10.1016/j.enpol.2009.02.007

Hatemi-J, A. (2012). Asymmetric Causality Tests with an application. *Empirical Economics*, *43*(1), 447–456. doi:10.100700181-011-0484-x

Hosoya, Y. (1991). The decomposition and measurement of the interdependence between second-order stationary process. *Probability Theory and Related Fields*, *88*(4), 429–444. doi:10.1007/BF01192551

Hosoya, Y. (2001). Elimination of third-series effect and defining partial measures of causality. *Journal of Time Series Analysis*, *22*(5), 537–554. doi:10.1111/1467-9892.00240

Khan, G., Kiani, A., & Ahmed, A. M. (2017). Globalization, endogenous oil price shocks and Chinese economic activity. *The Lahore Journal of Economics*, *22*(2), 39–64. doi:10.35536/lje.2017.v22.i2.a2

Lardic, S., & Mignon, V. (2008). Oil prices and economic activity: An asymmetric cointegration approach. *Energy Economics*, *30*(3), 847–855. doi:10.1016/j.eneco.2006.10.010

Moshiri, S. (2015). Asymmetric effects of oil price shocks in oil-exporting countries: The role of institutions. *OPEC Energy Review*, *39*(2), 222–246. doi:10.1111/opec.12050

Rodríguez, J. R., & Sánchez, M. (2005). Oil price shocks and real GDP growth: Empirical evidence for some OECD countries. *Applied Economics*, *37*(2), 201–228. doi:10.1080/0003684042000281561

Sarwar, S., Chen, W., & Waheed, R. (2017). Electricity consumption, oil price and economic growth: Global perspective. *Renewable & Sustainable Energy Reviews*, *76*, 9–18. doi:10.1016/j.rser.2017.03.063

Shahbaz, M., Sarwar, S., Chen, W., & Malik, M. N. (2017). Dynamics of electricity consumption, oil price and economic growth: Global perspective. *Energy Policy*, *108*, 256–270. doi:10.1016/j.enpol.2017.06.006

Syzdykova, A. (2018). The impact of oil prices on BRIC countries' stock markets. *International Journal of Economics. Business and Politics*, *2*(1), 1–20.

Toda, H. Y., & Yamamoto, T. (1995). Statistical inference in vector autoregressions with possibly integrated processes. *Journal of Econometrics*, *66*(1-2), 225–250. doi:10.1016/0304-4076(94)01616-8

Van Eyden, R., Difeto, M., Gupta, R., & Wohar, M. E. (2019). Oil price volatility and economic growth: Evidence from advanced economies using more than a century's data. *Applied Energy*, *233*, 612–621. doi:10.1016/j.apenergy.2018.10.049

Wani, F. A., Kirmani, M. M., & Saif, S. M. (2015). Impact of crude oil on Indian economy. *International Journal of Modern Management Sciences*, *4*(1), 11–26.

Wong, S. L. (2013). Energy consumption and energy in OECD: Perspectives from oil prices and economic growth. *Energy Policy*, *62*, 1581–1590. doi:10.1016/j.enpol.2013.07.025

Yao, F., & Hosoya, Y. (2000). Inference on one-way effect and evidence in Japanese macroeconomic data. *Journal of Econometrics*, *98*(2), 225–255. doi:10.1016/S0304-4076(99)00084-6

Yıldırım, D. Ç., Erdoğan, S., & Çevik, E. M. (2018). Regime-dependent effect of crude oil price on BRICS stock markets. *Emerging Markets Finance & Trade*, *54*(8), 1706–1719. doi:10.1080/1540496X.2018.1427062

KEY TERMS AND DEFINITIONS

Frequency Domain: The analytic space in which mathematical functions or signals are conveyed in terms of frequency, rather than time.

Granger Causality: A way to investigate causality between two variables in a time series. The method is a probabilistic account of causality; it uses empirical data to find patterns of correlation.

OPEC: The Organization of the Petroleum Exporting Countries (OPEC) is an intergovernmental agency of 13 nations, founded on 14 September 1960.

Structural Break: A point in a dataset where there is a divergence or change in the behavior of the data in question.

Unit Roots: A unit root test tests whether a time series variable is non-stationary and possesses a unit root.

Vector Autogression (VAR): A stochastic process model used to capture the linear interdependencies among multiple time series. They generalize the univariate autoregressive model (AR model) by allowing for more than one evolving variable.

ENDNOTES

1 The AIC suggests 3 lags.

2 AIC suggests 6 lags in the VAR model for China.

Chapter 2
Dynamics of the Relation Between Producer and Consumer Price Indices:
A Comparative Analysis in the U.S. Market

Özcan Ceylan
https://orcid.org/0000-0003-2924-2903
Özyeğin University, Turkey

ABSTRACT

The relation between the Producer Prices Index (PPI) and the Consumer Price Index (CPI) in the U.S. is analyzed for two sub-periods: one spanning from 1947 to 1982, the post-war period marked by demand-side economic policies, and the other one starting by 1983 when supply-side policies pioneered by the Reagan government came into effect. As the series in question are found to be cointegrated, a Vector Error Correction Model is employed for the analysis. Regarding the long-run equilibrium relationships, it is found that the loading for the PPI series are statistically significant for both periods, while the loading for the CPI is barely significant for the first period, and it is insignificant at any acceptable level for the second. Thus, the CPI represents the common trend in the system in both periods, but it does more clearly so in the second period.

DOI: 10.4018/978-1-7998-1093-3.ch002

INTRODUCTION

The relationship between the Producer Prices Index (PPI) and the Consumer Price Index (CPI) has long been an essential question for academic and policy-making purposes. Numerous empirical studies have investigated this relationship and identified unidirectional or bidirectional causal relations for different samples.

In early studies for the U.S. market, Colclough and Lange (1982) found a unidirectional causality from CPI to PPI (called Wholesale Price Index at the time) by using Sims and Granger causality tests, while Jones (1986) found a bidirectional causal relationship. Bloomberg and Harris (1995) and Clark (1995) reveal that the PPI does not help to predict the CPI. These empirical results casted doubt on the conventional wisdom according to which there is unidirectional causality running from producer to consumer prices.

The supply-side approach claims that there is a causal relationship from PPI to CPI. This conventional explanation is based on the well-known cost-push mechanism: through the production chain, increases in prices of raw materials and intermediary goods are reflected in the prices of finished goods. The causality from CPI to PPI is explained through a less intuitive mechanism: the demand-side approach refers to the demand-pull effect according to which increased demand for final goods leads to an increase in demand for inputs (Cushing & McGarvey, 1990; Caporale, Katsimi, & Pittis, 2002).

More recent empirical evidence is mixed as the results depend on both the method and the data used. Using Toda and Yamamoto's (1995) causality approach, Caporale, Katsimi and Pittis (2002) found that there is a unidirectional causality from PPI to CPI for the G7 countries for the period of 1976 to 1999. Unidirectional causality from PPI to CPI is also found by Ghazali, Yee, and Muhammed (2008) in their study on the Malaysian economy and by Sidaoui, Capistrán, Chiquiar and Ramos-Francia (2010) for Mexico. Moreover, Liping, Gang, and Jiani (2008) showed that there is a unidirectional causality from CPI to PPI in China.

Vector Autoregressive (VAR) models or Vector Error Correction (VEC) models are employed for these types of analyses where the variables in question are potentially interrelated. For VAR models to be reliable, the series should all be stationary. However, many empirical time-series tend to exhibit time-varying moments. Through differencing, non-stationary series may be transformed into stationary series that are suitable for VAR analysis at the expense of valuable information about long-term dynamics. Instead, cointegration analysis may be conducted to identify long-term stable relationships between variables. Identified cointegration relationships may then be integrated into the VAR model with differenced series to form a VEC model. Through a VEC model, it is possible to analyze not only how the variables react to any innovations but also how the system reverts to the long-run equilibrium after any deviance.

In this chapter, the relationship between the PPI and CPI in the U.S. is analyzed for two sub-periods: one spanning from 1947 to 1982, the post-war period marked by demand-side economic policies, and the other sub-period starting in 1983 when supply-side policies pioneered by the Reagan administration came into effect. The primary purpose of this chapter is principally pedagogical: through the empirical analysis, VAR and VEC models are exhibited, related statistical concepts such as stationarity and cointegration are explained, and econometrical tests that are employed to identify these statistical properties are presented in detail. The comparative analysis employed in this chapter is also expected to enhance the comprehension as it permits to expose how different results lead to different interpretations.

The remainder of the chapter is organized as follows. First, technical and non-technical explanations of VAR and VEC models along with the related statistical concepts are provided. Then, the data used in the empirical analysis are presented. The empirical application section introduces the econometrical tests and methods that are employed to identify the appropriate empirical model. Empirical results are then presented and interpreted.

VAR AND VEC MODELS

VAR and VEC models are widely used to analyze interrelationships between contemporaneous and lagged values of different time series. In these models, changes in each series are explained through an estimated system of lagged values of all the series in the analysis. Thus, this estimated system allows one to isolate the effect of a shock to any of the variables on each of the series through time. For a set of *n* time series variables, the basic VAR model may be represented as follows:

$$X_t = C + A_1 X_{t-1} + A_2 X_{t-2} + \dots A_p X_{t-p} + \varepsilon_t$$

where $X_t = \left(X_{1t}, X_{2t} \dots X_{nt}\right)'$ is the vector of time series variables, $C = \left(C_1, C_2 \dots C_n\right)'$ is a vector of constants, A_i's are (nxn) coefficient matrices, p is the lag order of the model and $\varepsilon_t = (\varepsilon_{1t}, \varepsilon_{2t}, \dots \varepsilon_{nt})'$ is the vector of error terms. ε_t's are assumed to be serially independent stochastic vectors with mean zero and with time-invariant, positive definite covariance matrix, $\varepsilon_t \sim (0, \Sigma_\varepsilon)$.

To assure reliable results, the variables of the model should meet the stationarity condition. Each variable should have constant mean, variance, and autocovariance functions throughout all of the estimation period. In economics and finance, variables are often non-stationary. Thus, the first step for modeling time-series would be to determine if the variables are stationary.

There are two main types of non-stationarity: trend-stationarity and random walk models. Trend-stationary variables vary linearly in time with a constant rate:

$$x_t = \alpha_0 + \alpha_1 t + u_t$$

where u_t is a zero-mean white noise error term, $E(x_t)=\alpha_0+\alpha_1 t$ and $Var(x_t)= Var(u_t)$. Thus, the series has a constant variance around a time-dependent mean which is characterized by a time-trend.

A random walk model may be represented as follows:

$$x_t = \mu + x_{t-1} + u_t$$

where μ is the drift term. The random walk model may be with or without drift. Assuming that at $t=0$, $x_t = x_0$, one can see that

$$x_t = t\mu + x_0 + \sum_{i=1}^{t} u_i$$

and that the shocks in this system never fade away as the coefficient of x_{t-1} is unity. Such a unit-root system has time-dependent mean and variance as $E(x_t)=x_0+\mu_t$ and $Var(x_t)= tVar(u_t)$.

The most popular test employed to determine if a variable is stationary is the Augmented Dickey-Fuller (ADF) test (Dickey & Fuller, 1979). The ADF test is based on the following autoregressive model:

$$\Delta x_t = \alpha_0 + \alpha_1 t + \beta x_{t-1} + \sum_{i=1}^{p-1} \phi_i \Delta x_{t-i} + u_t$$

Depending on the empirical case, α_1 or both α_0 and α_1 may be set to 0 referring to the models with and without constants, respectively. Given these model assumptions, the ADF test evaluates the unit root (non-stationarity) hypothesis, H_0: $\beta=0$, versus stationarity, H_a: $\beta<0$.

A non-stationary random walk series may be rendered stationary through differencing the series. Letting $\Delta x_t = x_t - x_{t-1}$, the first-differenced random walk series will be

$$\Delta x_t = \mu + u_t$$

which is now a stationary series with constant mean and constant variance as u_t is white noise.

A non-stationary series which needs to be differenced *d* times to induce stationarity is said to be integrated of order *d*. For the case above, x_t is integrated of order *1*, and this is generally shown as $x_t \sim I(1)$ or $\Delta x_t \sim I(0)$. When the series in question are integrated, one may then choose to take differences of each of the series until they are all *I(0)* and set a VAR model. Nevertheless, building the analysis on the differenced series only, one may miss important information that may be contained in the levels. A better way to proceed is to check if there is a linear combination of *I(1)* series which results in an *I(0)* series such as

$$z_t = \sum_{i=1}^{n} \gamma_i X_{it}$$

where z_t may also be taken as residual series of a regression where one of the non-stationary variables is regressed on the other(s):

$$X_{1t} = \sum_{i=2}^{n} \beta_i X_{it} + z_t$$

This equation may be rearranged to the following:

$$z_t = \left(1, -\beta_2, -B_3 \ldots - \beta_n\right)\left(X_{1t}, X_{2t}, X_{3t}, \ldots X_{nt}\right)'.$$

One can conclude that there is a cointegrating relationship between the variables if z_t is stationary. The vector β, $\left(1, -\beta_2, -\beta_{3, \ldots} \beta_n\right)'$, would then be called the cointegrating vector.

If a cointegrating relationship exists between series, this would be interpreted that the series move together over time, satisfying the long-run equilibrium defined by cointegrating relationship. Should there be any deviations from this relationship in the short-run, these cointegrating variables would adjust themselves to return to this equilibrium relationship in the long-run. The cointegration relationship, as it is a stationary series, can be added to the VAR model to develop a VEC model:

$$\Delta X_t = C + \alpha\beta' X_{t-1} + A_1 \Delta X_{t-1} + A_2 \Delta X_{t-2} + \ldots A_{p-1} \Delta X_{t-p+1} + \varepsilon_t$$

where α is a vector of coefficients that govern the speed of adjustment of each variable after any deviation from the long-run equilibrium. Thus, cointegrating relation, Π in a VEC model is composed of adjusting parameters and cointegration vectors. For example, for a model with three variables, the cointegrating relation will be

$$\Pi = \alpha\beta' = \begin{pmatrix} \alpha_1 \\ \alpha_2 \\ \alpha_3 \end{pmatrix} \begin{pmatrix} 1 & -\beta_2 & -\beta_3 \end{pmatrix}.$$

There may also be more than one cointegrating vector. For example, a model with three variables and two cointegrating vectors would lead to a cointegrating relation with rank 2.

$$\Pi = \alpha\beta' = \begin{pmatrix} \alpha_{11} & \alpha_{21} \\ \alpha_{12} & \alpha_{22} \\ \alpha_{13} & \alpha_{23} \end{pmatrix} \begin{pmatrix} 1 & -\beta_{12} & -\beta_{13} \\ 1 & -\beta_{22} & -\beta_{23} \end{pmatrix}$$

The rank of Π may be determined using the Johansen test[1]. As there are only two variables in the empirical analysis, PPI and CPI, there may be one cointegrating vector at most. Thus, the Johansen test may not be very useful for this specific application. Even so, the Johansen test will be applied to data, and the main aspects of the test will be briefly illustrated in the empirical application section.

DATA

The U.S. CPI and PPI data are acquired from the U.S. Bureau of Labor Statistics. Data spans from January 1947 through January 2019, containing 865 observations for each series. For the empirical analysis, the data are divided into two sub-periods, one spanning from 1947 to 1982, and the other one from 1983 through 2019. As expected, both series in both sub-periods exhibit an upward trend through time as shown in Figure 1. Based on the graphs, one may easily conclude that both series in both periods are not stationary as it is straightforward that the means of the series are not constant through time within each sub-period. Table 1 provides the descriptive statistics of the data. It may be seen that the PPI is generally slightly higher than the CPI during the first sub-period, whereas the CPI has been clearly higher than the PPI during the second sub-period (the beginning of which corresponds to the implementation of supply-side policies by the Reagan administration.

Figure 1. Time-series plots of PPI (solid line) and CPI (dotted line) for the sub-samples 1947-1982 and 1983-2019

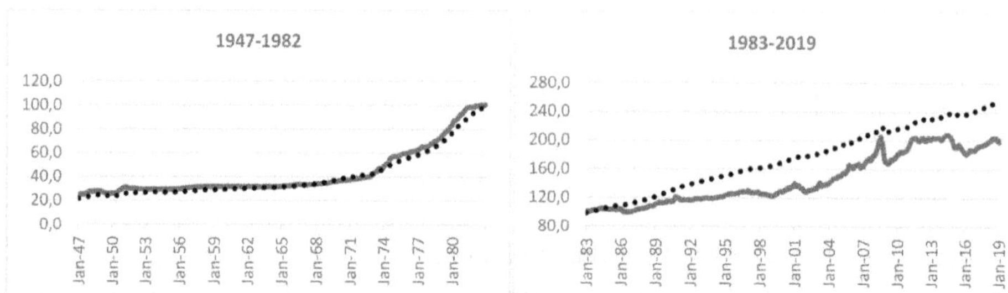

Table 1. Summary statistics of PPI and CPI for the full sample and the sub-samples

	Full Sample		1947-1982		1983-2019	
	PPI	CPI	PPI	CPI	PPI	CPI
# of observations	865	865	433	433	432	432
Mean	94.541	108.245	42.795	40.4	146.168	175.933
Std. Deviation	59.451	76.449	20.671	19.416	35.965	46.017
Skewness	0.3977	0.4053	1.5997	1.5313	0.4147	-0.0186
Excess Kurtosis	-1.1391	-1.304	1.3683	1.3859	-1.3496	-1.2437
Minimum	24.5	21.5	24.5	21.5	99.3	97.8
Quartile 1	31.85	31.2	30.3	26.9	117.4	138
Median	99.9	97.9	31.85	31.2	130.9	175.1
Quartile 3	131.5	175.45	48.63	46.5	183.8	218.01
Maximum	208.3	252.9	100.5	98.2	208.3	252.9

Even if the series clearly follows upward sloping patterns for each sub-sample, it would be wise to employ statistical tests to verify if the series are non-stationary. As stated previously, the ADF test is one of the most popular tests used to check for the stationarity of a series. This test may be performed in R using the package **fUnitRoots**. As an alternative, the DF-GLS test that has been developed by Elliot Rothenberg and Stock (1986) may also be employed to check for the unit-root problem in the series. The DF-GLS test transforms the series via a generalized least squares regression, and it outperforms the ADF test, especially when the series has an unknown mean or trend. The results of these unit-root tests are provided in Table 2.

ADF tests fail to reject the null hypothesis of stationarity for the PPI and CPI series as the p-values are found to be higher than any acceptable significance level. Both series in both sub-periods have unit roots. The next step would be to reveal the level of integration. To do so, the ADF test is applied for the first-differenced series. The results show that the first-differenced PPI and CPI series are stationary, indicating that both the PPI and CPI are *I(1)*.

Table 2. Unit root test results

1947-1982				1983-2019			
Test	**Series**	**p-Value**	**Result**	**Test**	**Series**	**p-Value**	**Result**
ADF	PPI	0.967	Unit root	ADF	PPI	0.500	Unit root
	CPI	0.963	Unit root		CPI	0.935	Unit root
DF-GLS	PPI	>0.10	Unit root	DF-GLS	PPI	>0.10	Unit root
	CPI	>0.10	Unit root		CPI	>0.10	Unit root
ADF	ΔPPI	<0.01	No unit root	ADF	ΔPPI	<0.01	No unit root
	ΔCPI	0.043	No unit root		ΔCPI	0.026	No unit root
DF-GLS	ΔPPI	<0.01	No unit root	DF-GLS	ΔPPI	<0.01	No unit root
	ΔCPI	<0.01	No unit root		ΔCPI	<0.01	No unit root

EMPRICAL APPLICATION

Having identified that both series are integrated of order 1, the series may be checked to determine if they are cointegrated. This step is essential to determine the empirical model. If the series are not cointegrated, a VAR model should be developed using the first-differenced series. The Johansen test may be performed to identify the rank of the cointegration relationship. As the rank of the cointegration relationship is equal to the number of existing cointegrating vectors, a test result which reveals that the cointegration rank is 1 would render a VEC model that contains the cointegration relationship between the variables appropriate.

As the Johansen test is based on a VEC model, one should first identify the VAR order, p, to identify the error correction lag order which will be a necessary input for the Johansen test. In R, there are several packages available for identifying the VAR order. In this study, the **MTS** package is used. R provides four options to determine the VAR order. Three of them are based on the information criteria (AIC, BIC, HQ). In addition, the sequential likelihood ratio test statistics, and their corresponding p-values are provided.

Based on the results, one would have two options to suggest as the VAR order *(p)* for the first sub-period: 14 (based AIC and the sequential ratio test)) and 3 (based on BIC and HQ). Researchers would be free to choose one of these options. In this study, considering that the model variables are macroeconomic variables with possibly longer serial dependencies, the lag order is set at 14 for this first sub-period. The same procedure is followed for the second sub-period, and the VAR order is set at 16. As both series are *I(1)*, the VEC order to be used in the Johansen cointegration tests would be *p-1*. In R, the Johansen test is found in the package **urca.** In this package, several options can be used to set the specifications of the test. The subcommand type allows users to choose how the maximum likelihood ratio test to be used to determine the cointegration rank will be specified. Specifically, the subcommands type="trace" and type="eigen" provide two alternative methods to estimate the test statistics for the cointegration rank tests. The subcommand spec is used to specify the error-correction model. The VEC model given previously may be chosen using the subcommand spec="transitory". As an alternative, the following error correction model may be provided by the subcommand spec="longrun":

$$\Delta X_t = C + A_1 \Delta X_{t-1} + A_2 \Delta X_{t-2} + \dots A_{p-1} \Delta X_{t-p+1} + \alpha\beta' X_{t-p} + \varepsilon_t$$

The constant in the model above may be specified using the subcommands ecdet="none", "const", or "trend."

Table 3 presents the Johansen cointegration test statistics and critical values for the two sub-periods.

Table 3. Johansen cointegration test results

Sub-Period	H_0	Test Statistics	Critical Values		
			10%	5%	1%
1947-1982	$r \leq 1$	2.35	7.52	9.24	12.97
	$r = 0$	27.32	13.75	15.67	20.20
1983-2019	$r \leq 1$	6.07	7.52	9.24	12.97
	$r = 0$	15.75	13.75	15.67	20.20

To determine the cointegration rank, one can compare the critical values that are set for different but commonly used significance levels and the test statistics that are estimated based on eigenvalues. First, the null hypothesis of no cointegration is tested. The test statistic is higher than the 1% critical value for the first sub-period, and it is slightly higher than the 5% critical value for the second. Thus, one can reject the null hypothesis of no cointegration and proceed to test if there is (at most) one cointegration relationship between the variables. The corresponding test statistics are lower than the critical values for all the significance levels. Thus, we can conclude that the cointegration rank is one. As a reminder, the cointegration rank cannot be more than one as there are one only two variables in the empirical model.

The Johansen test also suggests some cointegration vectors. These cointegration vectors are normalized to one of the variables of the model, and as such, they may be used to identify the cointegration relationship. However, when there are only two variables in the model, it would be possible to follow the Engle-Granger two-step approach (Engle & Granger, 1987) to specify alternative cointegration vectors. An example is imposing some theoretical restrictions on the coefficients of the cointegration vectors. The first step in this approach is to estimate the long-run equilibrium equation through a simple bivariate regression:

$$y_t = \delta + \beta x_t + u_t$$

where the OLS residuals, u_t, represent the long-run disequilibrium. If the series of residuals from an OLS regression between two *I(1)* is stationary, one can conclude that the series are cointegrated. As the equation above concerns a long-run relation between non-stationary variables, the residual series may have some serial correlations, and the t-ratios would not be interpretable. Thus, the stationarity of the residuals is the only concern in this step. As explained previously, the ADF test may be employed to check for the stationarity of the residual series. For both sub-periods, the PPI is regressed over the CPI to obtain the residuals. The regression results are estimated as

$$PPI = 1.0159002 * CPI + u_t$$

for first sub-period and

$$PPI = 0.9648337 * CPI + u_t$$

for the second. To check if these equations represent the long-run equilibria, it suffices to test the residual series for stationarity. The ADF test provides p-values of 0.022 and 0.016 for the first and second sub-periods, respectively. The residual series for both sub-periods are stationary. Thus, the estimated regressions represent cointegration relationships.

As the series are found to be cointegrated, the VEC model would be appropriate. Like the VAR models, VEC models may also be estimated using the **MTS** package in R. A necessary input for the estimation would be the expression of the residuals from the estimated cointegration relationships. When this expression is known, the VEC model can be estimated by the least-squares method. To illustrate, the estimated VEC model for the first sub-period may be expressed as follows:

$$\begin{bmatrix} \Delta PPIt \\ \Delta CPI_t \end{bmatrix} = \begin{bmatrix} -0.0145 \\ -0.00391 \end{bmatrix} \left(1 - 1.0159002\right) \begin{bmatrix} PPI_{t-1} \\ CPI_{t-1} \end{bmatrix} + \begin{bmatrix} 0.159 & 0.05475 \\ 0.143 & -0.00237 \end{bmatrix} \begin{bmatrix} \Delta PPI_{t-1} \\ \Delta CPI_{t-1} \end{bmatrix} + \dots$$

$$\dots + \begin{bmatrix} -0.0993 & -0.0991 \\ -0.0577 & 0.0691 \end{bmatrix} \begin{bmatrix} \Delta PPI_{t-13} \\ \Delta CPI_{t-13} \end{bmatrix} + \begin{bmatrix} \varepsilon_{PPIt} \\ \varepsilon_{CPIt} \end{bmatrix}, \Sigma_{\varepsilon} = \frac{1}{10^5} \begin{bmatrix} 3.924669 & -0.8732741 \\ 0.8732741 & 0.9311839 \end{bmatrix}$$

where the first vector on the right-hand side of the equation contains the adjusting parameters, the second vector is the cointegrating vector, the last vector contains the model residuals, and Σ_{ε} is the variance-covariance matrix.

Some of the estimated coefficients are not significant at the commonly used significance levels. Thus, the models may be refined by eliminating these spurious coefficients. However, when certain coefficients are set to zero, this would influence all the estimated coefficients in the model. As VAR and VEC models identify complex time-dependencies between the model variables, refining the model may give rise to significant cross-correlations between the residuals of the model at different lags. Thus, the refinement step should go hand-in-hand with the diagnostic checks. Too much refining, at the 5% or 1% significance levels for example, may lead to issues with the model fit. The Ljung-Box test is widely used to test the randomness of the residuals (Ljung & Box, 1978). Even if there are some significant cross-correlations between the residuals at certain lags, the model may still pass the test as the Ljung-Box test checks the model fit for the overall randomness of model residuals at a specified number of lags.

In this chapter, to obtain a reasonable balance between the model refinement and model fit, the significance level limit for the coefficients is set to 20%. In other words, the model coefficients with t-statistics that are less than 1.282 in modulus are set to 0. Diagnostic checks for the refined models are implemented at the same time, and the threshold t-statistic is used for model refinement only if the models pass the Ljung-Box test.

The Figure 2 shows the results of the Ljung-Box tests applied to the refined models for the first (the graph at the left) and the second (the one at the right) sub-periods. Blue, dotted lines represent the 5% levels, and circles represent p-values of the Ljung-Box tests applied on the residuals of the models. As the p-values of the tests are higher than 5% at all lags, it can be concluded that residuals at different lags are not correlated; thus, the refined models for both sub-periods fit the data well.

Figure 2. Ljung-Box test results for the first (left) and the second (right) sub-periods

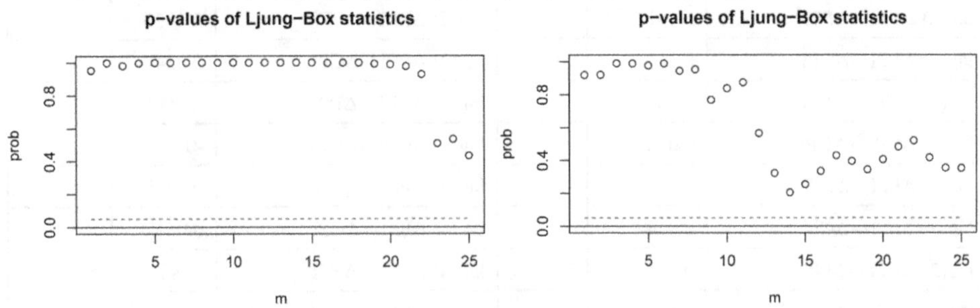

The estimation results of the refined VEC models for the two sub-periods are provided in the Table 4.

In the table, 1%, 5%, and 10% significance levels are shown by ***, **, and * respectively. The remaining coefficients are significant at the 20% significance level. The coefficients α_i are the crucial elements for the cointegration analysis. For instance, α_{PPI}, the adjustment parameter for the PPI, measures how the PPI would adjust to a long-run disequilibrium defined by the residuals of the cointegration equation. For example, the residuals equation of the cointegration relation for the first sub-period was identified as $z_t = PPI - 1.0159002 * CPI$. The long-run disequilibrium, z_t, would be negative (positive) when the PPI is lower (higher) than its equilibrium level, so that the product of $\alpha_{PPI} z_t$ would be positive (negative). Thus, increases in the PPI would be expected in the following periods until the long-run equilibrium is attained. It is important to note that the adjusting parameter for the CPI is very low and only barely significant (at the 20% level) for the first sub-period as well as not significant for the second sub-period. This result shows that the CPI is the main driver for the long-run equilibrium relationship, and the only adjusting variable is the PPI. This is especially true for the second period, where the CPI does not adjust at all after long-run disequilibria. Thus, it can be concluded that there is one-way long-run causality from the CPI to the PPI in the U.S. The remaining coefficients concern the short-run effects of a shock to lagged differenced variables. These transitory effects may be treated in the same manner as in a VAR model.

Table 4. Estimation results for the refined VEC models

1947-1982			1983-2019		
α_{PPI}	-0.0144	**	α_{PPI}	-0.0126	**
α_{CPI}	-0.00406		α_{CPI}	0	
lag(1) ΔPPI→ΔPPI	0.183	***	lag(1) ΔPPI→ΔPPI	0.2724	***
lag(1) ΔPPI→ΔCPI	0.143	***	lag(1) ΔPPI→ΔCPI	0.0662	***
lag(1) ΔCPI→ΔPPI	0		lag(1) ΔCPI→ΔPPI	0.355	
lag(1) ΔCPI→ΔCPI	0		lag(1) ΔCPI→ΔCPI	0.335	***
lag(2) ΔPPI→ΔPPI	0.181	***	lag(2) ΔPPI→ΔPPI	0.135	*
lag(2) ΔPPI→ΔCPI	0.1	***	lag(2) ΔPPI→ΔCPI	0.024	
lag(2) ΔCPI→ΔPPI	0.1833	*	lag(2) ΔCPI→ΔPPI	-0.249	
lag(2) ΔCPI→ΔCPI	0.0962	*	lag(2) ΔCPI→ΔCPI	-0.171	**
lag(3) ΔPPI→ΔPPI	0		lag(3) ΔPPI→ΔPPI	0.1495	**
lag(3) ΔPPI→ΔCPI	0.0344		lag(3) ΔPPI→ΔCPI	0.0327	
lag(3) ΔCPI→ΔPPI	0.181	*	lag(3) ΔCPI→ΔPPI	-0.465	*
lag(3) ΔCPI→ΔCPI	0.11	**	lag(3) ΔCPI→ΔCPI	-0.14	**
lag(4) ΔPPI→ΔPPI	-0.0907	*	lag(4) ΔPPI→ΔPPI	0	
lag(4) ΔPPI→ΔCPI	0		lag(4) ΔPPI→ΔCPI	0	
lag(4) ΔCPI→ΔPPI	0.155		lag(4) ΔCPI→ΔPPI	0.419	**
lag(4) ΔCPI→ΔCPI	0		lag(4) ΔCPI→ΔCPI	0	
lag(5) ΔPPI→ΔPPI	0.0811		lag(5) ΔPPI→ΔPPI	0	
lag(5) ΔPPI→ΔCPI	0.0476	*	lag(5) ΔPPI→ΔCPI	0	
lag(5) ΔCPI→ΔPPI	0		lag(5) ΔCPI→ΔPPI	-0.736	***
lag(5) ΔCPI→ΔCPI	-0.0866	*	lag(5) ΔCPI→ΔCPI	0	
lag(6) ΔPPI→ΔPPI	0.1356	**	lag(6) ΔPPI→ΔPPI	0	
lag(6) ΔPPI→ΔCPI	0.0559	**	lag(6) ΔPPI→ΔCPI	0	
lag(6) ΔCPI→ΔPPI	-0.178	*	lag(6) ΔCPI→ΔPPI	0	
lag(6) ΔCPI→ΔCPI	-0.115	**	lag(6) ΔCPI→ΔCPI	0	
lag(7) ΔPPI→ΔPPI	0		lag(7) ΔPPI→ΔPPI	0	
lag(7) ΔPPI→ΔCPI	0		lag(7) ΔPPI→ΔCPI	0	
lag(7) ΔCPI→ΔPPI	0		lag(7) ΔCPI→ΔPPI	0	
lag(7) ΔCPI→ΔCPI	0		lag(7) ΔCPI→ΔCPI	0.0481	
lag(8) ΔPPI→ΔPPI	0		lag(8) ΔPPI→ΔPPI	0	
lag(8) ΔPPI→ΔCPI	0		lag(8) ΔPPI→ΔCPI	0	
lag(8) ΔCPI→ΔPPI	0.167	*	lag(8) ΔCPI→ΔPPI	0	
lag(8) ΔCPI→ΔCPI	0.158	***	lag(8) ΔCPI→ΔCPI	0	

continues on following page

Table 4. Continued

1947-1982			1983-2019		
lag(9) ΔPPI→ΔPPI	0		lag(9) ΔPPI→ΔPPI	0	
lag(9) ΔPPI→ΔCPI	0		lag(9) ΔPPI→ΔCPI	0	
lag(9) ΔCPI→ΔPPI	0		lag(9) ΔCPI→ΔPPI	0	
lag(9) ΔCPI→ΔCPI	0.192	***	lag(9) ΔCPI→ΔCPI	0	
lag(10) ΔPPI→ΔPPI	-0.0489		lag(10) ΔPPI→ΔPPI	0	
lag(10) ΔPPI→ΔCPI	0		lag(10) ΔPPI→ΔCPI	0	
lag(10) ΔCPI→ΔPPI	0		lag(10) ΔCPI→ΔPPI	0.314	**
lag(10) ΔCPI→ΔCPI	0.116	***	lag(10) ΔCPI→ΔCPI	0.106	**
lag(11) ΔPPI→ΔPPI	0.0837	*	lag(11) ΔPPI→ΔPPI	0.0579	
lag(11) ΔPPI→ΔCPI	-0.0553	**	lag(11) ΔPPI→ΔCPI	0	
lag(11) ΔCPI→ΔPPI	0		lag(11) ΔCPI→ΔPPI	0	
lag(11) ΔCPI→ΔCPI	0.108	**	lag(11) ΔCPI→ΔCPI	0.118	**
lag(12) ΔPPI→ΔPPI	0.142	***	lag(12) ΔPPI→ΔPPI	-0.129	*
lag(12) ΔPPI→ΔCPI	0		lag(12) ΔPPI→ΔCPI	-0.116	***
lag(12) ΔCPI→ΔPPI	-0.219	**	lag(12) ΔCPI→ΔPPI	0.221	
lag(12) ΔCPI→ΔCPI	0		lag(12) ΔCPI→ΔCPI	0.498	***
lag(13) ΔPPI→ΔPPI	-0.1299	***	lag(13) ΔPPI→ΔPPI	0	
lag(13) ΔPPI→ΔCPI	-0.0554	**	lag(13) ΔPPI→ΔCPI	-0.0529	***
lag(13) ΔCPI→ΔPPI	0		lag(13) ΔCPI→ΔPPI	0	
lag(13) ΔCPI→ΔCPI	0.0748		lag(13) ΔCPI→ΔCPI	0	
			lag(14) ΔPPI→ΔPPI	0	
			lag(14) ΔPPI→ΔCPI	0.0514	***
			lag(14) ΔCPI→ΔPPI	0	
			lag(14) ΔCPI→ΔCPI	0	
			lag(15) ΔPPI→ΔPPI	-0.103	
			lag(15) ΔPPI→ΔCPI	0	
			lag(15) ΔCPI→ΔPPI	0.43	*
			lag(15) ΔCPI→ΔCPI	0.133	***

CONCLUSION

In this chapter, the relationship between the CPI and PPI for the U.S. is analyzed for two sub-periods, one ranging from 1947 through 1982, and the other one from 1983 to 2019. These two series are found to be cointegrated which allowed us to study the long-run relationship between these series through a cointegration analysis in a

VEC model. The results show that the CPI is the main driver in this relationship, and this is more clearly so in the more recent period. Based on the estimated adjustment coefficients, it is concluded that after deviations from the long-run equilibrium, the system reverts to the equilibrium through adjusting movements in the level of PPI. Thus, in the long run, there is a one-way causal relationship from the CPI to the PPI for the U.S., especially in the second sub-period.

These empirical results that are related to the long-run adjustment process support the demand side approach for the U.S., especially in the second sub-period of the analysis. The demand-pull mechanism may explain the long-run movements in the producer prices for this period. Demand-pull mechanism is especially effective in fast-growing economies. Abrupt increases in demand for final goods cause upward pressure on input prices. The U.S. economy has experienced a remarkable process of financialization in the second sub-period that starts by 1983 during which lower interest rates, increasing house prices, and financial gains from stock markets have led to important transformations in demand. While the level of disposable income has been increasing, it has also been more sensitive to financial fluctuations. Thus, in this period, it may be expected that the changes in demand and consumer prices have been more closely followed by producers and by monetary authorities and that firms adjust their prices based on the expected consumer prices. In addition, the Federal Reserve sets its target inflation rate based on the price index for personal consumption expenditures, and if backed by a credible monetary policy, these target inflation rates may anchor long-run expectations about inflation as well as provide a basis for wage-setting and determination of markups.

REFERENCES

Blomberg, S. B., & Harris, E. S. (1995). The commodity-consumer price connection: Fact or fable? *Federal Reserve Bank of New York Economic Policy Review, 1*(3), 21–38.

Caporale, G. M., Katsimi, M., & Pittis, N. (2002). Causality links between consumer and producer prices: Some empirical evidence. *Southern Economic Journal, 68*(3), 703–711. doi:10.2307/1061728

Clark, T. E. (1995). Do producer prices lead consumer prices? *Federal Reserve Bank of Kansas City Economic Review,* 25–39.

Colclough, W. G., & Lange, M. D. (1982). Empirical evidence of causality from consumer to wholesale prices. *Journal of Econometrics, 19*(2-3), 379–384. doi:10.1016/0304-4076(82)90012-4

Cushing, M. J., & McGarvey, M. G. (1990). Feedback between wholesale and consumer price inflation: A reexamination of the evidence. *Southern Economic Journal*, *56*(4), 1059–1072. doi:10.2307/1059891

Dickey, D. A., & Fuller, W. A. (1979). Distribution of the estimators for autoregressive time series with a unit root. *Journal of the American Statistical Association*, *74*, 427–431.

Elliott, G., Rothenberg, T. J., & Stock, J. H. (1996). Efficient tests for an autoregressive unit root. *Econometrica*, *64*(4), 813–836. doi:10.2307/2171846

Engle, R., & Granger, C. (1987). Cointegration and error correction: Representation, estimation and testing. *Econometrica*, *55*(2), 251–276. doi:10.2307/1913236

Ghazali, M. F., Yee, O. A., & Muhammed, M. Z. (2008). Do Producer Prices Cause Consumer Prices? Some Empirical Evidence. *International Journal of Business and Management*, *3*(11), 78–82.

Johansen, S. (1991). Estimation and hypothesis testing of cointegration vectors in Gaussian vector autoregressive models. *Econometrica*, *59*(6), 1551–1580. doi:10.2307/2938278

Johansen, S., & Juselius, K. (1990). Maximum likelihood estimation and inference on cointegration - With applications to the demand for money. *Oxford Bulletin of Economics and Statistics*, *52*(2), 169–210. doi:10.1111/j.1468-0084.1990.mp52002003.x

Jones, J. D. (1986). Consumer prices, wholesale prices, and causality. *Empirical Economics*, *11*(1), 41–55. doi:10.1007/BF01978144

Liping, H., Gang, F., & Jiani, H. (2008). CPI vs PPI: Which Drives Which? *Economic Research Journal*, *43*(11), 16–27.

Ljung, G. M., & Box, G. E. P. (1978). On a measure of lack of fit in time series models. *Biometrika*, *65*(2), 297–303. doi:10.1093/biomet/65.2.297

Sidaoui, J., Capistrán, C., Chiquiar, D., & Ramos-Francia, M. (2010). On the predictive content of the PPI on CPI inflation: The case of Mexico. *BIS Papers*, *49*, 249–257.

Toda, H. Y., & Yamamoto, T. (1995). Statistical inference in vector autoregressions with possibly integrated processes. *Journal of Econometrics*, *66*(1-2), 225–250. doi:10.1016/0304-4076(94)01616-8

KEY TERMS AND DEFINITIONS

Adjustment Parameter: A parameter that determines the adjustment speed of a variable when a long-run disequilibrium occurs. It is estimated within a VEC model.

Cointegration: Cointegration is a statistical property about the relationship between a group of integrated series. If there is a linear combination of several $I(d)$ series which results in an $I(b)$ series where $b<d$, the series are cointegrated. For instance, when there are two $I(1)$ series, while a linear combination of these series gives a stationary variable, then there is cointegration. This linear combination is generally normalized to one of the cointegrating variables to define the cointegration relation. The coefficients of the cointegration relation are included in a cointegrating vector.

Long-Run Disequilibrium: Any deviance of a cointegrating variable from the cointegrating relationship.

Order of Integration: The order of integration is a statistic about data indicating the number of unit roots in the series. A series that is integrated of order d is shown as $I(d)$. An $I(2)$ series, for instance, should be differenced twice to obtain a stationary, $I(0)$, series.

Stationarity: An important property in time-series econometrics. A time-series is stationary if it has a constant mean, a finite variance, and a constant auto-covariance structure throughout the sample. If any one of these conditions is not satisfied, the time-series would be non-stationary.

Unit-Root: A form of non-stationarity that can be easily coped with by differencing. Consider for instance a simple autoregressive process, $X_t=\alpha X_{t-1}+u_t$, where u_t is white noise. This equation may be rewritten as $(1-\alpha B)X_t=u_t$, where B is the backshift operator ($BX_t=X_{t-1}$). As u_t is a white noise process with mean 0, this equation has a unique root at $1/\alpha$. Thus, the process would have a unit root when $\alpha=1$. Note that this with unit root series will consist of the cumulative sum of the white noise series which would not be stationary, while the first difference of this series would be equal to the white-noise series, which is clearly stationary.

White Noise: A white noise process is also a stationary series but with additional strict conditions. A white noise series also has constant mean, constant and finite variance, and a constant auto-covariance structure, but the mean should be zero, and there should be no serial autocorrelations in white noise series.

ENDNOTE

1 See, for example, Johansen (1991), Johansen & Juselius (1990) for details.

Chapter 3
Autoregressive Distributed Lag Approach to External Credit and Economic Growth in Nigeria

Oluwasogo Sunday Adediran
Department of Economics and Development Studies, Covenant University, Nigeria

Philip O. Alege
Covenant University, Nigeria

ABSTRACT

The need for increasing external credit flows to boost economic activity has exposed Nigeria to the negative effects of external structural changes. Therefore, an important question of concern in this study is, how does the Nigerian economy grow when there is a decline in external credit? This study attempted to answer this question by comparing the flow of external credit to economic activities. This is a distinction from previous studies that had compared stock of external credit to economic activities. Using annual data covering 36 years for the period 1980-2016, the study adopted the neoclassical growth model and estimated the model using the Autoregressive Distributed Lag (ARDL) approach. The study argued that, to the extent that expenditure is credit financed, GDP should be a function of credit flow, which is new borrowing.

DOI: 10.4018/978-1-7998-1093-3.ch003

INTRODUCTION

The deep domestic economic crises that have ravaged the African economies since the early 1970s created considerable challenges for policymakers and economists. At each turn of events, efforts are being made to design and implement appropriate policy responses to these economic disequilibria. For instance, in the 1970s, the Nigerian economy expanded as a result of an increase in revenue of crude oil, and between 1981 and 1985, at the wake of the falling oil income, the economy declined, giving way to a rapid deterioration of Nigerians' standard of living. The subsequent periods were not too different as the economic implications of the preceding period dragged into the following periods. The various macroeconomic indicators point to the grave economic situations. Particularly, there were sharp fluctuations in the economic activities, chronic fiscal deficit, remarkable fluctuations in the inflation rate, high unemployment rate, consistent growing in size and composition of government spending, and slow growth of the domestic output.

Likewise, given that domestic savings in Nigeria is inadequate to address savings-investment gap, in order to bring about the needed investment for required steady growth, there is the need for increasing external credit flows to boost economic activity, while a decline of it may adversely impact the economic activity. An important question of concern in this study is the following: how does the economy grow when there is adverse external credit shock? This study attempted to answer this question by comparing the different flows of external credit to economic activities in Nigeria. This is a distinction from previous studies that compared stock of external credit to economic activities (see Ogun & Akinlo, 2010; Oluitan, 2012; Emecheta & Ibe, 2014; Fapetu & Obalade, 2015). The study argued that, to the extent that expenditure is credit financed, GDP should be a function of credit flow. The implication is that economic growth should be related to changes in the flow of credit rather than stock of credit. This is not to invalidate the argument that stock of credit is important for output because it determines the level of potential growth in an economy. However, focusing on credit stock misses the developments in the credit flow, which is more useful for understanding the business cycle.

In addition, credit growth in emerging economies is often associated with financial deepening, which is beneficial to long-term economic growth, but it is also related to boom-bust circles and financial crises (Kalema, 2013). As a result, the recent and rapid increase in credit growth witnessed in the last decade in Nigeria is easily traceable to some of the following factors: financial deepening, macroeconomic stability, real income gains, increase in capital inflows, developed monetary policy instruments, and economic growth. These factors explain the strong expansion of credit in Nigeria. While part of this credit expansion is traceable to the process of credit boom in the economy, the resulting evidence can be seen in the vulnerabilities of the economy to both external and internal financially adverse changes. During credit bubbles, lending standards may be loosened, which encourages excessive asset price bubbles and excessive allocation of capital resources to less productive sectors; such a circumstance can trigger financial crisis as evident in the period 2007 - 2009.

Hence, to address the issues raised, this chapter is divided into six sections. Section One is the introduction of the study, and the second section is the literature review. Section Three addresses the theoretical framework, and Section Four examines the model specification and data sources. Section Five focuses on the empirical results and discussion of findings, while Section Six focuses on a summary, policy implications, and a conclusion.

THE LITERATURE REVIEW

The analysis of credit shocks and their impacts have been extensively studied in the literature, with evidences to help stakeholders rightly understand the link between external credit shocks and economic fluctuations. Many organizations and individual researchers have analysed the relationship and the effects of these important variables on one another with the aid of diverse economic models in country specific and panel studies across various regional blocs. In the Nigeria case, although many studies have assessed the relationship between credit shocks and economic growth, different sample periods and choice of variables gave different results. Also, several of these studies did not account for the effect of the external credit shocks which has a major role to play in economic growth. For example, Akpansung and Babalola (2010) examined the relationship between banking sector credits and economic growth in Nigeria with the sample period of 1970 to 2008. A Granger causality test and two-stage least squares techniques were employed to empirically examine this relationship. They find a unidirectional relationship between GDP and private sector credits as well as industrial production index and GDP. Even though the study suggests more credit be allocated to the private sector at a minimal interest rate to enhance economic growth, the study did not consider that an increase in money supply without effective policy initiative could trigger inflation.

Likewise, Oluitan (2012) assesses the impact of real bank credits on real output growth in Nigeria using the econometric techniques of an Ordinary Least square and Granger causality test. He finds that bank credits Granger causes output. The study also finds that capital inflows and imports are linked to credit expansion. Therefore, the study concludes that credits stimulate international trade as well as capital flows into the non-oil sector. Meanwhile, Olokoyo and Ogunnaike (2011) examined the relationship between stock market crisis and Nigeria's economic growth, and the study further examined the interactive influence of movements in the major indicators of the performance of the Nigerian Stock Exchange Market to include: all share index; market capitalization, volume, and value of stock; number of deals; inflation; and total number of new issues on the Nigerian Gross Domestic Product using Ordinary Least Square (OLS) technique with data from 1985 to 2009. Although the result shows that the stock market crisis has a highly significant effect on Nigeria's economic growth, the influence of the external economy was not accounted for in the study, which could have given a broader perspective of the impact of the stock market crisis on the Nigerian economy.

In addition, Yakubu and Affoi (2013) analyzed the impact of commercial bank credits on economic growth in Nigeria using Ordinary Least Square within the period of 1992 to 2012. They discovered that commercial bank credits had a significant effect on economic growth in Nigeria, and therefore, they recommend that better and stronger credit culture be promoted and sustained, among others. Similarly, Balago (2014) examined the relationship between financial sector development and economic growth in Nigeria using time series data from 1990 to 2009 and various econometric techniques. He found that development in financial sector variables like banking sector credits, total market capitalization, and foreign direct investment positively affect economic growth. However, a sample period of less than 30 years was used by both Yakubu and Affoi (2013) and Balago (2014); when not using an ARDL co-integration approach, this might have biased their findings under valid econometrics assumptions.

In the light of the above arguments, it is noted that the theoretical strand through which external credit affects economic growth of developing economies has been studied extensively in the literature, and more studies are still ongoing. Some of the existing studies include: Adediran, George, Alege, and Obasaju (2019); Emecheta and Ibe (2014); Fapetu and Obalade (2015); Giwa, George, Okodua, and Adediran (2020); Léon (2018); Li (2017); Ogun and Akinlo (2010); Olowofeso, Adeleke, and Udoji (2015); and Song and Ryu (2016). However, there is no consistency in the finding of these studies for developing economies as could be found in developed economies (see Aysun (2016); Bernanke and Gertler (1989); Meeks (2009); Gilchrist and Zakrajsek (2012); Kim and Sohn (2017)). Thus, the great recession that followed the last global financial crisis has increased interest in assessing the real effects of changes in external credit. This creates a gap, which generates incentive for more enquiries into the impact of external credit on emerging economies. Therefore, this study seeks to examine the short and long-run effects of flow of external credit on economic growth in Nigeria, which may have important policy implications for designing a stable economic plan for both Nigeria and other proximate economies.

THEORETICAL FRAMEWORK

The study adopts the Neoclassical growth model of the Cobb-Douglas type. This provides the theoretical foundation for the study as it links credit to economic growth. Such specification has earlier been applied by Lucas (1988); Kiyotaki and Moore (1997); and Bernanke, Gertler, and Gilchrist (1998). It is specified as follows:

$$Y_t = A_t, f(K_t^{\alpha_1}, L_t^{\alpha_2}) \tag{3.1}$$

Where Y_t represents output, A_t is the total factor productivity, K_t is capital stock, L_t is the labor input, α_1 and α_2 are the elasticities. Also, equation (1) is further expanded with the addition of external credit and policy variables $(X_t^{\alpha_j})$, to represent factors that enhance productivity:

$$A_t = f(X_t^{\alpha_j}) \tag{3.2}$$

Where A_t is substituted into equation (3.1), we have

$$Y_t = f(K_t^{\alpha_1}, L_t^{\alpha_2}, X_t^{\alpha_i}) \tag{3.3}$$

Following the linearization of equation (3.3), the model representing the impact of external credit on economic growth of Nigeria becomes:

$$\ln rgdp = \alpha_0 + \alpha_1 \ln kap_t + \alpha_2 \ln lfpr_t + \sum_{i=6}^{3} \alpha_i \ln(X_t) + \varepsilon_t \tag{3.4}$$

where $rgdp_t$ is the growth rate of real GDP, kap_t is capital input, $lfpr_t$ is the proxy for labor input, X_i is a row vector, such that $X_t = f(mpr_t, crr_t, tsoc_t, tfoc_t)$. Hence, the variables in the equation (3.4) are described as follows:

1. Real Gross Domestic Products (rgdp): The growth of an economy as measured by growth of real GDP gets the attention of researchers and policymakers for its provision of broader coverage of the economy.
2. Capital input (kap): This is proxied by Gross Fixed Capital Formation. The empirical study of Chandran and Krishnan (2008) emphasizes the relevance of capital input to economic growth. For consistent, long-run growth to occur

in an economy, there is always a need for both government and private sectors to invest more in capital input.

3. Labor Force Participation Rate (lfpr): This is the proxy for labor input. Since the model is a production function, the inclusion of this variable is necessary due to its importance as a factor input in total production, which is GDP.
4. Monetary Policy Rate (mpr): This measures the rate at which the Central Bank lends to the Deposit Money Banks. The monetary policy rate as a proxy for the interest rate is the basic rate upon which other rates revolve in a mixed country like Nigeria and is a proxy rate for short-term interest.
5. Cash Reserve Requirement (crr): This represents a specified minimum fraction of the total deposits of customers, which Deposit Money Banks must hold as reserves, either in cash or as deposits with the Central Bank. It is a credit policy instrument that can play an important role during a global credit crisis, especially for emerging economies like Nigeria.
6. Total stock of external credit (tsoc): This is an important variable for economic output, and it is related to the stock of capital, which in turn determines the level of potential real GDP in an economy. The gap of domestic savings and investment in Nigeria lags, and external inflows of credit play an important role in economic growth. However, focusing basically on credit stock may miss the developments in credit flow, which is important for understanding credit shocks.
7. Total flow of external credit (tfoc): Real GDP growth is expected to be more related to changes in credit flow rather than credit flow. The focus of the study is on changes in credit flow relative to economic activity since the behavior of credit flow can differ from changes in credit stock.

Having described the relationship between external credit shocks and domestic real economic activity in Nigeria in an attempt to capture the objective of the study earlier stated, the study made use of Autoregressive Distributed Lag (ARDL) modeling approach.

MODEL SPECIFICATION

This chapter examines the short and long-run effects of external credit on economic growth in Nigeria, and the study adopted the Autoregressive Distributed Lag (ARDL) approach. This approach is also called the Bounds test as proposed in Pesaran, Shin, and Smith (2001). This cointegration test is more relevant in this context in comparison to Johansen and Juselius (1990) because it does not give a rigid classification of the independent variables to be of the same order of integration.

Following Pesaran *et al.* (2001), the study characterized the production function for the general framework for the ARDL model as:

$$rgdp_t = f(kap_t, lfpr_t, mpr_t, crr_t, tsoc_t, tfoc_t) \quad (4.1)$$

where *rgdp* represents the Nigerian real GDP growth rate, *kap* is capital input, *lfpr* is labor force participation rate, which is labor input, *mpr* is monetary policy rate, *crr* is cash reserve requirement, *tsoc* is total stock of external credit to Nigeria, and *tfoc* represents total flow of external credit to Nigeria. Although analyzing the influence of some other variables such as financial depth, institutional development and human capital could be interesting, quality and reliable data from the World Development Index and the Nigerian Statistical Bulletin on the series of the variables used proved sufficient. Therefore, from the above equation (4.1), the explicit form of the specification can be written as an Autoregressive Distributed Lagged, ARDL [p,q,r,s,v,w,x] model such as:

$$\begin{aligned}\Delta \ln rgdp_t &= a_0 + \sum_{i=0}^{p} a_{1i}\Delta \ln rgdp_{t-i} + \sum_{i=0}^{q} a_{2i}\Delta \ln kap_{t-i} + \sum_{i=0}^{r} a_{3i}\Delta \ln lfpr_{t-i} + \sum_{i=0}^{s} a_{4i}\Delta \ln mpr_{t-i} \\ &+ \sum_{i=0}^{v} a_{5i}\Delta \ln crr_{t-i} + \sum_{i=0}^{w} a_{6i}\Delta \ln tsoc_{t-i} + \sum_{i=0}^{x} a_{7i}\Delta \ln tfoc_{t-i} + c_1 \ln rgdp_{t-i} + c_2 \ln kap_{t-i} \\ &+ c_3 \ln lfpr_{t-i} + c_4 \ln mpr_{t-i} + c_5 \ln crr_{t-i} + c_6 \ln tsoc_{t-i} + c_7 \ln tfoc_{t-i} + \varepsilon_t\end{aligned} \quad (4.2)$$

where Δ is the first difference operator and ln is the natural logarithm of the respective variables in the model. From equation (4.2), it was tested if ln *rgdp* is co-moving with the regressors. In the ARDL model, the study tested if real GDP growth rate is co-moving with the regressors. To test for the absence of a long-run relationship between ln *rgdp* and the regressors, the study restricted the coefficients of c_1, c_2, c_3, c_4, c_5, c_6, and c_7 to be zero against the alternative by conducting a restricted F-test. Therefore, the null and alternative hypotheses are as follows:

H_0: $c_1=c_2=c_3=c_4=c_5=c_6=c_7=0$

(no long-run relationship between ln *rgdp* and the regressors)

H_1: $c_1 \neq c_2 \neq c_3 \neq c_4 \neq c_5 \neq c_6 \neq c_7 \neq 0$

(there is long-run relationship between ln *rgdp* and the regressors)

Drawing from Pesaran et al. (2001), the asymptotic distribution of the test statistics is non-standard irrespective of whether the variables are integrated of order

(0) or integrated of order (1). As a result, they computed two sets of asymptotic critical values where the first sets assume variables to be I (0) and the other I (1) which are regarded as lower bounds (LCB) and upper bounds (UCB) critical values, respectively. Decisions on whether or not cointegration exists between ln *rgdp* and its regressors were then made as consistent with the literature and based on the following: Computed F-statistics > UCB: Reject the null hypothesis; Computed F-statistics < LCB: Fail to reject the null hypothesis and Computed F-statistics value between LCB and UCB: Results are inconclusive (Chandran & Krishnan, 2008).

In the study, there was evidence of cointegration among the variables, and then, ln *rgdp* and its regressors have a stable long-run relationship. As a result, the study used the two-step strategy of the ARDL approach as proposed in Pesaran and Shin (1997) to estimate the long and short-run coefficients (elasticities) of the specified model. Hence, the long-run estimation follows this ARDL [p,q,r,s,v,ww,x] model:

$$\ln rgdp_t = a_0 + \sum_{i=0}^{p} a_{1i} \ln rgdp_{t-i} + \sum_{i=0}^{q} a_{2i} \ln kap_{t-i} + \sum_{i=0}^{r} a_{3i} \ln lfpr_{t-i} + \sum_{i=0}^{s} a_{4i} \ln mpr_{t-i} + \sum_{i=0}^{v} a_{5i} \ln crr_{t-i} + \sum_{i=0}^{w} a_{6i} \ln tsoc_{t-i} + \sum_{i=0}^{x} a_{7i} \ln tfoc_{t-i} + \delta_t \tag{4.3}$$

Constructing an Error Correction Mechanism (ECM) of the above equation to derive the short-run elasticities:

$$\Delta \ln rgdp_t = a_0 + \sum_{i=0}^{p} a_{1i} \Delta \ln rgdp_{t-i} + \sum_{i=0}^{q} a_{2i} \Delta \ln kap_{t-i} + \sum_{i=0}^{r} a_{3i} \Delta \ln lfpr_{t-i} + \sum_{i=0}^{s} a_{4i} \Delta \ln mpr_{t-i} + \sum_{i=0}^{v} a_{5i} \Delta \ln crr_{t-i} + \sum_{i=0}^{w} a_{6i} \Delta \ln tsoc_{t-i} + \sum_{i=0}^{x} a_{7i} \Delta \ln tfoc_{t-i} + \psi ECM_{t-i} + \lambda_t \tag{4.4}$$

Where the b`s are the elasticities relating to the short-run dynamics of the convergence to equilibrium, and ψ is the measure of the speed of adjustment. To estimate the model, the study used different lag lengths. To avoid the loss of degree of freedom, the maximum selection of lag did not exceed three. The Akaike Information Criterion (AIC) was used to choose the appropriate lag length for the ARDL model.

DATA SOURCES

The data employed for this study were annual data from 1980 to 2015 sourced from the World Development Indicator (WDI) database, International Financial Statistics by International Monetary Funds (IMF), and The Statistical Bulletin by Central Bank of Nigeria (CBN). These data were analyzed using E-views 9.0 and Stata 12

EMPRICAL RESULTS AND DISCUSSION OF FINDINGS

The summary statistics of the variables used for analyses are presented in Table 1. It outlines several properties of the variables used in the estimation processes. These properties include the mean, standard deviation, minimum, maximum, variance, skewness, kurtosis, and Jarque Bera statistics. The values taken by the last three statistics (skewness, kurtosis, and Jarque Bera statistics) are imperative in ascertaining the symmetric assumption of the series distribution. A critical observation reveals that external credit volatility tends to be extreme in Nigeria. Therefore, it is likely that the excess volatility exposes Nigeria to more external risks. Consequently, all variables exhibit a normal distribution as the alternate hypothesis of non-normality could not be accepted. The Jarque Bera test is a goodness-of-fit measure of departure from normality based on sample kurtosis and skewness and calculated as

$$JB = n.\left[\frac{s^2}{6} + \frac{\left(EK\right)^2}{24}\right]$$

with the H_0: normal distribution and H_1: non-normal distribution. A normal distribution is indicated by skewness of zero and excess kurtosis of zero (kurtosis of 3). The value obtained for skewness and kurtosis in each of the variables is largely between zero and three, respectively. This implies a normal distribution, which is similarly supported by the Jarque Bera statistics, as it failed to accept the alternative hypothesis.

Furthermore, the estimation procedure began by conducting a unit root test on the variables in the model. This enabled us to examine the time series property of the variables. Although there are several ways of testing for the presence of a unit root as proposed in macroeconomic literature, the study adopted the Phillips-Perron (PP) test. The PP test is sensitive to the structural change in the mean of a stationary variable which is captured in the test in order to avoid bias in the usual unit root test towards non-rejection of the null of unit root (Phillips & Perron, 1988). Using the PP method, all the series became stationary at first difference I (1) as the series were not all stationary at level I (0). Table 2 presents the summary of PP unit root test of the series. The results shows that not all the variables were stationary at levels since the absolute values of the PP test did not exceed the critical value at the 5 percent level of significance except for *ltfoc, lcrr* and *lrdgp*, but same became

Table 1. Summary statistics of variables

Variable	Measurement	Obs	Mean	Std. Dev	Min	Max	Skewness	Kurtosis	Jarque Bera	Prob*
ltsoc	Million $US	36	23.8519	0.413301	22.9136	24.40959	-0.765019	2.385626	4.077711	0.130180
Ltfoc	Million $US	36	1.32361	1.83211	-3.04736	3.840890	-0.649551	2.427430	3.023251	0.220551
Lmpr	Percentage	35	2.51048	0.33766	1.79176	3.258097	-0.339980	3.060666	0.679620	0.711906
Lcrr	Percentage	36	3.81572	0.21182	3.37074	4.175925	-0.167577	2.566343	0.450579	0.798285
Lkap	Million $US	35	23.9327	0.58476	23.2001	24.97741	0.607151	1.818302	4.186789	0.123268
Llfpr	Million person	35	4.02642	0.01112	4.00321	4.042420	-0.363228	2.149578	1.824310	0.401658
Lrgdp	Percentage	35	10.1944	0.51995	9.53092	11.14221	0.492623	1.862178	3.303633	0.191701

Source: Authors` computation using stata 12.0

Note: Measure represents Measurement

Table 2. Unit root @ 5 percent level of significance with constant

Variable	Log Level				Log First Difference			
	PP Observed Values	**PP Critical Values**	**Order of Integration**	**Remark**	**PP Observed Values**	**PP Critical Values**	**Order of Integration**	**Remark**
Legdp	-0.714	-12.820	I(0)	Non-Stat.	-21.039	-12.788	**Stationary**	**I(1)**
Ltsoc	-8.529	-12.820	I(0)	Non-Stat.	-24.989	-12.788	**Stationary**	**I(1)**
Ltfoc	-23.669	-12.500	**I(0)**	**Stationary**	-	-	-	-
Lmpr	-11.367	-12.788	I(0)	Non-Stat.	-38.346	-12.756	**Stationary**	**I(1)**
Lcrr	-19.442	-12.820	**I(0)**	**Stationary**	-	-	-	-
Lrer	-2.0875	-2.9484	I(0)	Non-Stat.	-4.3122	-2.9511	**Stationary**	**I(1)**
Lkap	-3.569	-12.788	I(0)	Non-Stat.	-22.844	-12.756	**Stationary**	**I(1)**
Llfpr	-5.214	-12.788	I(0)	Non-Stat.	-24.100	-12.756	**Stationary**	**I(1)**
Lrgdp	-14.186	-12.500	**I(0)**	**Stationary**	-	-	-	-

Note: The optimal lag length was chosen using Newey-West (1994) automatic lag selection, and Non-Stat. = Non-Stationary

Source: Authors` computation using Stata 12.0

stationary at first differencing, which is the main procedure for using Autoregressive Distributed Lag (ARDL).

Having conducted the unit root test as indicated in the previous sub-section, the study rests on the assumption that the variables are I (0) and I(1) as indicated in Table 2. Hence, in order to estimate the bounds test model, an appropriate maximum lag length of 2 was chosen to avoid loss of degree of freedom. The lag length was chosen using Akaike Information Criterion (AIC). Based on the bounds test result in Table 3, the computed F-statistic of 7.22 exceeds the upper-bound critical value of 3.61 at the 5 percent significance level. This indicates the rejection of the null hypothesis of no cointegration between *lrgdp* and the regressors. This established the fact that there is a strong indication that *lkap, llfpr, lmpr, lcrr, ltsoc* and *ltfoc* serve as the long-run forcing variables in explaining the growth of the Nigerian economy.

Table 3. Cointegration test based on bounds test

Test Statistic	Value	K
F-statistic	7.221392	6
	Critical Value Bounds	
Significance	**I0 Bound**	**I1 Bound**
10%	2.12	3.23
5%	2.45	3.61
2.5%	2.75	3.99
1%	3.15	4.43

Source: Authors` computation using E-views 9

Table 4 shows the estimated long-run coefficients for Autoregressive Distributed Lag (ARDL) model. In the long run, capital input (KAP) at 10.33 t-Statistic value, was found to have a positive value on the economic output of Nigeria. This higher contribution of capital attests to the fact that both the government and the private sectors are now investing in modern technology and infrastructure to improve productivity. Likewise, the labor force participation rate (LFPR), which is used to measure labor input, has a significant negative impact on the economic output with a value of -3.70 at the 5 percent level of significance. This explains that in the long run, additional labor input may not be enhancing economic growth because of the lack of skills, low productivity, and introduction of modern technology to the economy.

On the other hand, the monetary policy rate (MPR) was found to be positively related to economic growth, but it is not statistically significant. Meanwhile, the cash reserve requirement (CRR) is negative and statistically insignificant at -1.87.

Table 4. Estimated Long Run Coefficients @ 5 percent level of significance

Variable	Coefficient	Std. Error	t-Statistic	Prob.
LOG(KAP)	1.117323	0.108196	10.326848	0.0000
LOG(LFPR)	-64.719322	17.450040	-3.708835	0.0100
LOG(LMPR)	0.078795	0.883909	0.089144	0.9319
LOG(CRR)	-0.591486	0.315713	-1.873493	0.1101
LOG(TSOC)	0.975861	0.360047	2.710374	0.0351
LOG(TFOC)	-0.490972	0.155810	-3.151087	0.0198
C	224.159264	65.074763	3.444642	0.0137

Source: Authors` computation using E-views 9

This explains the weakness of the policy framework of the monetary authority in stabilizing the economy. A good illustration is when the Nigerian monetary authority failed to prevent the adverse effect of the last global financial crisis (2007-2009) on time. This experience exposed the Nigerian economy into the lagged effects of the global financial crisis, which almost crippled the financial system. The contribution of total stock of external credit (TSOC) towards economic growth is positive and statistically significant at the 5 percent level of significance. This is unlike total flow of external credit (TFOC), which has a negative impact on economic output, but was statistically significant. This could be a result of the inability of the economy to channel credit inflow to the productive sector, while unnecessary accumulation of credit inflow may not benefit the economy in the long run.

Table 5 shows the short-run dynamics and the adjustment towards the equilibrium at the long-run. The specification shows a good fit with the R^2 of 0.967, which suggests that 97 percent of the variation in economic growth is being explained by the regressors. As a whole, capital (KAP), labor (LFPR), and total stock of credit (TSOC) are positive and have a statistically significant (at the 10, 5, and 5 percent levels, respectively) impact on economic growth. On the other hand, cash reserve requirement (CRR) and total flow of credit (TFOC) are statistically significant and negative at 2.86 and 4.37, respectively. As expected, the lagged terms of LFPR (2.26), CRR (2.19), and TFOC (2.61) are all positive and statistically significant at the 5 percent level of significance in the short run. This is unlike TSOC (1.57) which is positive but not statistically significant. While KAP and MPR are negative

Table 5. Autoregressive distributed lag (ARDL) – ECM

Variable	Coefficient	Std. Error	t-Statistic	Prob.
DLOG(RGDP(-1))	-0.529857	0.223132	-2.374637	0.0552
DLOG(RGDP(-2))	-0.389578	0.179828	-2.166392	0.0734
DLOG(KAP)	0.077508	0.041338	1.874994	0.1099
DLOG(KAP(-1))	0.046005	0.033796	1.361257	0.2223
DLOG(KAP(-2))	-0.111478	0.042964	-2.594678	0.0410
DLOG(LFPR)	3.299557	1.296022	2.545912	0.0437
DLOG(LFPR(-1))	4.556530	2.015643	2.260584	0.0645
DLOG(LMPR)	-0.017426	0.049759	-0.350205	0.7382
DLOG(LMPR(-1))	0.125397	0.064866	1.933163	0.1014
DLOG(LMPR(-2))	-0.128049	0.052638	-2.432619	0.0510
DLOG(CRR)	-0.120602	0.042981	-2.805908	0.0309
DLOG(CRR(-1))	-0.054696	0.024652	-2.218691	0.0683
DLOG(CRR(-2))	0.049811	0.022764	2.188153	0.0713
DLOG(TSOC)	0.127117	0.027112	4.688589	0.0034
DLOG(TSOC(-1))	0.055343	0.035268	1.569213	0.1676
DLOG(TFOC)	-0.013196	0.003019	-4.370914	0.0047
DLOG(TFOC(-1))	0.014597	0.005797	2.517872	0.0454
DLOG(TFOC(-2))	0.014740	0.005642	2.612487	0.0400
Ecm_{t-1}	-0.231089	0.038895	-3.370314	0.0150
Ecm_{t-1} = LOG(RGDP) - (1.1173*LOG(KAP) -64.7193*LOG(LFPR) + 0.0788 *LOG(LMPR) -0.5915*LOG(CRR) + 0.9759*LOG(TSOC) -0.4910 *LOG(TFOC) + 224.1593)				
R-squared 0.967320 Mean dependent var 0.050193 Adjusted R-squared 0.831152 S.D. dependent var 0.035574 S.E. of regression 0.014618 Akaike info criterion -5.662151 Sum squared resid 0.001282 Schwarz criterion -4.471240 Log likelihood 116.5944 Hannan-Quinn criter. -5.267398 F-statistic 7.103872 Durbin-Watson stat 2.248597 Prob(F-statistic) 0.010728				

Source: Authors` computation using E-views 9

with -2.59 and -2.43, respectively, they have a statistically significant impact on economic growth. This further explains that capital and monetary policy normally responds slowly to the Nigerian economic growth in the short run.

The statistical significance of the ECM at -0. 23 confirms the presence of long-run equilibrium between economic growth and the independent variables, namely KAP, LFPR, LMPR, CRR, TSOC, and TFOC. This also confirms the previous ARDL cointegration analysis results. It is discovered that the ECM value is between 0 and -1 and is statistically significant at the 5 percent level of significance. This implies that the error correction mechanism converges to the equilibrium path slowly.

SUMMARY

Based on empirical analysis of the study with the Bounds test approach, it is found that both stock of external credit and flow of external credit play important roles in the Nigerian economic growth. As a result, the structural economic changes in the associated external economies could alter economic growth in Nigeria. For instance, the contribution of total stock of external credit (TSOC) towards economic growth is positive and statistically significant at the 5 percent level of significance. This is unlike the total flow of external credit (TFOC), which has a negative impact on economic output but was statistically significant. This could be a result of the inability of the economy to channel credit inflow to the productive sector, while unnecessary accumulation of credit inflow may not benefit the economy in the long run.

On the other hand, total flow of credit (TFOC) is statistically significant at the 5 percent level of significance in the short run, unlike TSOC which is positive but not statistically significant. This further explains that stock of external credit is always an important variable, whereas flow of external credit is more relevant during the period of economic crisis in the short run. This is because flow of external credit is more correlated with economic growth in Nigeria.

POLICY IMPLICATIONS AND CONCLUSION

The short and long-run effects of external credit on economic growth in Nigeria have been examined. The empirical results show that in the short run, external flow of credit is more significant to growth in the Nigerian economy, while stock of external credit is more significant in growing the economy in the long run. Therefore, the policy direction for Nigeria is that, to the extent that expenditure is credit financed,

GDP should be a function of credit flow (new borrowings) in the short run. The implication is that economic growth should be more related to changes in the flow of credit rather than stock of credit in the period of economic crisis.

ACKNOWLEDGMENT

The authors acknowledge the sponsorship contribution of this publication by the Centre for Research, Innovation and Development (CUCRID) and Centre for Economic Policy and Development Research (CEPDeR), Covenant University, Ota, Nigeria.

REFERENCES

Adediran, O., George, O., Alege, P., & Obasaju, O. (2019). Is there any relationship between monetary policy tools and external credit-growth nexus in Nigeria? *Cogent Economics & Finance*, *7*(1625100), 1–14.

Akinboade, O. A., & Makina, D. (2010). Econometric analysis of bank lending and business cycles in South Africa. *Applied Economics*, *42*(29), 3803–3811.

Akpansung, A., & Babalola, S. (2010). Banking sector credit and economic growth in Nigeria: An empirical investigation. *CBN Journal of Applied Statistics*, *2*(2), 51–62.

Aysun, U. (2016). Bank size and macroeconomic shock transmission: Does the credit channel operate through large or small banks? *Journal of International Money and Finance*, *65*, 117–139.

Balago, G. S. (2014). Financial sector development and economic growth in Nigeria: An empirical investigation. *International Journal of Finance and Accounting*, *3*(4), 253–265.

Bernanke, B., & Gertler, M. (1989). Agency costs, net worth and business fluctuations. *The American Economic Review*, *79*, 14–31.

Bernanke, B., Gertler, M., & Gilchrist. (1998). The financial accelerator in a quantitative business cycle framework in handbook of macroeconomics. *Handbooks in Economics, 15,* 1341-93.

Chandran, V. G., & Krishnan, G. (2008). Foreign direct investment and manufacturing growth: The Malaysian experience. *International Business Research*, *1*(3), 83–90.

Emecheta, B. C., & Ibe, R. C. (2014). Impact of bank credit on economic growth in Nigeria: Application of reduced vector autoregressive (VAR) Approach. *European Journal of Accounting. Auditing and Finance Research*, *2*(9), 11–21.

Fapetu, O., & Obalade, A. (2015). Sectoral allocation of banks' credit and economic growth in Nigeria. *International Journal of Academic Research in Business and Social Sciences*, *5*(6), 161–169.

Gilchrist, S., & Zakrajsek, E. (2012). Credit spreads and business cycle fluctuations. *The American Economic Review*, *102*(4), 1692–1720.

Giwa, B., George, E., Okodua, A., & Adediran, O. (2020). Empirical analysis of the effects of foreign direct investment inflows on Nigerian real economic growth: Implications for Sustainable Development Goal-17. *Cogent Social Sciences*, *6*(1), 1–11.

Johansen, S., & Juselius, K. (1990). Maximum likelihood estimation and inference on co-integration with applications to the demand for money. *Oxford Bulletin of Economics and Statistics*, *52*, 169–210.

Kalema, V. (2013). Managing the Downside Risks of Surging Capital Flows on Financial Stability for Sub-Saharan African Countries. *CBN Economic and Financial Review*, *15*(14), 129–143.

Kim, D., & Sohn, W. (2017). The effect of bank capital on lending: Does liquidity matter? *Journal of Banking & Finance*, *77*, 95–107.

Kiyotaki, N., & Moore, J. (1997). Credit cycles. *Journal of Political Economy*, *105*(2), 211–248.

Léon, F. (2018). Convergence of credit structure around the world. *Economic Modelling*, *68*, 306–317.

Li, Y. A. (2017). (forthcoming). Credit constraints and firm productivity: Macroeconomic evidence from China. *Research in International Business and Finance*. Advance online publication. doi:10.1016/j.ribaf.2017.07.142

Lucas, R. E. (1988). On mechanics of development. *Journal of Monetary Economics*, *22*, 3–42.

Meeks, R. (2009). *Credit shocks: Evidence from corporate spreads and defaults*. Working Paper 0906, Federal Reserve Bank of Dallas.

Newey, W., & West, K. (1994). Automatic lag selection in covariance matrix estimation. *The Review of Economic Studies*, *61*(4), 335–653.

Ogun, T. P., & Akinlo, A. E. (2010). The Effectiveness of Bank Credit Channel of Monetary Policy Transmission: The Nigerian Experience. *African Economic and Business Review*, *8*(2), 15–29.

Olokoyo, F. O., & Ogunnaike, O. O. (2011). An empirical analysis of the effect of stock market crisis on economic growth: The Nigerian Case. *Acta Universitatis Danubius*, *7*(2), 172–186.

Olowofeso, E., Adeleke, A., & Udoji, A. (2015). Impact of private sector credit on economic growth in Nigeria. *CBN Journal of Applied Statistics*, *6*(2), 81–101.

Oluitan, R. O. (2012). Bank credit and economic growth: Evidence from Nigeria. *Journal of International Business and Management*, *5*(2), 1–9.

Pesaran, M. H., & Shin, Y. (1997). An Autogressive Distributed Lag Modelling Approach to Cointegration Analysis. In S. Strom, A. Holly, & P. Diamond (Eds.), *Centennial Volume of Ragnar Frisch, Econometric Society Monograph*. Cambridge University Press. http: //www.econ.cam.ac.uk/faculty/pesaran

Pesaran, M. H., Shin, Y., & Smith, R. J. (2001). Bounds testing approach to the analysis of level relationships. *Journal of Applied Econometrics*, *16*(3), 289–326.

Phillips, P., & Perron, P. (1988). Testing for a unit root in time series regression. *Biometrika*, *75*(2), 335–346.

Song, J., & Ryu, D. (2016). Credit cycle and balancing the capital gap: Evidence from Korea. *Economic Systems*, *40*, 595–611.

Yakubu, Z., & Affoi, A. Y. (2013). An analysis of commercial banks' credit on economic growth in Nigeria. *Current Research Journal of Economic Theory*, *6*(2), 11–15.

KEY TERMS AND DEFINITIONS

Autoregressive Distributed Lag (ARDL): Are standard least squares regressions that include lags of both the dependent variable and explanatory variables as regressors. It is a method of examining cointegrating relationships between variables.

Economic Growth: An increase in the production of economic goods and services, compared from one period of time to another. It can be measured in nominal or real (adjusted for inflation) terms.

Emerging Market Economies: This is economy of a developing nation that is becoming more engaged with global markets as it continues to grow.

External Credit: It refers to money borrowed from a source outside the country.

Neoclassical Growth Model: This model shows how a steady economic growth rate that results from a combination of three driving forces: labor, capital, and technology. The theory also argues that technological change has a major influence on an economy, and economic growth cannot continue without technological advances.

Chapter 4
Macroeconomic Suprises and the Turkish Financial Market

Ayşegül İşcanoğlu Çekiç
https://orcid.org/0000-0002-3157-4635
Trakya University, Turkey

Havva Gültekin
https://orcid.org/0000-0002-3157-4635
Trakya University, Turkey

ABSTRACT

In the study, the authors investigate the impacts of macroeconomic news originating from Turkey, US, Euro Zone, and China on the Turkish financial market. They consider Purchasing Managers Indices and Gross Domestic Product growth rates as macroeconomic news. The study covers the period from May 4, 2015 to January 1, 2019, and six sectoral indices are included into the analysis. The findings show that impacts of macroeconomic surprises on abnormal returns are significant for all the sectors except Holdings and Investments and Insurance. The authors also provide evidence that the impacts of macroeconomic surprises on volatilities are significant for only Holdings and Investments and Technology.

INTRODUCTION

During the last few decades, scientific research studies concerning the impact of macroeconomic news on financial markets have increased significantly. Macroeconomic news provides information about economic strength and growth of a country for both economists and investors. Therefore, it is expected that this news

DOI: 10.4018/978-1-7998-1093-3.ch004

will have an impact on both local and international markets. Many empirical studies also show that the macroeconomic news has an impact on financial markets, and they further provide evidence for the existence of this impact. In particular, after the increase in globalization, emerging markets may be affected not only by the local macroeconomic news but also by the macroeconomic news of developed foreign countries. The traditional approach is to consider the macroeconomic variables as external factors in Arbitrage Pricing Theory (APT) (Ross, 1976). In this context, the effects of the macroeconomic news such as money supply, consumer price index (CPI), producer price index (PPI), employment and unemployment rates, growth rates, industrialization, foreign market indexes, inflation, interest rates, exchange rates, and risk premiums, among other factors, have been investigated by various researchers. Examples include Fama (1981, 1990), Pearce and Roley (1983), Fama and French (1989), Schwert (1990a), Ferson and Harvey (1991), McQueen and Roley (1993), Rigobon and Sack (2002), Wongswan (2006), Kim and Nguyen (2008, 2009), and Albuquerque and Vega (2009). These studies mainly focus on the effect of the macroeconomic news on the first moment (i.e., the return). On the other hand, recent studies focus not only on the first moment but also on the second moment, namely the volatility. The first study which examines the impact of macroeconomic news on volatility is conducted by Ederington and Lee (1993). Following these studies, Kim et al. (2004), Wongswan (2006), Andersen et al. (2007), Hanousek et al. (2009), Nowak et al. (2011), Korkmaz et al. (2012), Yi et al. (2013), Huang (2018), and Wang and Yang (2018) investigate the impact of macroeconomic news on the financial markets within a larger framework.

In this study, the impact of macroeconomic news[1] on the Turkish stock market's returns and volatility is investigated empirically. For this purpose, the BIST100 index and six sectoral indices of financial and technology companies are considered. These sectoral indices include the BIST Banks, the BIST Information Technology, the BIST Real Estate Invest Trusts, the BIST Holdings & Investments, the BIST Insurance, and finally, the BIST Technology. A comprehensive analysis of the daily stock market data, which covers the period from May 04, 2015 to January 01, 2019, is performed. In the analysis, the domestic effect within Turkey and the foreign country effects of the US, the Euro-Zone, and China on the Turkish financial market are discussed. As macroeconomic indicators, the Purchasing Managers Indices (PMI) and Gross Domestic Products (GDP) growth rates are considered. The motivation behind selecting these indicators hinges on the fact that these indicators provide a realistic insight about the future economic conditions of a country. The PMI is calculated by using the data collected from industrial surveys and indicates the attitude of purchasing managers towards economic developments. On the other hand, the GDP growth rate is a periodic measure of economic growth which is announced once per quarter. Since the GDP is announced quarterly, PMI is the primary indicator of economic strength in many countries.

Today, the productions of most developing countries such as Turkey depend on imported raw materials (Erdoğan & Acet, 2016). In the last decade, Turkey has imported mostly from Russia, China, and Germany, respectively. They are followed by US (United States of America) (TUIK, 2019). Therefore, any unexpected news from these counterparties may result in a depreciation in Turkey's economy. For example, in July 2018, Turkish money depreciated by 35% in 47 days because of a trade war between US and Turkey (Mansour-Ichrakieh & Zeaiter, 2019). Moreover, the US, the Euro-Zone, and China have the largest share of GDP among the world economies, and thus, these economies have the leading role in the world. Therefore, in this study, the PMI and the GDP growth rates of the US, the Euro-Zone, and China are also considered as the macroeconomic news.

This study contributes to the existing literature in various ways. First, this study contributes to the existent literature by considering the Turkish financial market on a sectoral basis. This study is important to emphasize the existence of different responses to the macroeconomic news announcement from different sectors. In addition, to the best of the authors' knowledge, the impact of the PMI news on return and conditional volatility of the Turkish financial markets on a sectoral basis has not yet been investigated. In this sense, this study fills this gap in the literature. Finally, the impact of macroeconomic news on both domestic and international levels is considered.

The chapter is organized as follows. In Section 2, a brief literature review is given. In Section 3, the data and methodology are introduced. The empirical results are given in Section 3. Section 4 closes the paper with conclusions and outlook.

LITERATURE REVIEW

In this section, the pioneering and recent studies on this subject are presented. Fama (1981) proposes a proxy hypothesis and aims to explain the negative relationships between inflation and stock returns. In the work, the relationships among inflation, interest rates, and expected returns for the period from 1953 to 1971 are analyzed by using the regression analysis. For this purpose, monthly, quarterly, and yearly datasets are used. According to the findings, evidence exists of a negative relationship between inflation and real activity measures. On the contrary, real stock returns are positively correlated with real activity measures. Moreover, stock returns and inflation rates are strongly related to the measures of future real activities. More specifically, for monthly, quarterly, and annual data when expected inflation is considered with growth rates of money and real activities, negative relationships between real stock returns and expected inflation rates are eliminated. As a result of the regression analysis performed with annual stock returns, it is stated that unexpected inflation loses its explanatory power when it joins the analysis with future real activities.

Pearce and Roley (1982) investigate the short-term effect of unexpected changes in money stock on weekly stock prices. The results show that an unexpected increase in the money stock has a negative effect on stock prices. Moreover, in the paper, it is shown that only a small portion of unexpected news on money stock causes fluctuations on financial markets, which indeed supports the effective market hypothesis.

Schwerth (1990) tests the real stock market and real activity relationship with the regression analysis for the period of 1889-1988 by replicating the study of Fama (1990). In the paper, the predictive powers of two production indices, namely the new industrial production index of Miron and Romer (1989) and the old index of Babson and Federal Reserve Board, are compared. According to the results, growth rates of Miron-Romer's index show much more volatility and smaller autocorrelations than that of Babson and Federal Reserve board. The results indicate weaker relationships with real stock returns on a monthly and quarterly basis. Furthermore, on an annual basis, both indices are unrelated with stock returns.

In their study, Ferson and Harvey (1991) examine the factors which have effects on monthly common stock and bond market returns. In the analysis, all the stocks listed on the New York Stock Exchange (NYSE) by using sectoral portfolios and the long-term government bond with six months to maturity are included in the analysis. A large portion of stock and bond returns can be explained by a multivariate stock pricing model. The results show that the most important factor in estimating the variations in stock portfolios is the stock market risk premium, and the most important factor in predicting bond returns is the premium related to the interest rates.

McQueen and Roley (1993), unlike previous studies, find that macroeconomic news and stock prices have stronger relationships. The paper provides evidence that the response of the stock market to the macroeconomic news depends on economic strength. When the economy is strong, surprisingly lower share prices are observed if real economic activities are higher than expected. On the contrary, when the economy is weak, higher stock prices are observed following the higher unexpected news. For weaker economies, unexpected increases in economic activity result in an increase in expectations about future economic activity and cash flows. However, in a strong economy, the same information does not yield higher expected cash flows.

Ederington and Lee (1993) examine the impact of 19 regulated macroeconomic news such as employment report, consumer price index (CPI), and producer price index (PPI), among others, on interest rates and foreign exchange markets. In this study, intraday data for the period from November 7, 1988 to November 29, 1991 are used. The findings show that the news is responsible for most of the volatility fluctuations depending on the time of the day and the day of the week.

Rigobon and Sack (2002) proposes a new estimator to determine the heteroscedasticity existing in high frequency data. In the paper, it is shown that the reaction of asset prices to changes in monetary policy can be determined by the increase in policy shocks which usually occur during the day of the Federal Open Market Committee (FOMC) meetings and on the day of the Chairman's semi-annual monetary policy testimony to the Congress. Moreover, findings also show that the increase in short-term interest rates causes a decrease in stock prices and an upward shift in the yield curve.

Kim et al. (2004) investigated the effects of six different macroeconomic news announcements on the US stock, bond, and foreign exchange markets. This study covers the period from January 2, 1985 to December 31, 1998. According to results, it is shown that these markets do not respond significantly to the government's news. For all three markets, it was found that the unexpected trade balance has the greatest impact on the average return on foreign exchange markets. Moreover, the news about the domestic economy has significant effects on the bond market. For the US stock market, the news about consumer and producer price indices is considered to be important. On the other hand, for the market volatility some macroeconomic news has greater impacts.

Wongswan (2006) investigated the impact of the American and Japanese macroeconomic news on the Korean and the Thai stock markets by using intraday data. This study covers the period of January 3, 1995 to December 26, 2000. In the analysis, he uses a GARCH(1,1) model with macroeconomic variables. His findings show that in the short-term, the macroeconomic variables of the developed economies have strong effects on emerging stock markets.

Andersen et al. (2007) examined the responses of stock, bond and foreign exchange markets of the US, Germany, and the UK to the real-time US macroeconomic news. For this purpose, the high-frequency dataset of future prices is used. In the analysis, a regression analysis is implemented. Results of the study show that the US macroeconomic news causes certain jumps to occur in the mean equations which addresses the existence of significant relationships between stock markets and macroeconomic news. In addition, it is also concluded that stock markets respond differently to macroeconomic news depending on the economic conditions. In particular, when the situation of the economy is considered, the stock and foreign exchange markets seem to be equally sensitive. Also, bond markets react most strongly to the macroeconomic news.

Kim and Nguyen (2008) investigated the response of the Australian financial markets to the news about interest rate targets of the Australian Reserve Bank (RBA) and the US Fed's starting from 1998 until 2006. Results of this study show that the RBA news has significant impacts on the first moments of market returns. Moreover, following a news release, the volatility of many markets has increased. In the Australian interest rate market, asymmetric reactions are observed following the news. Markets tend to react more strongly to unexpected rate increases than the decreases in those rates.

Kim and Nguyen (2009) investigated the spillover effects of the interest rate targets news of the US Fed and the European Central Bank (ECB) on 12 different financial markets. In the analysis, they considered the effects of these news on both returns and volatilities. This study covered the period of 1999-2006. According to the findings, in response to unexpected rate increases, significant decreases in returns are observed. Moreover, although markets show different adjustment periods for the Fed's news, in general, the adjustment periods of the markets for the ECB news are all slow. On the other hand, if one considers return volatilities, the increases in volatilities are observed in response to the interest rate news.

Hanousek et al. (2009) studied the effect of macroeconomic news on stock returns. For this purpose, they considered three European Union countries, namely Czech Republic, Hungary, and Poland for the period from June 2, 2003 to December 29, 2006. In the analysis, the intraday data and GARCH analysis were used. The results show evidence of significant spillovers from composite index returns of the EU, US and neighboring markets of these countries. Moreover, the composite index of Hungary shows the strongest spillovers, and the Czech Republic shows the least spillovers.

Albuquerque and Vega (2009) examined the responses of Portugal and the United States to domestic and foreign public news. The dataset of the study covers the period from January 4, 2002 to October 15, 2002. The findings show that the US macroeconomic news and Portugal's earnings do not have significant effects on co-movements. After the regression analysis, which is implemented between the US stock market returns and the US news, it is observed that the effects of the US Stock markets on the Portuguese market decrease sharply. Moreover, Portugal's macroeconomic news reduces the stock exchange co-operation.

Nowak et al. (2011) analyzed the volatility dynamics of the bond markets. They investigated the effects of macroeconomic news on prices and volatilities. In the analysis, intraday bond price data of four emerging markets, namely Brazil, Mexico Russia, and Turkey, were considered, and they used the US market as a benchmark for the period of October 1, 2006-February 20, 2008. The findings show that the surprises of macroeconomic news have significant effects on both returns and volatilities. In addition, impacts of macroeconomic news are more persistent for volatilities than returns.

Gümüş et al. (2011) studied the response of the Turkish stock market to the macroeconomic news of the US and Turkey. In the analysis, Consumer Price Index,

GDP growth, current account deficit, interest rate, and the US/TRY exchange rate are considered the Turkish macroeconomic news. Moreover, the Import Price Index, the Export Price Index, the Consumer Price Index, the Producer Price Index, and the Regional, State Employment and Unemployment are considered the US macroeconomic news. The study covers the period of 2002-2010. They provided evidence that domestic news has a greater impact on the Turkish stock market.

Fedorova et al. (2014) investigated the impact of euro area macroeconomic announcements on CIVETS (Colombia, Indonesia, Vietnam, Egypt, Turkey, and South Africa) stock markets. In the analysis, daily MSCI data are used for the period from 2007 to 2012. Consumer price index, industrial production index, GDP, retail sales, unemployment rate, liquidity by M3, PMI, and consumer confidence index are considered macroeconomic variables. The effects were analyzed using the EGARCH model. The findings show that impacts exist of Euro area macroeconomic news on stock volatility for all CIVETS countries, and impacts also exist of Euro area macroeconomic news on stock returns of Vietnam, Egypt, Turkey, and South Africa.

Cakan et al. (2015) examine the impact of the US macroeconomic news on 12 emerging markets. The inflation and unemployment rates are considered the macroeconomic news, and in the analysis, GARCH is used. According to the findings, the volatility is persistent and asymmetric. Moreover, asymmetric impacts of the macroeconomic news vary among countries. The US inflation and employment news are effective on many emerging markets. More specifically, the volatility of the Turkish stock market decreases depending on the good news of the US, and contrarily, it increases depending on the bad news of the US.

Chen et al. (2015) analyzed the impact of the domestic macroeconomic news releases on the China stock futures market. The study covered the intraday data for the period from January 2011 to May 2014. The Consumer Price Index (CPI), the Producer Price Index (PPI), the Total Retail Sales of Consumer Goods (RSCG), the Industrial Production (INP), and the Investment in Fixed Assets (IFA) were considered macroeconomic news. The findings of the study provide evidence that the CPI announcement has significant impacts on the price, liquidity, and volatility of futures. In addition, the futures market's response to the bad CPI news is much stronger than that of good news.

Gok and Topuz (2016) studied the impacts of Turkish and US macroeconomic news announcements on Turkish Stock market volatility. For this purpose, the volatility of the BIST100 index was analyzed. In the study, 13 US macroeconomic news namely, Dur. Goods Manufacturers' Ship., Inv. and Orders, Manufacturers' Shipments, Inventories and Orders, GDP, Construction Spending, Personal Income and Outlays, Int.Trade in Goods and Services, Sales For Retail And Food Services, Nonfarm Payroll Employment, Consumer Price Index, Producer Price Index, Manufacturing and Trade Inventories and Sales, New Residential Construction, and New Residential Sales as well as 8 Turkish macroeconomic news, namely, GDP, Business Tendancy Survey, Labor Force Statistics, House Sales, Industrial Production Index, Foreign Trade Statistics, Consumer Price Index, and Consumer Confidence Index, were used for the period from April 1, 2010 to December 31, 2015. The findings show that both Turkish and US GDP news and US House Sales have significant effects on BIST100 volatility.

Omokehinde and Akingunola (2018), analyzed the impacts of macroeconomic news announcements on Nigerian Stock Exchange market volatility. This study covered the period from 2000 to 2015. In the study, AR-EGARCH methodology is used under generalized error distributed innovations. Inflation rate, monetary policy rate, exchange rate, and crude oil price were investigated as macroeconomic variables. The findings show that the macroeconomic news has insignificant effects on stock returns.

Duangin et al. (2018) studied the effects of domestic macroeconomic news announcements on Thailand's stock market for the period from January 2011 to December 2016. Foreign trade export, foreign trade import, consumer price index, GDP, and trade balance were considered macroeconomic variables. In the paper, Markow Switching GARCH (MSGARCH) with jumps is augmented to news, and then, it is compared with the MSGARCH with jumps. The results show that MSGARCH with jumps has better performance in the estimations. Moreover, all the macroeconomic variables effects are the same.

Huang (2018) investigated the effects of macroeconomic news on both the US bond and the US stock market. In the study, the second moments are used by decomposing them into two components (i.e., the continuous volatility and the discrete jumps). In the analysis, the intraday data of future prices, which cover the period from January 3, 1994 to September 30, 2014, are included. The findings show that the market responses depend both on the surprises caused by the news and the forecasts of the agents. Furthermore, uncertainty has a stronger influence than disagreement on the second moment. The level of financial stress and the monetary policy have impacts on the second moment.

Ekinci et al. (2019) studied the impact of 18 US macroeconomic news on prices, returns, trading activity, and volatility of the Turkish stock market. They used the intraday data for the year of 2010 and a set of 18 macroeconomic variables to include Building Permits, Change in Nonfarm Payrolls, CPI MoM, Current Account Balance, Durable Goods Orders, Employment Cost Index, GDP Annualized QoQ, Housing Starts MoM, Initial Jobless Claims, Nonfarm Productivity, PCE Core MoM, Personal Consumption, Personal Income, Personal Spending, PPI MoM, Retail Sales Advance MoM, Trade Balance, and Unemployment Rate. In the paper, the differences between the release and non-release dates are compared by using

Student-t test. The results show evidence that the markets negatively respond to the macroeconomic news in a five-minute period.

Camilleria et al. (2019) examined the effects of fundamental macroeconomic variables, namely inflation, industrial production, interest rates, and money supply on Belgium, France, Germany, Netherlands and Portugal. The study focused on the lead-lag relationships among the stock prices and the selected variables. For this purpose, they considered lagged variables, and they used VAR analysis. They showed evidence of the lead-lag relationships among the stock prices and the macroeconomic variables. However, these relationships vary across countries.

Pal et al. (2019) analyzed the response of a set of Indian stock indices to monetary policy and macroeconomic surprises using data from April 1, 2004 to July 31, 2016. In the paper, GDP, World Production Index, Consumer Price Index, Industrial Production Index, and Current Account Deficit were considered macroeconomic variables, and the 91-day T-bill yield was used as a proxy of monetary policy. A VAR analysis was implemented, and the results show that that the monetary policy surprise has effects on the stock market more clearly than other macroeconomic surprises. Moreover, it is also found that firm size and response to shocks are directly proportional.

DATA AND METHODOLOGY

In this section, the dataset and the methodology which is adopted to conduct an extensive data analysis are presented.

Sectorial Indices

In this study, daily closing prices of six sectoral indices and the BIST100 index of Borsa Istanbul[2] are collected from https://tr.investing.com/. These indices include the BIST Banks (XBANK), the BIST Information Technology (XBLSM), the BIST Real Estate Invest Trusts (XGMYO), the BIST Holdings & Investments (XHOLD), the BIST Insurance (XSGRT) and the BIST Technology (XUTEK). The dataset covers the period from May 04, 2015 to January 01, 2019. The percentage log-return series for each index are used in the analysis, and all analysis functions are implemented in R Software (R Core Team, 2017)[3].

Percentage log-return series are calculated for each index by using Equation (1):

$$r_t = \ln\left(\frac{P_t}{P_{t-1}}\right) \times 100 \qquad (1)$$

Table 1 shows descriptive statistics, the Augmented Dickey Fuller (ADF) test for stationarity (Dickey and Fuller, 1979, 1981), the Jarque-Bera test for normality (Jarque and Bera, 1980), and the Ljung-Box Q*test for serial correlations (Ljung & Box, 1978) of return series. Moreover, the Ljung-Box test for squared returns are also given in Table 1.

Table 1. Descriptive statistics, stationarity, normality, and serial correlation tests

	XBANK	XBLSM	XGMYO	XHOLD	XSGRT	XUTEK
Minimum	-10.2957	-11.9679	-10.3998	-7.0929	-4.6071	-15.1518
Maximum	8.9466	5.9639	8.4653	3.9596	3.7827	7.2984
Mean	-0.0188	0.0076	-0.0322	0.0184	0.0487	0.0958
Stdev	1.9384	1.6235	1.3901	1.2810	0.8424	1.7982
Skewness	-0.3034	-0.6116	-0.6476	-0.3488	-0.2749	-0.9506
Kurtosis	2.9568	5.7773	6.9364	1.6740	2.1567	8.9648
ADF	-10.7**	-10.05**	-10.24**	-9.97**	-9.67**	-9.46**
Jarque-Bera	345.41**	1319.3**	1883.06**	124.99**	188.08**	3174.74**
Ljung-Box Q(10)						
Returns	5.261*	3.825	8.767**	0.033	0.066	1.623
Squ. Returns	53.434**	88.866**	41.809**	69.673**	73.559**	118.201**

Note: * shows significance at level α=0.05, ** shows significance at level α=0.01

Table 1 shows that return distributions of all sectors are left skewed,[4] and XBLSM, XGMYO, XUTEK index returns are leptokurtic. According to the ADF test results, all return series are stationary. In addition, the Jarque-Bera test results indicate the strong evidence of non-normality. The Ljung-Box Q* test results present the existence of serial correlations up to order ten in XBANK and XGMYO return series and in all squared return series.

The Macroeconomic News

In this study, the PMI and the GDP growth rate are considered the macroeconomic news indicators. The market announced values of the PMI and the GDP growth rate for three foreign markets (the US, the Euro-Zone, and China), and the domestic market data (Turkey) are obtained from https://tr.investing.com/. The PMI is released monthly, and the GDP growth rate is released quarterly. The descriptive statistics are shown in Table 2.

Table 2. Descriptive statistics of macroeconomic indicators

	PMI				GDP Growth Rate			
	Turkey	**US**	**Euro**	**China**	**Turkey**	**US**	**Euro**	**China**
Minimum	42.7	50	51.2	49	-0.018	-0.002	0.002	0.011
Maximum	55.7	57	60.6	52.4	0.111	0.042	0.006	0.018
Mean	50.1163	54.2091	54.574	50.7791	0.0475	0.0226	0.0043	0.0161
Stdev	2.9838	1.6193	2.660	0.850	0.0291	0.0119	0.0014	0.0021
Skewness	0.0208	-0.7289	0.589	-0.152	-0.0326	-0.1235	0.1541	-1.1360
Kurtosis	-0.3381	-0.147	-0.873	-1.292	0.6109	-0.8442	-1.5256	0.1454

Table 2 implies that according to the average PMI, the Euro-Zone one is expected to grow at the highest rate, and according to the GDP growth rate, Turkey is the fastest growing country. However, the PMI expectation for Turkey cannot be attained. Hence, one month lagged values are taken as the expectation.

In order to be able to make a standardized comparison among the sectoral indices and interpret the relevant results, a macroeconomic surprise variable, which is introduced by Balduzzi et al. (2001), is used. The macroeconomic surprise variable is given in Equation (2).

$$Suprise_i = \frac{A_i - M_i}{\sigma_i}, \tag{2}$$

where M_i is the expected value, A_i is the actual value, and σ_i is the standard deviation of the macroeconomic indicator *i*, respectively.

Methodology

This study aims to capture the impact of macroeconomic news on the sectoral indices. With this motivation, firstly one factor model (i.e., the Capital Asset Pricing Model (CAPM) introduced by Sharpe (1964)) is applied. The CAPM is given in Equation (3):

$$E\left(r_{it}\right) - r_{ft} = \beta_i \left(r_{mt} - r_{ft}\right) + \varepsilon_{it}, \forall i \in I \tag{3}$$

with r_{nt} being the daily percentage return of the BIST100 index and r_{ft} being the yield of the 10-year Turkish Government Bond. Subsequently, the abnormal returns, i.e. $AR_{it} = \varepsilon i_{t,}$ are calculated, and the analysis is proceeded with these abnormal returns.

In the analysis, the effects of macroeconomic news are examined under two different settings which are listed as follows:

1. Macroeconomic Surprises in the Mean Equation
2. Macroeconomic Surprises in the Variance Equation

For this purpose, the conditional mean model given in Equation (4) is considered:

$$Ar_{it} = \mu + \sum_{k=1}^{p} \phi_k Ar_{i,t-k} + \sum_{k=1}^{q} \theta_k \varepsilon_{it-k} + \varepsilon_{it}, \forall i \in I \tag{4}$$

where p and q denote the order of the ARMA model. Moreover, various conditional variance models such as GARCH, EGARCH, gjrGARCH, and APARCH, which are briefly introduced in Section 2.3.1 - 2.3.4, are implemented for five innovative distributions (e.g., Normal, Student-t, Generalized Error Distribution, Skewed Student-t, and Normal Inverse Gaussian Distribution).

The best model is selected by using the Akaike Information Criteria (AIC) (Akaike, 1974) and the Schwarz Information Criteria (BIC) (Schwarz, 1978). Finally, the effects of the macroeconomic surprises on the Turkish stock market are empirically tested.

GARCH(p, q)

The GARCH (Generalized Autoregressive Conditional Heteroscedasticity) model is a generalized version of the ARCH (Autoregressive Conditional Heteroscedasticity) model which is initially developed by Bollerslev (1986). Despite being simple, this model is widely accepted as the most robust model among the variance models.

The GARCH(p, q) model is given in Equation (5):

$$h_{i,t} = \omega + \sum_{i=1}^{p} \alpha_i \varepsilon_{i,t-i}^2 + \sum_{i=1}^{q} \beta_i h_{i,t-i}, \tag{5}$$

where, $\alpha_i \geq 0$, $\beta_i \geq 0$ are constant parameters.

The case where p=1 and q=1 is a special form of the GARCH model, which is denoted by GARCH(1,1). This model is usually sufficient to model financial series.

EGARCH(p,q)

Nelson (1991) proposed the Exponential GARCH (EGARCH) model in order to overcome certain drawbacks of the crude GARCH model. For instance, the asymmetric effects between negative and positive asset returns are not considered in the GARCH model. This has been improved in the EGARCH model. Thus, the EGARCH model is advantageous over the crude GARCH model. Moreover, since EGARCH models the logarithm of variance rather than the variance itself, in this model, the estimated variance is always positive.

The EGARCH(p, q) model is given in Equation (6)

$$\log h_t = \omega + \sum_{i=1}^{p} \alpha_i z_{t-i} + \sum_{i=1}^{p} \gamma_i \left(\left| z_{t-i} \right| - E\left| z_{t-i} \right| \right) + \sum_{i=1}^{q} \beta_i \log h_{t-i}, \qquad (6)$$

where α_i is the parameter for sign effect, γ_i is the parameter for size effect, and z_{it} stands for the standardized innovation.

GJR-GARCH (p,q)

The GJR-GARCH model, which is proposed by Glosten, Jagannathan, and Runkle (1993), is similar to the Threshold GARCH (TGARCH) model proposed by Zakoian (1994). The main advantage of this model is that it allows the leverage effect in volatility (Zivot, 2008).

The GJR-GARCH(p,q) model is given in Equation (7)

$$h_t = \omega + \sum_{i=1}^{p} \alpha_i \varepsilon_{t-i}^2 + \sum_{i=1}^{p} \gamma_i I_{t-i} \varepsilon_{t-i}^2 + \sum_{i=1}^{q} \beta_i h_{t-i}, \qquad (7)$$

where γ_i is the parameter for leverage effect, and $I_{i,t}$ is the indicator function given as follows:

$$I = \begin{cases} 1, for\ \varepsilon_{it} < 0 \\ 0, otherwise. \end{cases}$$

APARCH (p,q)

The APARCH (Asymmetric Power ARCH) model is developed by Ding, Granger, and Engle (1993), and this model is one of the standard models which is used to determine the asymmetry effect. Since it considers both the power of the volatility and the leverage effect, it has a rather generic structure which contains many other variance models.

The APARCH(p, q) is given in Equation (8):

$$h_t^{\delta} = \omega + \sum_{i=1}^{p} \alpha_i \left(\left| \varepsilon_{t-i} \right| - \gamma_i \varepsilon_{i,t-1} \right)^{\delta} + \sum_{i=1}^{q} \beta_i h_{t-i}^{\delta} \tag{8}$$

where $\delta \in \mathbb{R}^{+}$ is the parameter for power effect, and γ_i is the parameter for leverage effect.

Special cases of the APARCH(p,q) can be listed as follows (Ghalanos, 2017):

1. If $\delta=2, \gamma_i=0$, then the model is identical to the GARCH(p,q) model of Bollerslev (1986)
2. If $\delta=1$, $\gamma_i=0$, then the model corresponds to the Absolute Value GARCH (AVGARCH(p,q)) model of Taylor (1986) and Schwert (1990b)
3. If $\delta=2$, then the model is the gjrGARCH(p,q) model of Glosten et al. (1993)
4. If $\delta=1$, then the model is equal to the TGARCH(p,q) model of Zakoian (1994)
5. If $\gamma_i=0$, $\beta_i=0$, then the model yields to the Nonlinear ARCH(p) model of Higgins et al. (1992)
6. If $\delta \to 0$, then the model is the Log ARCH(q) model of Geweke (1986) and Pantula (1986).

Table 3. Estimation results of the CAPM

	XBANK	XBLSM	XGMYO	XHOLD	XSGRT	XUTEK
β	1.3701	0.8145	0.8506	0.8826	0.2857	0.8325
$se(\beta)$	0.0204	0.0319	0.0220	0.0150	0.0195	0.0371
t-stat	67.33**	25.56**	38.66**	58.81**	14.64**	22.42**
R^2	0.8342	0.4203	0.6238	0.7933	0.1921	0.358

Note that: * shows significance at level α=0.05, ** shows significance at level α=0.01 and *** shows significance at level α=0.001

EMPIRICAL RESULTS

In this section, the empirical results of the data analysis are presented. Initially, the CAPM model is considered. The estimation results of the CAPM are presented in Table 3.

From Table 3, it can be seen that the market beta coefficients of all indices are statistically significant. Accordingly, it is observed that the Banking sector is the most sensitive, and the Insurance Sector is the least sensitive sector against the fluctuations in the market. If the coefficient of determination is considered, then it is observed that the value of the Banking and Holding & Investments sector is over 70%. This means that 70% of the variability in returns of this sector is caused by the variability in the market. However, only a small portion of the variability in the insurance sector can be explained by the variability in the market.

Macroeconomic Surprises in the Mean Equation

It is known that the macroeconomic news is released on certain days. Therefore, it is important to investigate the effect of these surprises on and after the announcement days which are called simultaneous and spillover effects, respectively. In order to analyze the dynamics of surprise effects, the conditional mean equations via the ARMA models by using the macroeconomic surprise variables and their first order lags are estimated. Specifically, the conditional mean model is given in Equation (9):

$$r_{it} = \mu + \sum_{k=1}^{p}\phi_k r_{i,t-k} + \sum_{k=1}^{q}\theta_k \varepsilon_{it-k} + \sum_{k=1}^{s}\delta_k PMI_{kt}$$
$$+ \sum_{k=1}^{s}\tilde{\delta}_k PMI_{kt-1} + \sum_{k=1}^{s}\lambda_k GDP_{kt} + \sum_{k=1}^{s}\tilde{\lambda}_k GDP_{kt-1} + \varepsilon_{it}, \forall i \in I$$

$$h_{i,t}^{1/2} z_t, \varepsilon_{it} \sim \left(0, h_{it}\right) \tag{9}$$

Moreover, the serial correlations for abnormal returns are tested by applying the Ljung and Box Q*test for all lags up to 10. The results are reported in Table 4.

*Table 4. Ljung-Box Q*test results for abnormal returns*

	XBANK	XBLM	XGMYO	XHOLD	XSGRT	XUTEK
Test-stat	39.239	16.192	19.654	34.161	8.102	37.975
p.value	0.000***	0.094	0.033*	0.000***	0.619	0.000***

Table 4 indicates that the abnormal returns for the sectors of Banking, Real Estate Invest Trusts, Holdings & Investments, and Technology exhibit serial correlation up to lag 10. However, for Information Technology and Insurance sectors, the serial correlations are statistically not significant. Note that, in the analysis, p=10 and q=0 are assigned for the sectors exhibiting significant serial correlations and p=q=0 for other sectors. In Table 5, the estimated conditional mean models for each index are reported.

Table 5. Estimation results of conditional mean equation

	XBANK	XBLSM	XGMYO	XHOLD	XSGRT	XUTEK
μ	-0.0024	0.0052	-0.0366	-0.0019	0.0198	0.0734
$PMI_{Turkey,t}$	0.0797	-0.2108	-0.0786	0.0485	-0.0450	0.0556
$PMI_{China,t}$	-0.1018	0.2294	0.1535	-0.0240	0.0025	0.0241
$PMI_{US,t}$	-0.1492	-0.1605	-0.3313	0.0309	0.1676	-0.6228
$PMI_{Euro,t}$	0.0810	-2.4787	-0.2760	-0.1340	-1.5145	-0.9863
$GDP_{Turkey,t}$	0.1158	0.8528	-0.1041	-0.0711	0.2819	0.4451
$GDP_{China,t}$	-0.1085	0.0601	0.0062	-0.0286	-0.0305	0.0479
$GDP_{US,t}$	1.3294*	2.0219*	-0.4151	-0.0438	-0.7124	1.0098
$GDP_{Euro,t}$	0.2282	-0.0020	-0.6441*	0.0063	0.2122	-0.3899
$PMI_{Turkey,t-1}$	0.0428	-0.2044	-0.0856	0.0854	0.1944	-0.4594*
$PMI_{China,t-1}$	-0.1590	0.0525	-0.2853*	0.0687	-0.0570	0.0331
$PMI_{US,t-1}$	-0.2709	-0.5489	0.4051	-0.0953	0.1802	0.0377
$PMI_{Euro,t-1}$	-1.7414	-2.0931	-0.6455	0.0425	-1.1327	2.5821
$GDP_{Turkey,t-1}$	-0.7268*	-0.4853	-0.0807	0.0889	0.0353	0.2408
$GDP_{China,t-1}$	0.2689*	-0.1230	-0.0434	-0.1416	-0.1209	-0.0232
$GDP_{US,t-1}$	0.5769	-1.6296	-0.5990	-0.0347	-0.1535	-1.2140
$GDP_{Euro,t-1}$	-0.1696	-0.8545	-0.3642	0.2342	-0.5346	0.0570
ϕ_1	0.0165	-	-0.0493	-0.0873*	-	0.0414
ϕ_2	-0.0263	-	-0.0761*	-0.0569	-	-0.0783*
ϕ_3	0.0488	-	0.0070	-0.0463	-	-0.0250
ϕ_4	-0.0182	-	0.0317	-0.0474	-	0.0666
ϕ_5	-0.0722*	-	0.0216	0.0021	-	0.0578
ϕ_6	0.0222	-	-0.0555	-0.0130	-	0.0322
ϕ_7	0.0673*	-	0.0279	-0.0438	-	-0.0130
ϕ_8	0.0315	-	0.0377	-0.0360	-	-0.0166
ϕ_9	0.0333	-	-0.0264	-0.0165	-	0.0057
ϕ_{10}	0.1322***	-	-0.0390	0.0447	-	-0.0117

Note that: * shows significance at level α=0.05, ** shows significance at level α=0.01 and *** shows significance at level α=0.001

The results of the estimated conditional mean models suggest that macroeconomic surprises have different impacts on the abnormal returns of some sectoral indices. For example, the GDP-US, the GDP-Turkey, and the GDP-China have spillover effects on abnormal returns of the Banking sector. Abnormal returns of the Banking sector increase at the rate of 1.33% following a positive surprise in the GDP-US. Similarly, following a positive surprise in the GDP-China, the Turkish Banking sector returns increase by 0.27%. On the other hand, the GDP-Turkey has a negative effect on the Banking sector, meaning that it reduces returns at the rate of 0.73%. In addition, a single surprise originating in the GDP-US has strong positive spillover effect on the Information Technology sector. A surprise causes a rate of 2.02% increase in this sector. For the Real Estate Invest Trusts sector, the GDP-Euro surprise has a negative simultaneous effect on abnormal returns (0.64%), while the PMI-China surprise exhibits a negative spillover effect (0.29%). Moreover, abnormal returns of the Technology sector show a negative spillover from the PMI-Turkey (0.46%).

In the analysis, the statistically insignificant variables are removed from the conditional mean models, and the diagnostic tests are presented in Table 6.

Table 6. Diagnostic tests of conditional mean models

	XBANK	XBLSM	XGMYO	XHOLD	XSGRT	XUTEK
Breusch- Godfrey (10)	17.527	3.576	12.272	10.979	12.154	14.435
p.value	0.063	0.965	0.267	0.359	0.275	0.154
F-stat.	7.992	-	5.089	5.790	-	6.007
p.value (F –stat)	0.000	-	0.002	0.016	-	0.003
R^2	0.051	-	0.017	0.006	-	0.013

Table 6 implies that the reduced conditional mean models are statistically significant to measure the abnormal returns. The Breusch and Godfrey tests (Breusch, 1978; Godfrey, 1978) for serial correlation confirm that the models are correctly specified.

Then, the GARCH models are estimated by using residuals of the conditional mean models. Guided by AIC and BIC, the most appropriate conditional variance models are selected among four GARCH models with six innovative distributions. Suggested models are reported in Table 7.

Results given in Table 7 state that the suggested conditional variance models are standard GARCH(1,1) models, and all the suggested innovative distributions are Student-t except for the Holdings and Technology sectors. The variance models

Table 7. Conditional variance models

	AIC	BIC
XBANK	GARCH(1,1)-std	GARCH(1,1)-std
XBLSM	GARCH(1,1)-std	GARCH(1,1)-std
XGMYO	GARCH(1,1)-std	GARCH(1,1)-std
XHOLD	GJR-GARCH(1,1)-std	GARCH(1,1)-std
XSGRT	GARCH(1,1)-std	GARCH(1,1)-std
XUTEK	EGARCH(1,1)-sstd	EGARCH(1,1)-sstd

suggested by AIC are evaluated. Table 8 reports the conditional variance model estimates and the diagnostic tests for each index.

The results given in Table 8 show that the estimates of α_1 and β_1 are significant. Moreover, $\alpha_1+\beta_1$ ranges from 0.5868 (XBLSM) to 1.0119 (XHOLD). In fact, this implies nonstationarity in conditional variance of the Holdings & Investments sector. However, significant leverage effect helps to reduce the persistency in this conditional variance. On the other hand, for the Banking and Technology sectors, $\alpha_1+\beta_1$ value is over 0.979 which refers to a high persistency level in conditional variances. In addition, the leverage effect is also significant for the Technology sector. Considering the diagnostics, the suggested models seem to perform well for all sectors.

Table 8. Conditional variance estimates and diagnostic tests

	Variance Parameter Estimates				Weighted Ljung-Box Test on Stand. Resid. Q*(1)		Weighted Ljung-Box Test on Stand. Squared Resid. Q*(1)	
	ω	α_1	β_1	γ_1	Stat.	p.Val.	Stat.	p.Val.
XBANK	0.0104	0.0560**	0.9232***	-	1.126	0.289	1.812	0.178
XBLSM	0.6680***	0.2171***	0.3697**	-	0.802	0.371	0.056	0.812
XGMYO	0.2262*	0.1133*	0.5655***	-	0.275	0.600	0.242	0.623
XHOLD	0.0027*	0.0408***	0.9711***	0.0366**	0.124	0.725	0.562	0.453
XSGRT	0.1601**	0.1591**	0.5717***	-	1.46	0.227	0.051	0.822
XUTEK	0.0251	0.0473	0.9430***	0.2447**	2.28	0.131	1.86	0.173

Macroeconomic Surprises Are in the Variance Equation

By following the similar approach given in Section 3.1, the dynamics of surprise effects are analyzed by considering the conditional variance equations with macroeconomic surprise variables and their first lags. First, the serial correlations in the abnormal returns are eliminated by using the ARMA models. Then, p=10 and q=0 are assigned for the sectors exhibiting significant serial correlations. Estimation results of the conditional mean equations are reported in Table 9.

Table 9. Estimation results of conditional mean equation

	XBANK	XGMYO	XHOLD	XUTEK
μ	-0.0173	-0.0583*	0.0021	0.0745
ϕ_1	0.0083	-0.0485	-0.0881**	0.0389
ϕ_2	-0.0353	-0.0713*	-0.0560	-0.0833*
ϕ_3	0.0547	0.0084	-0.0441	-0.0186
ϕ_4	-0.0188	0.0285	-0.0452	0.0674*
ϕ_5	-0.0688*	0.0148	0.0041	0.0650
ϕ_6	0.0185	-0.0538	-0.0140	0.0330
ϕ_7	0.0700*	0.0374	-0.0424	-0.0108
ϕ_8	0.0315	0.0422	-0.0357	-0.0241
ϕ_9	0.0296	-0.0232	-0.0181	0.0061
ϕ_{10}	0.1407***	-0.0358	0.0423	-0.0101

Note that: * shows significance at level α=0.05, ** shows significance at level α=0.01 and *** shows significance at level α=0.001

The results in Table 9 indicate that the abnormal returns of the Banking sector show fifth, seventh, and tenth orders of serial correlations. Abnormal returns of the Real Estate Invest Trusts Banking sector and Holdings & Investments sector show second and first order serial correlations, respectively. In addition, the Technology sector has second and fourth order serial correlations. For these sectors, models are reduced by excluding the insignificant lags, and the diagnostic tests are reported in Table 10.

F statistics given in Table 10 indicate that the reduced conditional mean models are statistically significant. The Breusch and Godfrey tests for serial correlation confirm that models are sufficient to capture the current serial correlations.

Table 10. Diagnostic tests of conditional mean models

	XBANK	XGMYO	XHOLD	XUTEK
Breusch- Godfrey (10)	18.366	12.363	10.979	10.079
p.value	0.0500	0.2615	0.3592	0.4336
F-stat.	10.4700	4.6960	5.7900	5.4740
p.value (F –stat)	0.0000	0.0305	0.0163	0.0043
R^2	0.0341	0.0052	0.0639	0.0121

For the sectors with serial correlations, the residuals from the reduced conditional mean models are used in conditional variance models. On the other hand, for the sectors which do not have serial correlation, the conditional variance models are estimated directly. In the estimations, the macroeconomic variables and their first lags are included in the conditional variance model as external variables. Afterwards, the most appropriate conditional variance models are selected by applying AIC and BIC. The selected models are reported in Table 11.

Table 11. Conditional variance models

	AIC	BIC
XBANK	EGARCH(1,1)-sstd	EGARCH(1,1)-std
XBLSM	EGARCH(1,1)-sstd	EGARCH(1,1)-sstd
XGMYO	EGARCH(1,1)--std	EGARCH(1,1)-std
XHOLD	EGARCH(1,1)-sstd	EGARCH(1,1)-std
XSGRT	EGARCH(1,1)-std	GARCH(1,1)-std
XUTEK	EGARCH(1,1)-sstd	EGARCH(1,1)-std

As seen in Table 11, EGARCH(1,1) is suggested for all sectors by AIC, and similarly, for all sectors except for the Insurance sector, EGARCH(1,1) is suggested by BIC. Furthermore, the variance models suggested by AIC are estimated, and the conditional variance model estimates are reported in Table 12.

The results given in Table 12 indicate that the estimates of β_1 and γ_1 are significant. The positive estimates of γ_1 show the existence of leverage effects. Also, the value of $\alpha_1+\beta_1$ ranges from 0.5222 (XBLSM) to 1.0179 (XUTEK). Since $\alpha_1+\beta_1=1.0179$ for the Technology sector, a nonstationarity in conditional variance is observed. However, significant leverage effect helps to reduce the amount of persistency. Moreover, for the Banking and Holdings & Investments sectors, $\alpha_1+\beta_1$ is greater than

Table 12. Conditional variance estimates

	XBANK	XBLSM	XGMYO	XHOLD	XSGRT	XUTEK
ω	0.0010	0.1763*	-0.1510	-0.0044	-0.2301*	-0.0079
α_1	-0.0005	0.0022	0.0247	-0.0032	0.0263	0.0517*
β_1	0.9997***	0.5200***	0.6457***	0.9979***	0.6153***	0.9662***
γ_1	0.0870***	0.3853***	0.2708***	0.0541***	0.3309***	0.1490**
$PMI_{Turkey,t}$	0.1113	-0.0537	-0.0477	-0.0879	0.0179	0.5671*
$PMI_{China,t}$	0.0594	0.5539	0.1112	0.1902	-0.0996	0.2811
$PMI_{US,t}$	-0.0550	0.6140	-0.2517	-0.1212	0.1545	-0.5079
$PMI_{Euro,t}$	0.1971	-0.0949	2.0344	-1.7141	0.3684	-1.9006
$GDP_{Turkey,t}$	-0.5589	0.1486	0.8350	-0.1493	-0.3559	-0.6353
$GDP_{China,t}$	-0.1080	-0.1699	-0.1952	-0.4440	-0.1742	0.1781
$GDP_{US,t}$	-1.0879	0.7717	-1.9509	0.7440	0.5885	1.0528
$GDP_{Euro,t}$	-0.2526	0.3006	0.7475	-1.1856	0.1475	0.3700
$PMI_{Turkey,t-1}$	0.0338	0.0288	0.0823	0.0528	0.2551	-0.6581*
$PMI_{China,t-1}$	-0.3033	-0.1196	0.0612	-0.1661	-0.1075	-0.1743
$PMI_{US,t-1}$	0.4085	-0.7441	0.2175	0.0698	-0.2830	0.0734
$PMI_{Euro,t-1}$	1.7190	-2.3316	3.4335	3.0985	-2.7576	2.6830
$GDP_{Turkey,t-1}$	0.8157	-0.1192	-0.2331	0.2024	0.1719	1.4579*
$GDP_{China,t-1}$	0.1221	0.3620	0.3503	0.3517	0.0323	0.0554
$GDP_{US,t-1}$	0.3290	-0.4890	-1.1117	-1.4674	-0.0084	-0.1196
$GDP_{Euro,t-1}$	-0.0131	-1.1672	-0.2122	1.3037*	0.7219	0.3720

0.995 which refers to a high persistency level in conditional variances. In addition, if the estimation results in terms of macroeconomic surprises are considered, it can be observed that the impact of macroeconomic surprises on conditional variances are not strong. In particular, for the sectors of Banking, Information Technology, Real Estate Invest Trusts, and Insurance, the macroeconomic surprises do not have any simultaneous or spillover effects on the conditional variances. For the Holdings & Investments sector, a single surprise in the GDP originating from Euro-Zone might cause a spillover effect, and the conditional variance increases by 1.3037. Moreover, the Technology sector shows both domestic PMI and domestic GDP spillovers. A single surprise in the PMI-Turkey causes a decrease in conditional variance about a rate of 0.6851, and a surprise in the GDP-Turkey yields an increase in conditional variance by 1.4579.

Finally, Table 13 reports the diagnostic tests of the conditional variance models.

Table 13. Conditional variance models diagnostic tests

	Weighted Ljung-Box Test on Stand. Resid. Q*(1)		Weighted Ljung-Box Test on Stand. Squared Resid. Q*(1)	
	Statistics	**p.Value**	**Statistics**	**p.Value**
XBANK	0.2639	0.6074	2.187	0.1392
XBLSM	0.02259	0.8805	0.003561	0.9524
XGMYO	1.929	0.1648	0.2622	0.6086
XHOLD	0.2155	0.64248	1.072	0.3004
XSGRT	1.282	0.2576	0.004127	0.9488
XUTEK	2.231	0.1352	2.182	0.1397

Considering the Ljung-Box*Q test results, it is observed that in the residuals, there is evidence of serial correlation or the ARCH effects. Therefore, the conditional variance models seem to perform well.

CONCLUSION

In this study, the impact of macroeconomic surprises on abnormal returns and volatilities of the Turkish financial market (e.g., Borsa Istanbul) has been investigated. In addition, an extensive empirical analysis with respect to several sectoral levels is presented. For this purpose, six sectoral indices of Borsa Istanbul have been considered (e.g., the BIST Banks, the BIST Information Technology, the BIST Insurance, the BIST Holdings & Investments, the BIST Industrials, the BIST Real Estate Invest Trusts, and the BIST Technology). The dataset covers the period from May 4, 2015 to January 1, 2019.

In the analysis, the impact of both domestic and foreign surprises has been considered. For this purpose, the US, the Euro-Zone, and China which have strong economical and international relations with Turkey have been included. The PMI and the GDP have been used as macroeconomic indicators. The reason for selecting these variables is their ability to represent the economic conditions of their countries of origin.

During the data analysis, the descriptive statistics of return series are initially presented, and then, a one factor CAPM model is applied in order to remove the market effect from the sectoral returns. The CAPM estimations imply that the Banking sector is the most sensitive sector, and the Insurance sector is the least sensitive sector. Subsequently, in order to examine the impact of macroeconomic surprises on these sectors, the first and second moments of the sectoral indices are considered. Hence, the macroeconomic surprises in the conditional mean equation are analyzed, and then, the impact of macroeconomic surprises is considered in conditional volatility.

Estimation results of the conditional mean models show that all sectors, except for the Holdings & Investments and Insurance sectors, have been affected by the macroeconomic surprises. The Banking sector is the most integrated sector with foreign countries. This sector responds to both the US and the Chinese macroeconomic surprises as well as the Turkish surprises. On the other hand, the Information Technology sector is the most sensitive sector. This sector's response to the GDP-US surprises is quite large and simultaneous.

Conditional volatility estimates involving the macroeconomic surprises and their first lags indicate that the most appropriate model for all indices is the EGARCH(1,1). This supports the existent literature (e.g., Fedorova et al., 2014, Omokehinde & Akingunola, 2018) which uses the EGARCH model to show the impact of macroeconomic news on stock markets. Furthermore, the results have revealed that the effects of the macroeconomic surprises on volatilities are not strong. In particular, apart from the Holdings & Investments and Technology sectors, the macroeconomic news has no significant impact on the market volatility.

The evidence of existing effects from the GDP surprises originating from the US to the Banking and Information Technology sectors is consistent with the leading role of the US in finance and information technologies. Interestingly, the Technology sector only reacts to domestic surprises. This might be a result of the fact that the activities of this sector are directly related to Turkey's economic power and expectations.

The findings of the study support the view that foreign country surprises may have an impact on the Turkish financial market, and these effects may vary among sectors. This study has also provided evidence that the Turkish financial market is more responsive to the GDP surprises than the PMI surprises. These results are consistent with the results of Fedorova et al. (2014) and Gok and Topuz (2016) which show the existence response of the Turkish stock market to GDP news. In general, this study supports the low response of the Turkish financial market to macroeconomic news at the sectoral level. The Insurance sector especially shows low sensitivity to both the market conditions and the macroeconomic surprises. As a final outcome of this study, it can be concluded that the Turkish financial market offers opportunities to develop various investment strategies.

REFERENCES

Akaike, H. (1974). A new look at the statistical model identification. *IEEE Transactions on Automatic Control*, *19*(6), 716–723. doi:10.1109/TAC.1974.1100705

Albuquerque, R., & Vega, C. (2009). Economic News and International Stock Market Co-Movement. *Review of Finance*, *13*(3), 401–465. doi:10.1093/rof/rfn020

Andersen, T. G., Bollerslev, T., Diebold, F. X., & Vega, C. (2007). Real-Time Price Discovery in Global Stock, Bond and Foreign Exchange Markets. *Journal of International Economics*, *73*(2), 251–277. doi:10.1016/j.jinteco.2007.02.004

Balduzzi, P., Elton, E., & Green, T. (2001). Economic News and Bond Prices: Evidence from the U.S. Treasury Market. *Journal of Financial and Quantitative Analysis*, *36*(4), 523–543. doi:10.2307/2676223

Bollerslev, T. (1986). Generalized Autoregressive Conditional Heteroskedasticity. *Journal of Econometrics*, *31*(3), 307–327. doi:10.1016/0304-4076(86)90063-1

Breusch, T. S. (1978). Testing for Autocorrelation in Dynamic Linear Models. *Australian Economic Papers*, *17*(31), 334–355. doi:10.1111/j.1467-8454.1978.tb00635.x

Cakan, E., Doytch, N., & Upadhyaya, K. P. (2015). Does U.S. Macroeconomic News Make Emerging Financial Markets Riskier? *Borsa Istanbul Review*, *15*(1), 37–43. doi:10.1016/j.bir.2014.10.002

Camilleria, S. J., Sciclunaa, N., & Bai, N. (2019). Do Stock Markets Lead or Lag Macroeconomic Variables? Evidence from Select European Countries. *The North American Journal of Economics and Finance*, *48*, 170–186. doi:10.1016/j.najef.2019.01.019

Chen, J., Liu, Y.-J., Lu, L., & Tang, Y. (2015). Investor Attention and Macroeconomic News Announcements: Evidence from Stock Index Futures. *Journal of Futures Markets*, *36*(3), 240–266. doi:10.1002/fut.21727

Dickey, D. A., & Fuller, W. A. (1979). Distribution of The Estimators for Autoregressive Time Series with Unit Root. *Journal of the American Statistical Association*, *74*, 427–431.

Dickey, D. A., & Fuller, W. A. (1981). Likelihood Ratio Statistics for Autoregressive Time Series with a Unit Root. *Econometrica*, *49*(4), 1057–1072. doi:10.2307/1912517

Ding, Z., Granger, C. W. J., & Engle, R. F. (1993). A Long Memory Property of Stock Market Returns and a New Model. *Journal of Empirical Finance*, *1*(1), 83–106. doi:10.1016/0927-5398(93)90006-D

Duangin, S., Yamaka, W., Sirisrisakulchai, J., & Sriboonchitta, S. (2018). Macroeconomic News Announcement and Thailand Stock Market. In *Integrated Uncertainty in Knowledge Modelling and Decision Making. IUKM 2018. Lecture Notes in Computer Science*, (vol 10758). Springer. 10.1007/978-3-319-75429-1_34

Ederington, L. H., & Lee, J. H. (1993). How markets process information: News releases and volatility. *The Journal of Finance*, *48*(4), 1161–1191. doi:10.1111/j.1540-6261.1993.tb04750.x

Ekinci, C., Akyıldırım, E., & Corbet, S. (2019). Analysing the Dynamic Influence of US Macroeconomic News Releases on Turkish Stock Markets. *Finance Research Letters*, *31*, 155–164. doi:10.1016/j.frl.2019.04.021

Erdoğan, S., & Acet, H. (2016). Cari İşlemler Dengesi ve Ekonomik Büyüme Arasındaki Ilişki: Türkiye Örneği (2003-2015). *The International Journal of Social Sciences (Islamabad)*, 51.

Fama, E. F. (1981). Association Stock Returns, Real Activity, Inflation, and The American. *Economic Review (Federal Reserve Bank of Atlanta)*, *71*(4), 545–565.

Fama, E. F. (1990). Stock Returns, Expected Returns and Real Activity. *The Journal of Finance*, *14*(4), 1089–1108. doi:10.1111/j.1540-6261.1990.tb02428.x

Fama, E. F., & French, K. R. (1989). Business Conditions and Expected Returns on Stocks and Bonds. *Journal of Financial Economics*, *25*(1), 23–49. doi:10.1016/0304-405X(89)90095-0

Fedorova, E., Wallenius, L., & Collan, M. (2014). The Impact of Euro Area Macroeconomic Announcements on CIVETS Stock Markets. *Procedia Economics and Finance*, *15*, 27–37. doi:10.1016/S2212-5671(14)00442-0

Ferson, W. E., & Harvey, C. R. (1991). Variation of Economic Risk Premiums. *Journal of Political Economy*, *99*(2), 385–415. doi:10.1086/261755

Geweke, J. (1986). Modelling the Persistence of Conditional Variances [Comment]. *Econometric Reviews*, *5*, 57–61. doi:10.1080/07474938608800097

Ghalanos, A. (2017). *Introduction to The Rugarch Package*. Retrieved from https://cran.r-project.org/web/packages/rugarch/vignettes/Introduction_to_the_rugarch_package.pdf

Ghalanos A. (2019). *rugarch: Univariate GARCH models*. R package version 1.4-1.

Glosten, L. R., Jagannathan, R., & Runkle, D. E. (1993). On the Relation Between the expected Value and The Volatility of The Nominal Excess Return on Stocks. *The Journal of Finance*, *48*(5), 1779–1801. doi:10.1111/j.1540-6261.1993.tb05128.x

Godfrey, L. G. (1978). Testing Against General Autoregressive and Moving Average Error Models when the Regressors Include Lagged Dependent Variables. *Econometrica*, *46*(6), 1293–1301. doi:10.2307/1913829

Gok, İ. Y., & Topuz, S. (2016). The Impact of the Domestic and Foreign Macroeconomic News Announcements on The Turkish Stock Market. Studii Financiare (Financial Studies), Centre of Financial and Monetary Research. *Victor Slavescu*, *20*(3), 95–107.

Gümüş, G. K., Yücel, A. T., Karaoğlan, D., & Çelik, Ş. (2011). The Impact of Domestic and Foreign Macroeconomic News on Stock Market Volatility: Istanbul Stock Exchange. *Boğaziçi Journal*, *25*(1), 123–137. doi:10.21773/boun.25.1.5

Hanousek, J., Kocenda, E., & Kutan, A. M. (2009). The Reaction of Asset Prices to Macroeconomic Announcements in New EU Markets: Evidence from Intraday Data. *Journal of Financial Stability*, *5*(2), 199–219. doi:10.1016/j.jfs.2008.01.003

Higgins, M. L., & Bera, A. K. (1992). A Class of Nonlinear ARCH Models. *International Economic Review*, *33*(1), 137–158. doi:10.2307/2526988

Huang, X. (2018). Macroeconomic News Announcements, Systemic Risk, Financial Market Volatility and Jumps. *Journal of Futures Markets*, *38*(5), 513–534. doi:10.1002/fut.21898

Jarque, C., & Bera, A. (1980). Efficient Tests for Normality Homoscedasticity and Serial Independence of Regression Residuals. *Economics Letters*, *6*(3), 255–259. doi:10.1016/0165-1765(80)90024-5

Kim, S. J., Mckenzie, M. D., & Faff, R. W. (2004). Macroeconomic News Announcements and The Role of Expectations: Evidence for US Bond, Stock and Foreign Exchange Markets. *Journal of Multinational Financial Management*, *14*(3), 17–232. doi:10.1016/j.mulfin.2003.02.001

Kim, S. J., & Nguyen, D. Q. T. (2008). The Reaction of the Australian Financial Markets to the Interest Rate News from the Reserve Bank of Australia and The U.S. Fed. *Research in International Business and Finance*, *22*(3), 378–395. doi:10.1016/j.ribaf.2008.02.001

Kim, S. J., & Nguyen, D. Q. T. (2009). The Spillover Effects of Target Interest Rate News from The U.S. Fed and the European Central Bank on the Asia-Pacific Stock Markets. *Journal of International Financial Markets, Institutions and Money*, *19*(3), 415–431. doi:10.1016/j.intfin.2008.12.001

Korkmaz, T., Cevik, E. I., & Atukeren, E. (2012). Return and Volatility Spillovers among CIVETS Stock Markets. *Emerging Markets Review*, *13*(2), 230–252. doi:10.1016/j.ememar.2012.03.003

Ljung, G. M., & Box, G. E. P. (1978). On a Measure of a Lack of Fit in Time Series Models. *Biometrika*, *65*(2), 297–303. doi:10.1093/biomet/65.2.297

Mansour-Ichrakieh, L., & Zeaiter, H. (2019). The Role of Geopolitical Risks on The Turkish Economy Opportunity or Threat. *The North American Journal of Economics and Finance*, *50*, 50. doi:10.1016/j.najef.2019.101000

McQueen, G., & Roley, V. V. (1993). Stock Prices, News, and Business Conditions. *Review of Financial Studies*, *6*(3), 683–707. doi:10.1093/rfs/5.3.683

Miron, J., & Romer, C. (1990). A New Monthly Index of Industrial Production, 1884-1940. *The Journal of Economic History*, *50*(2), 321–337. doi:10.1017/S0022050700036469

Nelson, D. B. (1991). Conditional Heteroskedasticity in Asset Returns: A New Approach. *Econometrica*, *59*(2), 347–370. doi:10.2307/2938260

Nowak, S., Andritzky, J., Jobst, A., & Tamirisa, N. (2011). Macroeconomic Fundamentals, Price Discovery, and Volatility Dynamics in Emerging Bond Markets. *Journal of Banking & Finance*, *35*(10), 2584–2597. doi:10.1016/j.jbankfin.2011.02.012

Omokehinde, J. O., & Akingunola, R. O. (2018). Macroeconomic News Announcements and Asymmetric Volatility of Stock Returns: The Nigerian Case. *The IEB International Journal of Finance*, *17*, 146–163.

Pal, S., Garg, A. K., & Tokic, D. (2019). Macroeconomic Surprises and Stock Market Responses-A Study on Indian Stock Market. *Cogent Economics and Finance, 7*(1).

Pantula, S. G. (1986). Modelling the Persistence of Conditional Variances [Comment]. *Econometric Reviews*, *5*, 71–73. doi:10.1080/07474938608800099

Pearce, D. K., & Roley, V. V. (1982). *The Reaction of Stock Prices to Unanticipated Changes in Money.* NBER Working Paper Series.

R Core Team. (2017). *R: A Language and Environment for Statistical Computing*. R Foundation for Statistical Computing. Retrieved from https://www.R-project.org/

Rigobon, R., & Sack, B. (2002). *The Impact of Monetary Policy on Asset Prices.* NBER Working Paper Series, 8794.

Ross, S. A. (1976). The Arbitrage Theory of Capital Asset Pricing. *Journal of Economic Theory, 13*(3), 341–360. doi:10.1016/0022-0531(76)90046-6

Schwarz, G. E. (1978). Estimating the dimension of a model. *Annals of Statistics, 6*(2), 461–464. doi:10.1214/aos/1176344136

Schwert, G. W. (1990a). Stock Returns and Real Activity: A Century of Evidence. *The Journal of Finance, 45*(4), 1237–1257. doi:10.1111/j.1540-6261.1990.tb02434.x

Schwert, G. W. (1990b). Stock Volatility and the Crash of 87. *Review of Financial Studies, 3*(1), 77–102. doi:10.1093/rfs/3.1.77

Sharpe, W. F. (1964). Capital Asset Prices: A Theory of Market Equilibrium Under Conditions of Risk. *The Journal of Finance, 19*(3), 425–442.

Taylor, S. (1986). *Modelling financial time series*. Wiley.

Trapletti A., & Hornik K. (2019). *tseries: Time Series Analysis and Computational Finance*. R package version 0.10-47.

TUIK. Türkiye İstatistik Kurumu. (2019). *Dış Ticaret İstatistikleri*. Retrieved from http://www.tuik.gov.tr/UstMenu.do?metod=temelist

Wang, Y., & Yang, X. (2018). *Asymmetric Response to PMI Announcements in China's Stock Returns. Statistical Finance*. Econometrics.

Wongswan, J. (2006). Transmission of Information Across International Equity Markets. *Review of Financial Studies, 19*(4), 1157–1189. doi:10.1093/rfs/hhj033

Yi, Y., Qi, W., & Wu, D. (2013). Are CIVETS the Next BRICS? A Comparative Analysis from Scientometrics Perspective. *Scientometrics, 94*(2), 615–628. doi:10.100711192-012-0791-9

Zakoian, J. M. (1994). Threshold Heteroskedastic Models. *Journal of Economic Dynamics & Control, 18*(5), 931–955. doi:10.1016/0165-1889(94)90039-6

Zeileis, A., & Grothendieck, G. (2005). zoo: S3 Infrastructure for Regular and Irregular Time Series. *Journal of Statistical Software, 14*(6), 1–27. doi:10.18637/jss.v014.i06

Zivot, E. (2008). *Practical Issues in the Analysis of Univariate GARCH Models. In Handbook of Financial Time Series*. Springer.

KEY TERMS AND DEFINITIONS

Akaike Information Criterion (AIC): An estimator of out-of-sample prediction error and thereby relative quality of statistical models for the underlying sample of data. It estimates the relative amount of information lost by a model, so the less information a model loses, the higher the quality of that model.

Capital Asset Pricing Model (CAPM): A model used to determine a theoretically appropriate required rate of return of an asset, to make decisions about adding assets to a well-diversified portfolio.

GARCH: Generalized Autoregressive Conditional Heteroskedasticity (GARCH) process is an econometric term developed in 1982 by Robert F. Engle to describe an approach to estimate volatility in financial markets.

GDP Growth: The gross domestic product (GDP) growth rate measures how fast the economy is growing by comparing a quarter of the country's gross domestic product to the previous quarter.

Jarque-Bera (JB) Test: A goodness-of-fit-test to determine if a sample of data have the skewness and kurtosis that matches a normal distribution. The test is named after Carlos Jarque and Anil K. Bera.

Schwarz Information Criterion (BIC): Also known as the Bayesian information criterion. It is a criterion for model selection among a finite set of models. A model with the lowest BIC is preferred. This is determined on a likelihood function for a distribution and it is closely related to the Akaike information criterion.

ENDNOTES

1. Throughout the study, the macroeconomic news and the macroeconomic surprises can be used interchangeably.
2. Borsa Istanbul provides a unified market place which brings together all the exchanges operating in the Turkish capital markets. The exchanges operated in the Borsa Istanbul include capital markets instruments, foreign currencies, precious metals and gems, and other contracts, documents, and assets approved by the Capital Markets Board of Turkey.
3. Additional *R* packages are "zoo" (Zeileis & Grothendieck, 2005), "tseries" (Trapletti & Hornik, 2019), "rugarch" (Ghalanos, 2019).
4. The skewness and kurtosis statistics of the normal distribution is equal to 0 and 3, respectively.

Chapter 5
The Convergence Behind the Curtain:
An Examination of Crime Rates in Pennsylvania Counties

Olivia A. Habacivch
Indiana University of Pennsylvania, USA

Ryan A. Redilla
Indiana University of Pennsylvania, USA

James J. Jozefowicz
https://orcid.org/0000-0002-6543-2504
Indiana University of Pennsylvania, USA

ABSTRACT

This chapter extends applications of unconditional and conditional β-convergence and unconditional σ-convergence analysis to Part I crime rates in a panel data sample of Pennsylvania counties during the period 1990-2015. Temporal structural breaks at specific points in the business cycle during the time frame and spatial breakpoints between rural and urban counties in Pennsylvania are acknowledged in the analysis in order to avoid spurious inferences regarding convergence behavior. Unit-root testing is performed on measures of dispersion as well as directly on the underlying crime-rate series via panel-data tests for non-stationarity. The findings support the existence of both unconditional and conditional β-convergence in the pooled, urban, and rural samples during 1990-2015. Visual and statistical evidence reveals the presence of σ-convergence in the three samples across the time span as well. The comprehensive convergence analysis of appropriately disaggregated data performed in this study offers strong support for the predictions of modernization theory.

DOI: 10.4018/978-1-7998-1093-3.ch005

INTRODUCTION

In the context of crime, convergence refers to the tendency of existing differences in crime rates across cross-sectional units or time periods to dissipate and effectively close the gap. In other words, disparities in rates of criminal activity will be transitory rather than permanent. The study of crime rate convergence is a relatively new undertaking for researchers in economics (Cook & Winfield 2013, 2016). Empirical results have been mixed thus far, with some studies showing both β-convergence and σ-convergence (Cook & Winfield, 2013), others finding only one of the two present, and still others revealing crime divergence (Cook & Winfield, 2016). Several important facets of crime rate convergence remain understudied, and no single crime theory of convergence (e.g., modernization theory, conflict theory) has distinguished itself as having the most explanatory power. Despite a dearth of empirical investigation, understanding crime rate convergence is important for policy direction and implementation, since criminal behavior remains a matter of ongoing concern for law enforcement officials and policymakers at all geographic levels. Cook and Winfield's (2013, 2016) findings on crime rate convergence have birthed new empirical questions, because there is ambiguity surrounding the policy implications of crime rate convergence. Questions like, "Is the convergence of crime rates favorable or unfavorable?" and "Can crime convergence be increased or limited?" remain unsatisfactorily answered.

Determining whether or not crime rate convergence exists across time and region may better inform crime rate predictions and offer new avenues of inquiry for criminological theory and ultimately crime-rate-reduction strategies. This research is motivated accordingly and acknowledges both temporal and spatial structural breaks. Cook and Cook (2011) argue that analyses of crime convergence over time that ignore breakpoints resulting from fluctuations in economic conditions, significant social shifts, and governmental regime changes may yield misleading results. They note that the persistent assertions of non-stationary U.S. crime rates in the existing literature may arise from overlooked structural breaks in the underlying series and, consequently, run the risk of advancing spurious inferences. Thus, the analysis separately considers the convergence behavior of crime rates across the expansionary and contractionary phases of the business cycle when structural changes occur. In addition, this study includes separate analyses of rural and urban regions based on a structural break between rural and urban counties in Pennsylvania, because criminal activity is a function of the features of a specific geographic location as emphasized by Buonanno and Montolio (2008). This approach to understanding crime rates in rural and urban Pennsylvania counties is consistent with previous literature (Cook & Winfield, 2016; Frederick & Jozefowicz, 2018), and it heeds the warning that equivalently treating non-metropolitan and metropolitan areas risks a sample selection bias toward finding convergence (Drennan, Lobo, & Strumsky, 2004). If convergence in crime rates varies by levels of economic activity and/or geographic area, then further analysis on the structural differences between rural and urban areas and the facets of business cycle fluctuations is in order.

Heavily disaggregated data repeatedly has been shown to provide more precise results in crime studies. Chilton and Chambliss (2014) stress the importance of disaggregating data according to race when studying crime trends. Disaggregated religion data also has been shown to be more informative when measuring hate crimes ("Comprehensive and Disaggregated Data," 2016). Geographically disaggregated data additionally is more palpable when formulating theories than national or international data (Frederick & Jozefowicz, 2018). Among the arguments for selecting counties rather than states or countries as the appropriate unit of observation are: (1) greater homogeneity than states; (2) more time-invariant structural factors; (3) consistent borders; and (4) diminished risk of aggregation bias (Phillips & Land, 2012; Wells & Weisheit, 2012). In reality, counties represent the location where most activities of daily living take place, and Brown and Kandel (2006) laud counties, because they "actually present fewer problems than most geographies" (p. 14). Finally, according to Jenkins (2014), concentrating on counties within a single state is appropriate since crime-fighting measures are implemented locally in the U.S. Thus, in accordance with Cook and Winfield (2016), who stress the importance of using disaggregated data when measuring crime rate trends, this study utilizes a panel data sample of 67 Pennsylvania counties in order to provide a more accurate view of crime rate behavior over time.

This chapter extends the applications of convergence analysis utilized by Cook and Cook (2011), Cook and Winfield (2013, 2016), and Drennan et al. (2004) to crime rates in Pennsylvania counties from the period 1990-2015. It contributes to the debate regarding which convergence theories have the most explanatory power by reviewing various theories and discussing which theory best explains the results. Furthermore, the policy implications of the crime convergence findings are discussed, and opportunities for future extensions of the research are identified. A unique feature of this study is the comprehensive investigation of convergence behavior in crime rates via different approaches with a more recent data sample.

In order to fill in some of the gaps in the existing crime rate convergence literature, the following objectives are pursued: (1) determining whether or not unconditional β-convergence exists in the crime rate series; (2) determining whether or not conditional β-convergence exists in the crime rate series; (3) visually determining whether or not unconditional σ-convergence exists using crime-rate measures of dispersion; (4) statistically determining whether or not unconditional σ-convergence exists via unit-root testing on crime-rate measures of dispersion; and (5) statistically determining whether or not unconditional σ-convergence exists via the direct application of panel unit-root tests to the crime rate series.

BACKGROUND

There are two primary criminological theories that seek to explain crime rate convergence. Modernization theory asserts that modernization brings with it an uncomfortable transition period that requires letting go of traditional values and practices and replacing them with more equitable and individualistic ones (Neuman & Berger, 1988). This transition period increases crime rates, and "anomie," which, according to Durkheim's institutional anomie theory, is a widening of the gap between society's value of wealth and the means available to obtain wealth. This disequilibrium between goals and the means of attaining goals creates a more criminogenic setting even after the transition period to modernization is completed. Modernization theory predicts that crime rates will completely converge once all nations are fully modernized. Studies testing modernization theory have shown mixed results. Arthur's (1991) research on development and crime in Africa found that only minor property crime rate results were consistent with modernization theory.

The second theory commonly used when discussing crime rate convergence is conflict theory. Conflict theory emerged in the 1990's and asserts that the laws governing society are created inequitably by the rich and powerful elite class in order to repress the lower classes and to maintain their own status. This theory is in direct opposition to consensus theory, which asserts that the laws governing society reflect a general consensus on what is "right" or "wrong," criminal or noncriminal behavior. Conflict theory predicts that crime rates will diverge across developing/ poor nations and developed/wealthy nations in time.

LaFree (2016), in his study analyzing cross-national homicide victimization trends, offers a third theoretical explanation in which only highly industrialized, wealthy, elite nations will show signs of crime convergence. His results generally support his predictions. Neuman and Berger (1988) offer still other theoretical explanations for crime rate convergence in their examination of Marxian-world and ecological-opportunity theories in addition to modernization theory and find that modernization theory is largely unsupported.

Convergence Measures

To better understand an important property of crime rates in Pennsylvania counties, two different types of convergence are considered in the analysis (Cook & Winfield, 2016). The presence of unconditional β-convergence suggests that counties with high initial levels of crime tend to experience slower crime growth in the future, while those regions with initially less criminal activity witness more rapid growth going forward (i.e., a catch-up effect). Bernard and Durlauf (1996) identify this phenomenon with cross-sectional convergence. On the other hand, σ-convergence indicates a narrowing of the county-level (i.e., cross-sectional) distribution of crime rates across time observations. This version is associated with the idea of time-series convergence, which is considered to be a more stringent form of convergence (Bernard & Durlauf, 1996). It is important to note that while β-convergence is a necessary condition for σ-convergence, it is not a sufficient condition (Cook & Winfield, 2013, 2016). In contrast, σ-convergence is both a necessary and a sufficient condition for β-convergence (Cook & Winfield, 2013; Young, Higgins, & Levy, 2008).

LITERATURE

Drennan et al. (2004) analyzed U.S. metropolitan-area data from the years 1969-2001 to test for σ-convergence in income. They used per capita personal income and average wage per job covariates, which they gathered from the Bureau of Economic Analysis' Regional Economic Information Systems. Using 318 metropolitan areas, they employed the Augmented Dickey-Fuller test to check for unit roots and were unable to reject the null of a unit root in the data sample. Rather than finding evidence of income σ-convergence, their results showed evidence for income divergence beginning in the mid-1970's. One possible reason for this finding is offered by Borts (1960) who claimed that areas with strong export demands, such as metropolitan areas, will grow faster than low-income areas if the demand continues to grow.

The two types of convergence, σ- and β-convergence, were examined by Higgins, Levy, and Young (2006). Using U.S. county-level data and personal income variables gathered from the Bureau of Economic Analysis, the authors estimated a model using three-stage least squares regression analysis. They found that there was β-convergence, which they asserted was a necessary but not sufficient condition for σ-convergence. Young et al. (2008) emphasized that σ-convergence was more telling than β-convergence in terms of income equality. Consistent with Drennan et al. (2004), Young et al. (2008) found evidence of significant σ-divergence from 1970-1998 contrary to prediction.

Cook and Winfield's (2016) study analyzed both U.S. state and county-level data to measure Part I crime rate convergence across regions and demonstrated the importance of disaggregated data and the variation between rural and urban areas, which increases as the data is further disaggregated. There was some inconsistency across results. Both violent and property crime rates showed significant unconditional β-convergence. Additionally, though σ-convergence was present for violent crimes, σ-divergence was evident for property crimes. In the county-level data sample, the presence of σ-convergence was lower than in the state-level data.

Cook and Winfield (2013) applied convergence analysis to U.S. crime rates from 50 U.S. states between the years of 1965-2009. They used Part I crime data gathered from the FBI's Uniform Crime Report (UCR) and found significant unconditional β-convergence in crime rates for their entire state-level sample. They also tested for σ-convergence, which was greatest and most significant for property crimes such as larceny. Inconsistent with the rest of the findings, σ-convergence for motor vehicle theft was nonexistent. Cook and Winfield (2013) also noted that σ-convergence rates seem to have sped up from the mid-1970's to 1980 for all crimes aside from motor vehicle theft and assault.

Cook and Watson (2013) examined convergence in crime rates using national trends in U.S. regional crime rates from 1965 to 2009. By analyzing z-statistics and their corresponding two-sided p-values, they concluded that as crime fluctuated over time, the crime rates have narrowed. These narrowing crime rates are due to myriad factors such as increased arrest rates, improved policing strategies, increased incarceration, and decreased alcohol and cocaine consumption. In summary, Cook and Watson (2013) found that while the discussion of crime convergence is appropriate in general, it must be qualified according to the specific form of crime and sample period considered.

Cook and Cook (2011) drew upon changes in the temporal patterns of crime to explore unit-root processes of U.S. crime rates from 1960 to 2007. Using annual observations obtained from the FBI's UCR, they analyzed natural logarithmic values of violent crimes and property crimes with Dickey-Fuller and GLS-DF tests. They also identified breakpoints in the crime series to better depict and describe the evolution of crime over time. Overall, Cook and Cook (2011) assert that crime rates in the U.S. are not best classified as unit-root processes, but rather can be characterized by stationary processes fluctuating about broken deterministic trends. Their findings stand in contrast to the existing literature on U.S. crime rates, which they attribute to a lack of appropriately recognizing structural breaks in the samples.

HYPOTHESES

Despite the inconsistent support for modernization theory in some prior convergence research, the authors of this study accept its primary propositions. This study, therefore, tests the following hypotheses:

Hypothesis One: Crime rate convergence does exist across Pennsylvania counties.

Hypothesis Two: The phases of the business cycle have a significant impact on crime rate convergence.

Hypothesis Three: Rural and urban regional differences have a significant impact on crime rate convergence.

Hypothesis Four: σ-convergence is a necessary and sufficient condition for β-convergence.

CONVERGENCE ANALYSIS

Data Sample

In accordance with Cook and Winfield (2013), the dependent variable is the Part I crime rate (CRIME) for the 67 counties in the Commonwealth of Pennsylvania observed over the 1990-2015-time frame. Analyzing county-level crime rates results in 67 total annual observations which, despite their popularity in the literature as noted by Cook and Winfield (2016), exceeds the samples utilized in similar state-level studies (Becsi, 1999; Chen, 2008; DeFina & Arvanites, 2002; Marvell & Moody, 1998, 2001; Smith, 1997, 2004; Spelman, 2008; Winsberg, 1993; Zhang, Maxwell, & Vaughn, 2009). In addition, by analyzing a sample that ends in 2015 rather than 2010, this study offers a more recent assessment of convergence than Cook and Winfield (2016) and incorporates a larger portion of the recovery from the Great Recession.

The Part I crime rate measures the number of reported crimes per 100,000 people, and it encompasses murder, nonnegligent manslaughter, forcible rape, robbery, assault, burglary, larceny-theft, motor-vehicle theft, and arson. The data was collected from the Pennsylvania State Police Uniform Crime Reports similar to Cook and Winfield (2016). According to Grugan (2014), Part I infractions more accurately depict crime trends, because they are reported to law enforcement authorities to a greater extent than other offenses. Furthermore, Ehrlich (1996) argues that any reporting biases in crime data can be ameliorated with logarithms, since the natural logarithm of crime rates probably is proportional to the actual level of criminal activity.

In Table 1, an examination of the descriptive statistics for the Part I crime rates at different points in the sample reveals how the variation is changing over time. In 1990, the county with the largest crime rate (6933.1) was 743% greater than the county with the smallest rate of criminal activity (933.1). That disparity had fallen to 487% in 2015 for the pooled sample. Considering the urban counties, the maximum crime rate in 1990 was 404% larger than the minimum, and that difference fell to 340% by the end of the study time frame. Rural areas possessed a maximum crime rate of 6277.9 in 1990, which was 673% higher than the minimum of 933.1 in that

Table 1. Descriptive statistics for CRIME in the pooled, urban, and rural samples

	1990	2000	2010	2015
Pooled				
Mean	2466.87	1998.90	1867.16	1681.10
Standard Deviation	1107.68	847.73	616.20	512.71
Median	2142.90	1857.0	1751.10	1625.50
Maximum	6933.10	6531.0	4442.90	4206.60
Minimum	933.10	759.0	925.70	863.20
Observations	67	67	67	67
Urban				
Mean	3174.30	2493.84	2340.47	2032.98
Standard Deviation	1225.57	1172.40	722.21	640.34
Median	2900.30	2413.0	2038.20	1934.40
Maximum	6933.10	6531.0	4442.90	4206.60
Minimum	1717.60	1152.0	1560.60	1239.00
Observations	19	19	19	19
Rural				
Mean	2186.85	1802.98	1679.81	1541.82
Standard Deviation	930.23	586.96	455.00	377.13
Median	1991.0	1793.0	1635.70	1517.45
Maximum	6277.90	4266.0	2756.10	2455.80
Minimum	933.10	759.0	925.70	863.20
Observations	48	48	48	48

same year. By 2015, rural counties had witnessed a decline in that gap to 284%. It is apparent from these values that the range of crime-rate values across the samples of Pennsylvania counties has decreased over the 26-year period under consideration.

While there is no prevailing agreement on a "complete" list of control variables in the existing literature, the controls included here reflect those used by other researchers (Arvanities & DeFina, 2006; Cantor & Land, 1985; Phillips & Land, 2012). UNEMP is the county-level unemployment rate. NONWHITE is the percent of the population that is not Caucasian, and YOUNG is the percent of the population between 18 and 24 years old. POVERTY measures the percent of the population below the poverty line. Deterrence variables include: ARREST, which represents the number of Part I crime arrests; CLEARANCE, which is the number of crimes cleared by charges being filed divided by the number of Part I crimes reported; and POLICE, which is the total number of police officers divided by the population.

Convergence Analysis Methods

In order to assess the existence of unconditional β-convergence in crime rates in Pennsylvania counties, a simple OLS regression model along the lines of Cook and Winfield (2013, 2016) is estimated:

$$\Delta \ln(CRIME_{iT}) = \alpha + \beta \ln(CRIME_{i0}) + \varepsilon_{\mathrm{i}} \quad (1)$$

where the dependent variable represents the change in the natural logarithm of the Part I crime rate in county i across the entire study period (i.e., from 1990 to 2015) while the key independent variable is the natural logarithm of the county-level crime rate in 1990, which marks the beginning of the time period (i.e., the initial level of crime in county i). Conditional β-convergence analysis acknowledges the "heterogeneity of places" by also incorporating control variables representing varying initial conditions in equation (1) (Drennan et al., 2004 p. 584; Higgins et al., 2006; Rey & Montouri, 1999; Young et al., 2008). Given this specification, β-convergence is indicated by a negative and statistically significant coefficient on the initial level of crime. Due to heteroskedasticity concerns, the regression results are based on White heteroskedasticity-corrected standard errors consistent with Cook and Winfield (2013, 2016).

Determining whether or not σ-convergence exists involves calculating a measure of dispersion, such as the coefficient of variation (i.e., the ratio of the standard deviation to the mean) or the standard deviation of the natural logarithm of a series, for each year for all of the counties in the sample. In other words, the level of variation is computed across the counties for 1990, 1991, and so on, resulting in a total of 26 values. It is possible to identify σ-convergence either via visual inspection of a plotted measure of dispersion or more formally by testing for the presence of a unit root in the underlying time series (Bernard & Durlauf, 1996; Drennan et al., 2004; Young et al., 2008). If a data series is determined to be non-stationary (i.e., has a unit root) then it is highly unlikely that σ-convergence exists, because any shocks will persist indefinitely into the future (Drennan et al., 2004; Rey & Montouri, 1999).

Structural Breaks

Cook and Cook (2011) warn against ignoring the existence of structural breaks in samples of crime rates. Since the period of study includes the then-longest post-WWII expansion in the United States in addition to the entirety of the Great Recession, as well as, the initial several years of the subsequent recovery, it is conceivable that structural breaks exist between different phases of the business cycle (Bushway & Reuter, 2002; Phillips & Land, 2012). The plethora of unemployment-crime relationship analyses in the existing literature (Cantor & Land, 1985; Phillips & Land, 2012) firmly establishes a link between aggregate economic activity and criminal behavior. Chow tests performed on the panel data sample confirm that breakpoints are evident between the 1990-1999 (i.e., expansion) and 2000-2009 (i.e., recession) periods, and between the 2000-2009 (i.e., recession) and 2010-2015 (i.e., recovery) time frames.

In addition, it is reasonable to assume that the impact of economic upturns/downturns differentially may impact illegal activities across regions of different types. Wells and Weisheit (2012) question whether existing analyses of criminal activity are as applicable to non-metropolitan areas as they are for metropolitan locales, both because policymakers seek to combat crime across diverse regions and because the limited scope of strictly urban-focused analyses of crime potentially renders crime-fighting approaches impotent in other settings. Albeit in the context of income convergence, Drennan et al. (2004) asserts that equivalently treating urban and rural areas may bias the results toward convergence. In the case of Pennsylvania, 48 of its 67 counties are classified as rural by the Center for Rural Pennsylvania (2014), and Frederick and Jozefowicz (2018) find that rural-urban differences in crime exist in the state. Consequently, periods of economic expansion, recession, and recovery are analyzed separately for rural and urban Pennsylvania counties. Other studies of rural-urban regional variation in illegal activities include Lyerly and Skipper (1981), Weisheit and Donnermeyer (2000), and Wells and Weisheit (2004).

β-CONVERGENCE RESULTS

Unconditional β-Convergence Findings

Table 2 presents the results of estimating Equation (1) in order to detect the existence of unconditional β-convergence in the crime rate during the period of study. For the pooled Pennsylvania sample (i.e., all 67 counties), statistically significant negative coefficients are obtained indicating β-convergence across the 1990-2015 time frame consistent with Cook and Winfield (2016), as well as, separately during the expansion, recession, and recovery phases of the business cycle. The estimated coefficients on the initial value of crime are significant at the 1% level based on one-tailed t-tests except during the period of economic upturn when the significance level is 5%. These findings offer strong evidence of β-convergence across the business cycle with the greatest degree of convergence occurring for the entire sample period (-0.58) followed closely by the 2000-2009 recessionary period (-0.45). Cook and Winfield (2013) obtained a comparable coefficient of -0.51 based on state-level violent crime rates, while Cook and Winfield (2016) estimated the equivalent coefficient to be -0.57

Table 2. Unconditional beta convergence results: Pooled sample

Variables	Pooled 1990-2015	Pooled 1990-1999	Pooled 2000-2009	Pooled 2010-2015
	Model 1	**Model 2**	**Model 3**	**Model 4**
Constant	4.1665***	0.9786	3.4445***	1.7186***
	(4.95)	(1.58)	(5.23)	(3.18)
$\ln(CRIME_{i0})$	-0.5835***	-0.1505**	-0.4529***	-0.2426***
	(-5.30)	(-1.89)	(-5.21)	(-3.37)
$\bar{R}^2$	0.48	0.05	0.32	0.18

Notes: A one-tailed t-test was used for the $ln(CRIME_{i0})$ covariate. t-statistics in parentheses are based on White heteroskedasticity-consistent standard errors. ***, **, * denote coefficient significant at 1%, 5%, and 10% levels, respectively. *Source: authors' calculations.*

using county-level observations. In contrast, the expansionary period in Pennsylvania witnesses the least convergence of crime rates with a coefficient of -0.15.

In the case of the urban Pennsylvania counties (i.e., 19 counties) in Table 3, negative coefficient estimates, which are significant at the 1% level with a one-tailed test, support the existence of unconditional β-convergence over the full time frame and during the economic downturn. However, in terms of magnitude, β-convergence occurs to a somewhat larger extent during the recession years (i.e., 200-2009) than during 1990-2015 (i.e., -0.62 vs. -0.44). Cook and Winfield (2016) found unconditional β-convergence of -0.67 for metropolitan-area violent crime rates during 1977-2010. Cook and Winfield (2013) and Drennan et al. (2004) point out that convergence may require lengthy periods of time to emerge, and Rey and Montouri (1999) emphasize that convergence corresponds to a long-run movement toward equalization, so the apparent lack of convergence during the expansion and recovery phases for urban counties may arise from the short time frames analyzed herein.

In contrast, the rural subsample (i.e., 48 counties) in Pennsylvania experiences unconditional crime-rate β-convergence in all cases as observed in Table 4, strongly mirroring the pooled sample. Significance levels also are consistent with 1% significance evident in all instances except for the upturn, which reflects a 5% level. The largest amount of convergence once again belongs to the 1990-2015 segment followed by the recession. However, while the degree of β-convergence during the downturn is very comparable across the pooled and rural samples (i.e., -0.45 vs. -0.48), the rural counties experience considerably more convergence during 1990-2015 than the full 67-county sample (i.e., -0.73 vs. -0.58). Cook and Winfield (2016) found unconditional β-convergence of about -0.6 among non-metropolitan areas in their study. Although the expansionary time frame accounts for the least convergence

Table 3. Unconditional beta convergence results: Urban sample

Variables	Urban 1990-2015	Urban 1990-1999	Urban 2000-2009	Urban 2010-2015
	Model 1	Model 2	Model 3	Model 4
Constant	3.1318***	-0.6710	4.8515***	0.3760
	(2.20)	(-0.46)	(3.69)	(0.53)
$\ln(CRIME_{i0})$	-0.4444***	0.0558	-0.6200***	-0.0668
	(-2.52)	(0.31)	(-3.69)	(-0.72)
$\bar{R}^2$	0.34	-0.05	0.54	0.0034

Notes: A one-tailed t-test was used for the $ln(CRIME_{i0})$ covariate. t-statistics in parentheses are based on White heteroskedasticity-consistent standard errors. ***, **, * denote coefficient significant at 1%, 5%, and 10% levels, respectively. *Source: authors' calculations.*

Table 4. Unconditional beta convergence results: Rural sample

Variables	Rural 1990-2015	Rural 1990-1999	Rural 2000-2009	Rural 2010-2015
	Model 1	Model 2	Model 3	Model 4
Constant	5.2381***	1.5513**	3.5971***	2.4214***
	(5.10)	(2.03)	(4.53)	(3.16)
$\ln(CRIME_{i0})$	-0.7281***	-0.2258***	-0.4795***	-0.3384***
	(-5.37)	(-2.27)	(-4.45)	(-3.26)
$\bar{R}^2$	0.55	0.12	0.29	0.20

Notes: A one-tailed t-test was used for the $ln(CRIME_{i0})$ covariate. t-statistics in parentheses are based on White heteroskedasticity-consistent standard errors. ***, **, * denote coefficient significant at 1%, 5%, and 10% levels, respectively. *Source: authors' calculations.*

in both the pooled and rural samples, the crime rate in rural Pennsylvania counties converges more than that of the entire sample (-0.23 vs. -0.15) during the 1990's. These findings lie in contrast with Cook and Winfield (2016), who found the greatest degree of convergence among large metropolitan areas across the United States.

Conditional β-Convergence Findings

The results of estimating Equation (1) with the addition of control and deterrence variables to investigate the possibility of conditional β-convergence in Pennsylvania appear in Tables 5-7. For the pooled 1990-2015 sample, conditional β-convergence is evident in Table 5. The coefficient for the initial level of crime is negative and

Table 5. Conditional beta convergence results: Pooled sample

Variables	Pooled 1990-2015	Pooled 1990-1999	Pooled 2000-2009	Pooled 2010-2015
	Model 1	Model 2	Model 3	Model 4
Constant	5.5382***	2.6952***	4.0562***	3.0278***
	(4.91)	(3.05)	(4.58)	(3.70)
$\ln(CRIME_{i0})$	-0.7417***	-0.3825***	-0.5500***	-0.3805***
	(-5.42)	(-3.53)	(-4.52)	(-3.93)
UNEMP	0.0070	0.0000195	-0.0080	-0.0435*
	(0.35)	(0.0009)	(-0.17)	(-1.85)
NONWHITE	0.0230**	-0.0086	0.0154*	-0.0000720
	(1.99)	(-0.59)	(1.80)	(-0.01)
YOUNG	-0.0151*	-0.0101	0.0027	-0.0185***
	(-1.92)	(-1.20)	(0.26)	(-2.76)
POVERTY	0.0117*	-0.0058	0.0120	0.0224***
	(1.79)	(-0.77)	(0.71)	(3.42)
POLICE	28.0607	168.4788**	-35.8253	7.8132
	(0.33)	(2.47)	(-1.22)	(0.21)
ARREST	-0.0000172	0.0000194	-0.0000122	0.0000119
	(-1.24)	(0.88)	(-0.72)	(0.97)
CLEARANCE	-0.0098**	-0.0002	-0.0005	-0.0004
	(-2.23)	(-0.05)	(-0.15)	(-0.16)
$\bar{R}^2$	0.59	0.16	0.32	0.32

Notes: A one-tailed t-test was used for the *ln(CRIME$_{i0}$)* covariate. t-statistics in parentheses are based on White heteroskedasticity-consistent standard errors. ***, **, * denote coefficient significant at 1%, 5%, and 10% levels, respectively. *Source: authors' calculations.*

statistically significant at the 1% level with a one-tailed t-test. This finding is robust across the expansion, recession, and recovery phases of the business cycle for the entire 67-county Pennsylvania sample, and it is consistent with the unconditional β-convergence results.

In the urban sample in Table 6, conditional β-convergence occurs across the 1990-2015 period at a 5% significance level. However, there is no evidence of β-convergence during the expansion among urban counties in Pennsylvania once control and deterrence covariates are included in the model. Based on a coefficient of -0.96, which is significant at the 1% level, there is very strong conditional β-convergence apparent during the recessionary years. Urban areas also experience β-convergence

Table 6. Conditional beta convergence results: Urban sample

Variables	Urban 1990-2015	Urban 1990-1999	Urban 2000-2009	Urban 2010-2015
	Model 1	Model 2	Model 3	Model 4
Constant	3.0464*	-1.9918	7.6323***	0.8406
	(1.77)	(-0.78)	(4.82)	(0.85)
$\ln(CRIME_{i0})$	-0.4864**	0.2465	-0.9628***	-0.1928*
	(-2.58)	(0.74)	(-4.74)	(-1.62)
UNEMP	0.2120***	0.0763	0.0310	0.0394
	(5.22)	(0.89)	(0.21)	(1.39)
NONWHITE	0.0242	-0.0018	0.0364**	0.0015
	(1.25)	(-0.06)	(2.24)	(0.47)
YOUNG	-0.0122	0.0118	-0.0320	-0.0036
	(-0.66)	(0.24)	(-0.83)	(-0.35)
POVERTY	-0.0244**	-0.0337*	0.0666	0.0042
	(-2.65)	(-1.84)	(1.37)	(0.41)
POLICE	-192.9108*	-83.5344	-197.5931	-37.0105**
	(-1.72)	(-0.38)	(-1.30)	(-2.23)
ARREST	0.0000107	0.0000289	-0.0000455***	0.00000957
	(0.65)	(0.98)	(-2.95)	(1.27)
CLEARANCE	-0.0040	-0.0073	-0.0112	0.0063**
	(-0.41)	(-0.35)	(-1.11)	(2.18)
$\bar{R}^2$	0.81	-0.33	0.78	0.57

Notes: A one-tailed t-test was used for the $ln(CRIME_{i0})$ covariate. t-statistics in parentheses are based on White heteroskedasticity-consistent standard errors. ***, **, * denote coefficient significant at 1%, 5%, and 10% levels, respectively. *Source: authors' calculations.*

during the recovery period, but the negative coefficient is only significant at the 10% level. Furthermore, its magnitude of -0.19 provides the weakest evidence of conditional β-convergence for urban counties. These results are broadly consistent with the unconditional β-convergence outcomes for metropolitan areas.

Strong conditional β-convergence takes place during 1990-2015 in rural counties based on a coefficient of -0.88 in Table 7, which is statistically significant at the 1% level. Although it is roughly 50% weaker than during the 1990-2015 time frame, β-convergence does occur during the expansionary phase of the business cycle in rural Pennsylvania. The rural counties witness degrees of β-convergence roughly comparable to the upturn during the recession and recovery years. Those

Table 7. Conditional beta convergence results: Rural sample

Variables	Rural 1990-2015	Rural 1990-1999	Rural 2000-2009	Rural 2010-2015
	Model 1	Model 2	Model 3	Model 4
Constant	6.2998***	2.9959***	3.8314***	3.5609***
	(5.99)	(3.13)	(4.88)	(4.06)
$\ln(CRIME_{i0})$	-0.8760***	-0.4430***	-0.5287***	-0.4456***
	(-6.86)	(-3.62)	(-4.82)	(-3.80)
UNEMP	0.0201	0.0106	-0.0345	-0.0560*
	(1.10)	(0.54)	(-0.80)	(-1.88)
NONWHITE	-0.0089	-0.0211	0.0009	-0.0007
	(-0.40)	(-0.73)	(0.08)	(-0.11)
YOUNG	-0.0157*	-0.0116	0.0062	-0.0185**
	(-1.91)	(-1.37)	(0.48)	(-2.01)
POVERTY	0.0133	-0.0022	0.0259	0.0210***
	(1.60)	(-0.31)	(1.23)	(2.72)
POLICE	79.5284	196.5209**	-25.6463	41.1768
	(0.91)	(2.50)	(-0.76)	(0.94)
ARREST	0.0004***	0.0002*	0.0003*	0.0001
	(4.08)	(1.85)	(1.90)	(1.59)
CLEARANCE	-0.0123***	-0.0014	-0.0036	-0.0014
	(-2.68)	(-0.23)	(-0.80)	(-0.46)
$\bar{R}^2$	0.69	0.26	0.30	0.34

Notes: A one-tailed t-test was used for the $\ln(CRIME_{i0})$ covariate. t-statistics in parentheses are based on White heteroskedasticity-consistent standard errors. ***, **, * denote coefficient significant at 1%, 5%, and 10% levels, respectively. *Source: authors' calculations.*

negative coefficients also are significant at the 1% level. Thus, both the conditional β-convergence and the unconditional β-convergence findings are consistent with each other in rural areas in Pennsylvania, but remain at odds with Cook and Winfield (2016).

It is notable that the degrees of conditional β-convergence exceed those of unconditional β-convergence for the 1990-2015 period across the pooled, urban, and rural samples in Pennsylvania. In particular, the 67-county sample's conditional β-convergence coefficient is -0.74 as opposed to -0.58 for the unconditional model. Urban areas have a conditional estimate of -0.48 versus -0.44 for the unconditional analysis. The coefficient for rural counties is -0.88 in the presence of control and deterrence variables, and it is -0.73 in the absence of them. The differences between the conditional and unconditional β-convergence coefficients suggest that the latter may suffer from omitted variable bias. These findings call into question the magnitudes of the unconditional β-convergence reported by other researchers (Cook & Winfield, 2013, 2016).

VISUAL INSPECTION σ-CONVERGENCE RESULTS

Coefficient of Variation

Figure 1 presents the plot of the standardized (i.e., adjusted so that the initial value is equal to 1) coefficients of variation for the pooled sample of the 67 Pennsylvania counties across 1990-2015 in accordance with Cook and Winfield (2013, 2016). When the standardized final value in the time frame under consideration is less than unity, σ-convergence is apparent (Cook & Winfield, 2013, 2016). Despite the vagaries of the coefficients of variation observed, it is apparent that σ-convergence exists based on the ending value of 0.68, which mirrors the results of Cook and Winfield (2013) using state-level crime data. However, Cook and Winfield (2016) identify much milder σ-convergence for violent crimes among counties. In Table 8, a regression of the pooled coefficient of variation for 1990-2015 on a constant and time trend confirms the existence of a negative trend, which is significant at the 1% level with a one-tailed t-test.

Figure 1. Standardized coefficient of variation: Pooled sample, 1990-2015
Source: authors' calculations.

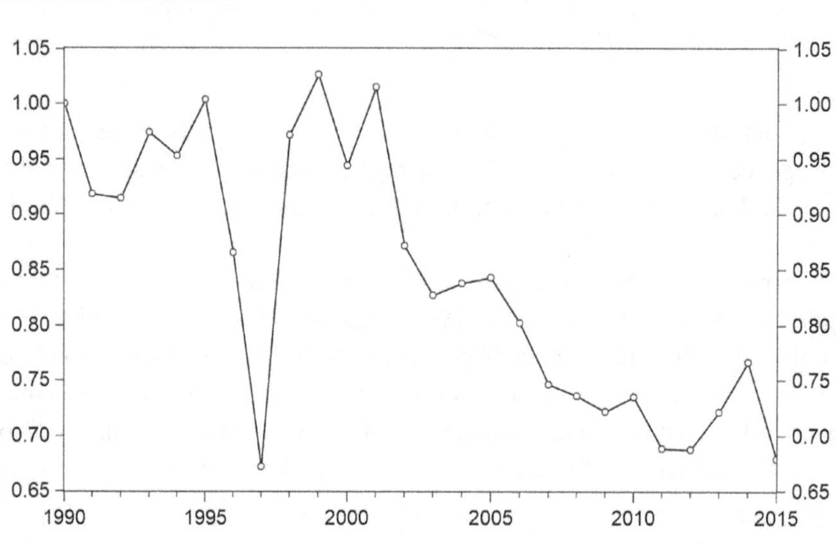

Examining sub-periods based on the phases of the business cycle, the pooled sample exhibits convergence in the early 1990s with some divergence evident into the middle of that decade. However, steep convergence followed by steep divergence characterizes the end of the expansionary period. In fact, the scaled coefficient of variation in 1999 reaches 1.03. Moving into the recessionary phase, a slight blip of divergence occurs going into 2001, but the remainder of the time frame supports steady convergence in Pennsylvania similar to the σ-convergence analysis of state-level violent crime rates performed by Cook and Winfield (2013). During the recovery, observations vary from convergence to divergence to convergence again. Overall, while the upturn and recovery offer somewhat mixed evidence, the downturn clearly shows a pattern of σ-convergence among the crime rates in the 67 counties of Pennsylvania.

Turning attention to Figure 2, which displays the graph of the coefficients of variation for the urban sample of 19 counties from 1990 to 2015, σ-convergence exists, but to a lesser degree than that of the pooled sample, with an ending value of 0.82. This observation is consistent with Cook and Winfield (2016). Much like the pooled sample of 67 counties, variation between convergence and divergence early in the 1990s leads to significant convergence followed by considerable divergence in the latter portion of the expansionary period. In fact, at the end of the expansion, the standardized coefficient of variation equals 1.2. Convergence dominates the recession and recovery periods with only a few minor instances of divergence. Overall, the urban Pennsylvania counties may converge less than the pooled sample, but their pattern is less volatile. The results of a regression in Table 8 do not support the existence of a statistically significant trend across 1990-2015 in urban areas. However, Drennan et al. (2004) argues that such a preliminary finding should be formally confirmed via unit-root testing.

Examining the standardized coefficients of variation in Figure 3, the greatest degree of σ-convergence across 1990-2015 among the three samples is observed for the rural sample of 48 counties. The ending value for the coefficient of variation is 0.58 in contrast to final values of 0.68 and 0.82 for the pooled and urban samples, respectively. The degree of σ-convergence apparent in Pennsylvania rural counties exceeds what was found by Cook and Winfield (2016) with a nationwide sample of counties. While there is movement between convergence and divergence across the period, it is much more muted than what is observed in the pooled and urban plots. An uptick in the coefficient of variation in 2000 is the most notable feature in the graph. A negative time trend significant at the 1% level is apparent from regression results in Table 8 for the rural sample during the 1990-2015 period.

Figure 2. Standardized coefficient of variation: Urban sample, 1990-2015
Source: authors' calculations.

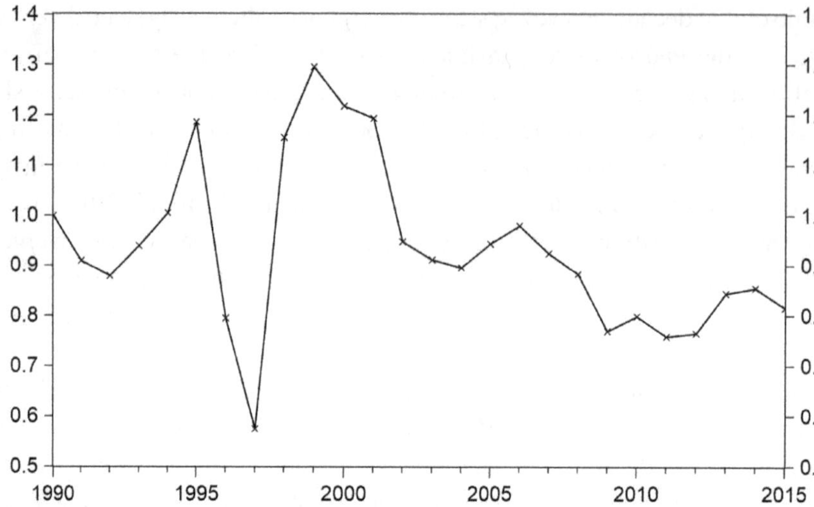

Figure 3. Standardized coefficient of variation: Rural sample, 1990-2015
Source: authors' calculations.

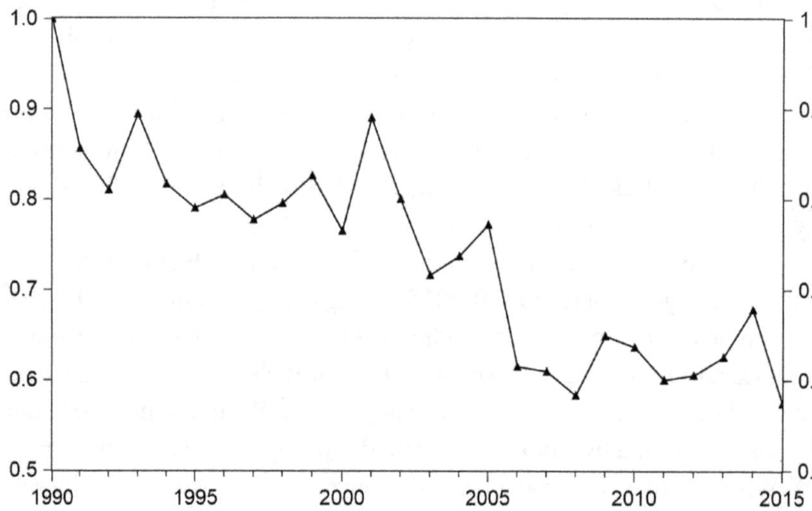

Table 8. Trend analysis with coefficient of variation

Variables	Pooled 1990-2015	Urban 1990-2015	Rural 1990-2015
	Model 1	Model 2	Model 3
Constant	0.4123***	0.3731***	0.3669***
	(39.23)	(11.05)	(24.37)
TREND	-0.0049***	-0.0040	-0.0042***
	(-4.91)	(-1.05)	(-4.36)
$\bar{R}^2$	0.66	0.24	0.62

Source: authors' calculations.

Standard Deviation of ln(CRIME)

The coefficient of variation and the standard deviation of the logarithm of the crime rate are highly correlated for the pooled, urban, and rural samples. In fact, the pairwise simple correlation coefficients are at least 0.9 in magnitude. To gauge the robustness of the visual σ-convergence findings based on the coefficient of variation, a similar inspection of the plots of the standard deviations for the three samples is undertaken. Figures 4-6 depict the pooled, urban, and rural standard deviation series for the natural log of the crime rate, respectively. A decline in the dispersion of the crime rate across the 1990-2015 span is visually evident in all three series for Pennsylvania. However, the results of regressions with the standard deviation as the dependent variable and a constant and time trend on the right-hand-side (with appropriate serial correlation corrections) in Table 9 reveal negative time trends significant at the 1% level only for the pooled and rural samples in much the same fashion as the regressions using the coefficient of variation as the regressand.

Table 9. Trend analysis with standard deviation of ln(CRIME)

Variables	Pooled 1990-2015	Urban 1990-2015	Rural 1990-2015
	Model 1	Model 2	Model 3
Constant	0.4461***	0.4029***	0.3749***
	(22.69)	(9.55)	(32.01)
TREND	-0.0054***	-0.0034	-0.0050***
	(-4.18)	(-1.23)	(-6.48)
$\bar{R}^2$	0.56	0.21	0.73

Source: authors' calculations.

Figure 4. Standard deviation of ln(CRIME): Pooled sample, 1990-2015
Source: authors' calculations.

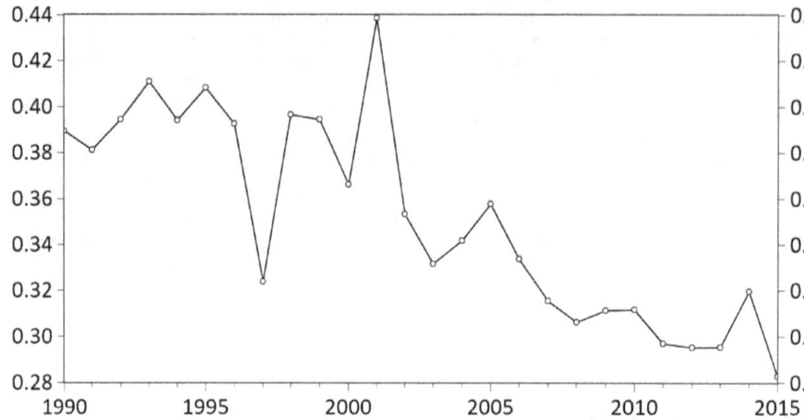

Figure 5. Standard deviation of ln(CRIME): Urban sample, 1990-2015
Source: authors' calculations.

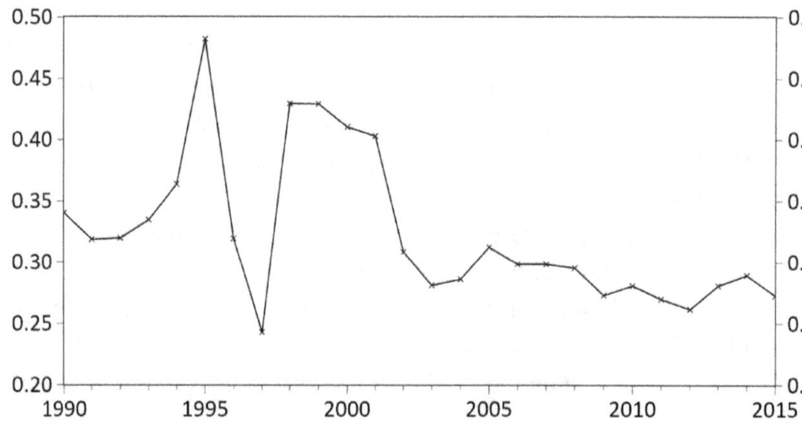

STATISTICAL ANALYSIS σ-CONVERGENCE FINDINGS

In order to formally test for unconditional σ-convergence in Pennsylvania, Augmented Dickey-Fuller (ADF) and Dickey-Fuller GLS (DF-GLS) tests for the presence of a unit root are conducted in accordance with Drennan et al. (2004). Critical values and one-sided p-values for the ADF tests are provided by MacKinnon (1996). Cook and Cook (2011) argue that identifying whether or not a crime series is a unit-root process is of the utmost importance for comprehending the evolution of crime over time. Furthermore, they assert that the unit-root testing equations for crime series

Figure 6. Standard deviation of ln(CRIME): Rural sample, 1990-2015
Source: authors' calculations.

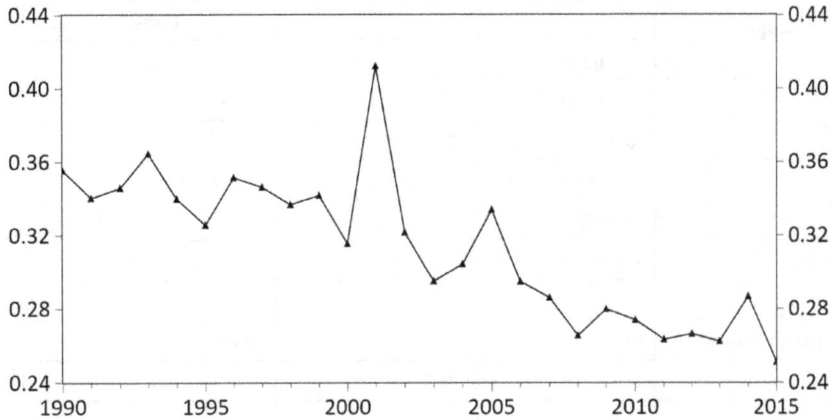

should be specified with a constant and a time trend consistent with the existing literature, and that same approach is adopted herein. However, with only 26 years in the sample, it is not prudent to separately analyze sub-periods reflecting different phases of the business cycle for unit roots (Drennan et al., 2004). Furthermore, even using a sample of 33 years, Drennan et al. (2004) urges caution in interpreting unit-root test results.

Augmented Dickey-Fuller Unit-Root Testing

Considering the pooled sample in Table 10, ADF tests based on the t-statistic and the z-statistic reject the presence of a unit root at the 5% and 1% significance levels, respectively, when analyzing the coefficient of variation. These outcomes are robust in Table 11 when considering the standard deviation of the logarithm of the crime rate as the underlying series instead. Thus, σ-convergence is confirmed for the full 67-county Pennsylvania sample.

In Table 10, ADF t-tests and z-tests also reject non-stationarity for the urban sample of 19 Pennsylvania counties based on the MacKinnon (1996) finite sample p-values when testing the coefficient of variation. Alternatively, when the standard deviation is used as the measure of dispersion in Table 11, comparison to the Dickey-Fuller critical values indicates that the null hypothesis of non-stationarity also is rejected.

While the ADF t-test fails to reject the unit root in the coefficient of variation for the rural sample of 48 counties in Table 10, the ADF z-test does reject the null at the 5% level of significance. Drennan et al. (2004) suggests that such a finding may be an aberration if, for instance, the underlying data-generating process has

Table 10. Unit-root test results for coefficient of variation of ln(CRIME)

Sample	Augmented Dickey-Fuller Unit-Root Test		Dickey-Fuller GLS Unit-Root Test
	t-Stat (*k*)	**z-Stat (*k*)**	**t-Stat (*k*)**
Pooled	-3.709 (1)	-32.232 (1)	-3.881 (1)
	(0.0413)	(0.00004)	
Urban	-3.859 (1)	-34.262 (1)	-4.011 (1)
	(0.0306)	(0.000009)	
Rural	-3.044 (1)	-22.021 (1)	-2.981 (1)
	(0.1415)	(0.0089)	
Critical Values	**t-Stat**	**z-Stat**	**t-Stat**
1%	-4.394	-21.729	-3.77
5%	-3.612	-17.234	-3.19
10%	-3.243	-14.963	-2.89

Notes: MacKinnon approximate (finite sample) one-sided p-values for ADF in parentheses below test statistics. *k* denotes the degrees of augmentation in the underlying test equations.

Table 11. Unit-root test results for standard deviation of ln(CRIME)

Sample	Augmented Dickey-Fuller Unit-Root Test		Dickey-Fuller GLS Unit-Root Test
	t-Stat (*k*)	**z-Stat (*k*)**	**t-Stat (*k*)**
Pooled	-3.922 (1)	-32.181 (1)	-3.766 (1)
	(0.0269)	(0.00004)	
Urban	-4.037 (1)	-35.467 (1)	-4.035 (1)
	(0.0213)	(0.000003)	
Rural	-3.549 (1)	-28.191 (1)	-3.611 (1)
	(0.0565)	(0.0005)	
Critical Values	**t-Stat**	**z-Stat**	**t-Stat**
1%	-3.394	-21.729	-3.77
5%	-3.612	-17.234	-3.19
10%	-3.243	-14.963	-2.89

Notes: MacKinnon approximate (finite sample) one-sided p-values for ADF in parentheses below test statistics. *k* denotes the degrees of augmentation in the underlying test equations.

not remained stable throughout the time frame under investigation. In contrast, examining the ADF test statistics for the standard deviation of the crime series in rural counties in Table 11 reveals that both the t-statistic and the z-statistic reject the unit root at the 10% and 1% levels, respectively.

Dickey-Fuller Generalized Least Squares Unit-Root Testing

Due to concerns about the low power of the ADF test and the corresponding weakness associated with its rejection of a random walk, DF-GLS tests are performed on the pooled, urban, and rural samples (Cook & Cook, 2011; Drennan et al., 2004). According to Drennan et al. (2004), the null hypothesis of the DF-GLS test is consistent with the series following a random walk, potentially with an accompanying drift, which suggests the existence of divergence. Drennan et al. (2004) notes that the power of unit-root tests hinges on the duration of the sample rather than the size in terms of the number of time periods included.

In Table 10, based on the appropriate critical values and the p-values, the unit root is rejected for all three Pennsylvania samples when analyzing the coefficient of variation with the DF-GLS test. It is noteworthy that the pooled and urban samples achieve significance at the 1% level while the unit root is rejected in the rural counties at only the 10% level. Turning attention to the DF-GLS tests of the standard deviation of the natural logarithm of the crime rate in Table 11, the null hypothesis of non-stationarity is rejected at a 1% level with the urban counties while the significance level is 5% for the pooled and rural samples. These outcomes are consistent with the results of Cook and Cook (2011) and cast serious doubt on the possibility of random walk in either the coefficient of variation or the standard deviation series. Rather, the test results support the conclusion that the series are stationary around a linear trend (Drennan et al., 2004). Thus, the existence of unconditional σ-convergence in Pennsylvania as indicated by stationarity of these series provides statistical support to accompany the visual inspection of the plotted dispersion measures. Cook and Cook (2011) explain that the absence of a unit root in a crime series casts doubt on the possibility of an ever-rising expected rate of illegal behavior.

Panel Data Unit-Root Testing

Finally, Drennan et al. (2004) recommend panel data unit-root tests of the underlying natural logarithm of the crime rate series to further investigate the existence of unconditional σ-convergence. There are two broad types of panel data unit-root tests, which differ depending upon whether the null hypothesis assumes a common unit-root process or an individual unit-root process. Based on p-values equal to zero, the results in Table 12 for the Levin, Lin, and Chu and Breitung tests reject the null of a common unit root in the panel-data sample. Similarly, the Im, Pesaran, and Shin test, the ADF test, and the Phillips and Perron test all reject the null of an individual unit root for the natural logarithm of the Part I crime rate in the 67-county Pennsylvania panel for the 1990-2015 time span. These uniform findings of stationarity are in keeping with Cook and Cook (2011). Furthermore, these unit-root results do not waver when separately considering the urban and rural subsamples of the panel as shown in Table 12. Thus, the finding of unconditional σ-convergence persists with the direct application of panel data unit-root tests to this sample.

Table 12. Panel unit-root test results for ln(CRIME)

Sample	Tests for Common Unit-Root Process		Tests for Individual Unit-Root Process		
	Levin, Lin & Chu t-Stat	**Breitung t-Stat**	**Im, Pesaran & Shin W-Stat**	**ADF Fisher Chi-Square**	**Phillips-Perron Fisher Chi-Square**
Pooled	-20.8510	-18.9738	-17.9192	529.892	531.203
	(0.00)	(0.00)	(0.00)	(0.00)	(0.00)
Urban	-10.9808	-10.3301	-9.94193	158.266	151.898
	(0.00)	(0.00)	(0.00)	(0.00)	(0.00)
Rural	-17.7287	-15.9147	-14.9120	371.626	379.305
	(0.00)	(0.00)	(0.00)	(0.00)	(0.00)

Notes: Parentheses contain p-values. The p-values for Fisher tests are calculated using an asymptotic Chi-square distribution, but the other tests assume asymptotic normality.

SOLUTIONS AND RECOMMENDATIONS

Evidence for crime rate convergence in Pennsylvania counties suggests that criminal justice policy be developed and implemented at the state and local levels to fit the needs of the specific population as noted by Cook and Winfield (2016). National criminal justice policy may not be widely applicable to disaggregated levels, and the varying degrees of convergence across rural and urban areas in Pennsylvania provide support for this claim. Furthermore, Cook and Winfield (2016) aver that while criminal behavior in metropolitan areas may reflect national trends, the same cannot be said of non-metropolitan locales. Commensurately, Frederick and Jozefowicz (2018) and Wells and Weisheit (2012) warn against a one-size-fits-all approach to crime fighting in a state.

Another dimension of policy development to consider revolves around fluctuations in levels of economic activity. Since convergence behavior appears to vary somewhat depending upon whether there is an upturn or a downturn in the state of the economy, the assertion by Saridakis and Spengler (2012) that good economic policy simultaneously serves as good crime-fighting policy due to the destabilizing impact of illegal activity on the economy is relevant.

As is true across the United States, law enforcement in Pennsylvania primarily is the domain of local municipalities (Jenkins, 2014). The Pennsylvania State Police provide a baseline of protection across the commonwealth, but it is incumbent upon community governments to augment those services. Pennsylvania is characterized by unique structural features, including having more police departments than the rest of the states, with 1,117 state and local police departments having jurisdiction exclusively in the commonwealth versus an average of 353 such agencies for other states. Additionally, among its largest outlays, the typical municipality in Pennsylvania devotes one-third of its budget to law enforcement expenditures, and real local police expenditures in Pennsylvania are $2.12 billion, which contrasts to a mean of $1.56 billion across all states (United States Census Bureau, 2009; Jenkins, 2014; Reaves, 2008).

In the context of convergence, the constituents who fare worse are those subject to the accelerating crime-rate growth in the initially low-crime areas, and it is their welfare that policymakers need to consider. Constituents witnessing the development of relatively greater crime rates over this time period essentially face three options: (1) choose to accept the rising crime rates and the risk associated with doing so; (2) elect sympathetic officials and garner sufficient community agreement to pass property tax increases at the local level to pay for enhanced law enforcement services; or (3) resort to private-market solutions, such as installing home security systems, fencing and exterior lighting, to ameliorate their concerns about climbing crime rates. In light of local government budget implications of the COVID-19 pandemic, the policy avenue of passing higher tax rates to provide for increased policing likely is less feasible for the foreseeable future.

FUTURE RESEARCH DIRECTIONS

In future research, it would be interesting to analyze the convergence behavior of crime rates for counties in different states and/or to expand the coverage to encompass all of the counties across the nation while allowing for structural breaks across time and geography. Additionally, the sample could be updated to include observations prior to 1990 and/or after 2015. This study includes assessment of conditional and unconditional β-convergence, visual and statistical σ-convergence analysis, and the application of panel unit-root tests to Pennsylvania counties. This type of comprehensive convergence analysis could be extended to all counties in the United States.

Finally, future studies specifically should examine why convergence trends exist at all and whether the crime rates are converging on lower or higher levels of criminal activity. A related question emerges: If convergence in the crime rate does exist, as this research suggests, then can it be influenced? If so, how? From a policy perspective, it would be beneficial to better understand the role played by deterrence measures in the crime-rate convergence phenomenon.

CONCLUSION

The findings for β-convergence and σ-convergence in this analysis are consistent with Drennan et al. (2004) and Young et al. (2008). In particular, β-convergence reveals itself to be a necessary, but not a sufficient condition for σ-convergence. Meanwhile, σ-convergence proves to be both a necessary and a sufficient condition for β-convergence in support of Hypothesis Four. Both β-convergence and σ-convergence exist for the 1990-2015 time frame across the pooled, urban, and rural samples in accordance with the prediction of Hypothesis Three.

Consistent with Hypothesis Two, business-cycle fluctuations seem to influence the convergence of crime rates across counties of different types. Although both unconditional and conditional β-convergence are observed for the pooled and rural samples across all phases of the business cycle, urban counties lack any kind of β-convergence during periods of economic expansion. A visual analysis of σ-convergence for the pooled and urban samples offers similar findings. However, the same cannot be said for the visual inspection of the rural sample. These differing outcomes may provide anecdotal evidence in support of a bias toward convergence in cases in which non-metropolitan and metropolitan areas are identically treated (Drennan et al., 2004).

It is worthwhile to note that these results are obtained using an entirely comprehensive approach that addresses several shortcomings in the existing literature on crime-rate convergence. Specifically, to the authors' knowledge, no other analysis of convergence in crime rates has applied visual and statistical testing of σ-convergence, as well as, unconditional and conditional statistical analysis of β-convergence. In fact, it is within the realm of possibility that previous researchers' conclusions regarding β-convergence (Cook & Winfield, 2013, 2016) suffer from omitted variable bias due to their sole application of unconditional β-convergence techniques. With respect to σ-convergence, Cook and Winfield (2013, 2016) only consider the coefficient of variation as a dispersion measure neglecting the standard deviation of the natural logarithm of the crime rate series. In the present study, both measures of dispersion are analyzed in order to gauge the robustness of the findings. The direct application of panel unit-root tests to the underlying natural logarithm of the crime rate series, as recommended by Drennan et al. (2004), affords even greater support for these convergence findings than previous literature offers (Cook & Winfield, 2013, 2016).

In general, the findings of both β-convergence and σ-convergence across time (i.e., 1990-2015) and space (i.e., pooled, urban, and rural counties) are robust, supporting the existence of a trend toward crime-rate convergence in Pennsylvania as conjectured in Hypothesis One. However, it is salient that several aspects make Pennsylvania counties a unique sample that perhaps is not representative of other states. Those characteristics specifically include several pockets of highly dense population concentration, strong rural county representation, and high levels of police per capita. Therefore, like crime rates in general, perhaps crime-rate convergence behavior also varies across states and nations.

Finally, from a criminology standpoint, modernization theory is robustly supported in these findings despite prior literature showing mixed support for it. Consequently, this new evidence in favor of modernization theory can be used to evaluate its explanatory power relative to other criminological explanations, especially as it relates to disaggregated data samples. Modernization theory's prediction that convergence will occur once regions fully have modernized is particularly consistent with the statistical results for σ-convergence based on unit-root tests performed here. The convincing rejection of unit roots in favor of stationarity across the samples implies that any crime shocks will be transitory and dissipate over time, which can be interpreted in a manner akin to modernization. In other words, as explained by Drennan et al. (2004), neither the coefficient of variation nor the standard deviation of the natural logarithm of the Part I crime rate follows a random walk over time. As noted by Bernard and Durlauf (1996), this type of time-series analysis represents a stricter notion of convergence than a cross-sectional test is able to assess, and adds strength to its support of modernization theory.

REFERENCES

Arthur, J. A. (1991). Socioeconomic predictors of crime in rural Georgia. *Criminal Justice Review, 16*(1), 29-41. doi: 10.1177%2F073401689101600106

Arvanites, T. M., & Defina, R. H. (2006). Business cycles and street crime. *Criminology*, *44*(1), 139–164. doi:10.1111/j.1745-9125.2006.00045.x

Becsi, Z. (1999). Economics and crime in the states. *Economic Review*, *84*(1), 38–56.

Bernard, A. B., & Durlauf, S. N. (1996). Interpreting tests of the convergence hypothesis. *Journal of Econometrics, 71*(1-2), 161–173. doi:10.1016/0304-4076(94)01699-2

Borts, G. H. (1960). The equalization of returns and regional economic growth. *The American Economic Review, 50*(3), 319–347. https://www.jstor.org/stable/i331461

Brown, D. L., & Kandel, W. A. (2006). Rural America through a demographic lens. In W. A. Kandel & D. L. Brown (Eds.), *Population Change and Rural Society* (pp. 3–23). Springer. doi:10.1007/1-4020-3902-6_1

Buonanno, P., & Montolio, D. (2008). Identifying the socio-economic and demographic determinants of crime across Spanish provinces. *International Review of Law and Economics, 28*(2), 89–97. doi:10.1016/j.irle.2008.02.005

Bushway, S. D., & Reuter, P. (2002). Labor markets and crime risk factors. In L. W. Sherman, D. P. Farrington, B. C. Welsh, & D. L. MacKenzie (Eds.), *Evidence-Based Crime Prevention* (pp. 198–240). Routledge. doi:10.4324/9780203166697_chapter_6

Cantor, D., & Land, K. C. (1985). Unemployment and crime rates in the post-World War II United States: A theoretical and empirical analysis. *American Sociological Review, 50*(3), 317–332. doi:10.2307/2095542

Center for Rural Pennsylvania. (2014). *County profiles*. Retrieved from http://www.ruralpa.org/count_profiles.cfm

Chen, E. Y. (2008). Impacts of "Three Strikes and You're Out" on crime trends in California and throughout the United States. *Journal of Contemporary Criminal Justice, 24*(4), 345-370. doi: 10.1177%2F1043986208319456

Chilton, R., & Chambliss, W. J. (2014). Urban homicide in the United States, 1980-2010. *Homicide Studies, 19*(3), 257–272. doi:10.1177/1088767914534241

Comprehensive and disaggregated data critical for developing effective responses to hate crimes and intolerance, say participants in OSCE/ODIHR workshop. (2016, December 6). Retrieved from https://www.osce.org/odihr/286401

Cook, J., & Cook, S. (2011). Are US crime rates really unit root processes? *Journal of Quantitative Criminology, 27*(3), 299–314. doi:10.100710940-010-9124-4

Cook, S., & Watson, D. (2013). Breaks and convergence in U.S. regional crime rates: Analysis of their presence and implications. *Journal of Social Sciences, 2*(3), 180–190. doi:10.3390ocsci2030180

Cook, S., & Winfield, T. (2013). Crime across the states: Are US crime rates converging? *Urban Studies (Edinburgh, Scotland)*, *50*(9), 1724–1741. doi:10.1177/0042098012466602

Cook, S., & Winfield, T. (2016). The urban–rural divide, regional disaggregation and the convergence of crime. *Applied Economics*, *47*(47), 5072–5087. doi:10.1080/00036846.2015.1042143

DeFina, R., & Arvanites, T. (2002). The weak effect of imprisonment on crime: 1971–1998. *Social Science Quarterly*, *83*(3), 635–653. doi:10.1111/1540-6237.00106

Drennan, M. P., Lobo, J., & Strumsky, D. (2004). Unit root tests of sigma income convergence across U.S. metropolitan areas. *Journal of Economic Geography*, *4*(5), 583–595. doi:10.1093/jnlecg/lbh035

Ehrlich, I. (1996). Crime, punishment, and the market for offenses. *The Journal of Economic Perspectives*, *10*(1), 43–67. doi:10.1257/jep.10.1.43

Frederick, S. A., & Jozefowicz, J. J. (2018). Rural-urban differences in the unemployment-crime relationship: The case of Pennsylvania. *Atlantic Economic Journal*, *46*(2), 189–201. doi:10.100711293-018-9581-y

Grugan, S. T. (2014). Hate crime. In J. S. Albanese (Ed.), *The Encyclopedia of Criminology and Criminal Justice* (pp. 1–5). Blackwell. doi:10.1002/9781118517383.wbeccj037

Higgins, M. J., Levy, D., & Young, A. T. (2006). Growth and convergence across the United States: Evidence from county-level data. *The Review of Economics and Statistics*, *88*(4), 671–681. doi:10.1162/rest.88.4.671

Jenkins, M. J. (2014). Law enforcement in Pennsylvania. In M. P. Brewster & H. R. Dammer (Eds.), *Pennsylvania's Criminal Justice System* (pp. 89–110). Carolina Academic Press.

LaFree, G. (2016). Evidence for elite convergence in cross-national homicide victimization trends, 1956 to 2000. *The Sociological Quarterly*, *46*(1), 191–211. doi:10.1111/j.1533-8525.2005.00009.x

Lyerly, R. R., & Skipper, J. K. (1981). Differential rates of rural-urban delinquency: A social control approach. *Criminology*, *19*(3), 385–399. doi:10.1111/j.1745-9125.1981.tb00424.x

MacKinnon, J. G. (1996). Numerical distribution functions for unit root and cointegration tests. *Journal of Applied Econometrics*, *11*(6), 601–618. doi:10.1002/(SICI)1099-1255(199611)11:6<601::AID-JAE417>3.0.CO;2-T

Marvell, T., & Moody, C. (1998). The impact of out-of-state prison population on state homicide rates: Displacement and free-rider effects. *Criminology*, *36*(3), 513–536. doi:10.1111/j.1745-9125.1998.tb01257.x

Marvell, T., & Moody, C. (2001). The lethal effects of three-strikes laws. *The Journal of Legal Studies*, *30*(1), 89–106. doi:10.1086/468112

Neuman, W. L., & Berger, R. J. (1988). Competing perspectives on cross-national crime: An evaluation of theory and evidence. *The Sociological Quarterly*, *29*(2), 281–313. doi:10.1111/j.1533-8525.1988.tb01255.x

Phillips, J., & Land, K. C. (2012). The link between unemployment and crime rate fluctuations: An analysis at the county, state, and national levels. *Social Science Research*, *41*(3), 681–694. doi:10.1016/j.ssresearch.2012.01.001 PMID:23017802

Reaves, B. A. (2008). *Census of state and local law enforcement agencies, 2008*. Retrieved from https://www.bjs.gov/content/pub/pdf/csllea08.pdf

Rey, S. J., & Montouri, B. D. (1999). US regional income convergence: A spatial econometric perspective. *Regional Studies*, *33*(2), 143–156. doi:10.1080/00343409950122945

Saridakis, G., & Spengler, H. (2009). Crime, deterrence and unemployment in Greece: A panel data approach. *The Social Science Journal*, *49*(2), 167–174. doi:10.1016/j.soscij.2011.08.005

Smith, K. (1997). Explaining variation in state-level homicide rates: Does crime policy pay? *The Journal of Politics*, *59*(2), 350–367. doi:10.1017/S0022381600053482

Smith, K. (2004). The politics of punishment: Evaluating political explanations of incarceration rates. *The Journal of Politics*, *66*(3), 925–938. doi:10.1111/j.1468-2508.2004.00283.x

Spelman, W. (2008). Specifying the relationship between crime and prisons. *Journal of Quantitative Criminology*, *24*(2), 149–178. doi:10.100710940-008-9042-x

United States Census Bureau. (2009). *Crime Rates by State and Type* [Data file]. Retrieved from https://www.census.gov/library/publications/2009/compendia

Weisheit, R. A., & Donnermeyer, J. F. (2000). Change and continuity in crime in rural America. *Criminal Justice*, *1*(2), 309–357. https://www.ncjrs.gov/criminal_justice2000/vol_1/02g.pdf

Wells, L. E., & Weisheit, R. A. (2004). Patterns of rural and urban crime: A county-level comparison. *Criminal Justice Review*, *29*(1), 1–22. doi:10.1177/073401680402900103

Wells, L. E., & Weisheit, R. A. (2012). Explaining crime in metropolitan and non-metropolitan communities. *International Journal of Rural Criminology, 1*(2), 153–183. doi:10.18061/1811/53700

Winsberg, M. (1993). Are crime waves in the United States regional or national? *Journal of Criminal Justice, 21*(5), 517–520. doi:10.1016/0047-2352(93)90036-M

Young, A., Higgins, M., & Levy, D. (2008). Sigma convergence versus beta convergence: Evidence from U.S. county-level data. *Journal of Money, Credit and Banking, 40*(5), 1083–1093. doi:10.1111/j.1538-4616.2008.00148.x

Zhang, Y., Maxwell, C., & Vaughn, M. (2009). The impact of state sentencing policies on the U.S. prison population. *Journal of Criminal Justice, 37*(2), 190–199. doi:10.1016/j.jcrimjus.2009.02.012

ADDITIONAL READING

Andresen, M. A. (2013). Unemployment, business cycles, crime, and the Canadian provinces. *Journal of Criminal Justice, 41*(4), 220–227. doi:10.1016/j.jcrimjus.2013.05.006

Batabyal, S. (2011). Temporal causality and the dynamics of crime and delinquency. *Atlantic Economic Journal, 39*(4), 421–441. doi:10.100711293-011-9289-8

Cook, P., & Zarkin, G. (1985). Crime and the business cycle. *The Journal of Legal Studies, 14*(1), 115–128. doi:10.1086/467767

DiCecio, R., & Gascon, C. S. (2008). Income convergence in the United States: A tale of migration and urbanization. *The Annals of Regional Science, 45*(2), 365–377. doi:10.100700168-008-0284-1

Glaeser, E. L., & Sacerdote, B. (1999). Why is there more crime in cities? *Journal of Political Economy, 107*(6), S225–S258. doi:10.1086/250109

Guetat, I., & Serranito, F. (2005). Using panel unit root tests to evaluate the income convergence hypothesis in middle East and North Africa countries. *Cahiers de la Maison des Sciences Economiques*, bla05003. Retrieved from https://ideas.repec.org/p/mse/wpsorb/bla05003.html

Ladbrook, D. A. (1988). Why are crime rates higher in urban than in rural areas?—Evidence from Japan. *Australian and New Zealand Journal of Criminology, 21*(2), 81–103. doi:10.1177/000486588802100203

Liska, A., & Bellair, P. (1995). Violent-crime rates and racial composition: Convergence over time. *American Journal of Sociology, 101*(3), 578–610. doi:10.1086/230754

KEY TERMS AND DEFINITIONS

β-Convergence: A cross-sectional phenomenon in which a unit with a lower initial endowment grows faster than a unit with a higher initial endowment until the former "catches up" to the latter.

σ-Convergence: A time-series phenomenon in which a reduction in the dispersion measures of a variable occurs across time.

Augmented Dickey-Fuller (ADF) Test: A test for the presence of a unit root in a time series of observations while incorporating lags of the dependent variable.

Business Cycle: The fluctuating periods of expansion and contraction in the level of economic activity in an economy around a long-term growth trend.

Dickey-Fuller Generalized Least Squares (DF-GLS) Test: A test for the presence of a unit root in which the time series of observations is transformed via a generalized least squares (GLS) regression before performing the test.

Part I Crime Rate: A measure of the number of reported crimes of murder, nonnegligent manslaughter, forcible rape, robbery, assault, burglary, larceny-theft, motor-vehicle theft, and arson per 100,000 people.

Stationarity: The case when the statistical properties, such as mean, variance, etc., of a time series of observations are all constant over time.

Unit Root: Its presence indicates that a time series is non-stationary.

Chapter 6
An Analysis of Gender Inequality in Professional Tennis:
A Study of the Cozening Sport

Hannah C. Mercer
Indiana University of Pennsylvania, USA

Patrick S. Edwards
Indiana University of Pennsylvania, USA

ABSTRACT

This paper examines the gender wage gap in professional sports using a pooled cross-section of professional tennis players across the years 2011-2017. The dependent variable is the prize money earned by the top fifty male and top fifty female ranked tennis players throughout the world. This prize money is measured in 2017 real dollar value. The independent variables include: number of tournaments played, age, rank differentiation, gender, country and WTA/ATP score. Gender inequality is measured by determining the wage gap shown through the mean prize money earned by the professional tennis players from 2011-2017. While prize money for men and women has recently become equal in the Grand Slam tournaments, there is evidence to show that women's prize money is considerably lower in the less-publicized tournaments. Results of the ordinary least squares (OLS) regressions suggest that there is evidence for a gender-related pay disparity in professional tennis due to a number of statistically significant variables including WTA/ATP score (+), age (+), country (+) and the gender (-) and year (+) dummies.

DOI: 10.4018/978-1-7998-1093-3.ch006

INTRODUCTION

Feminism is the general belief that women and men should be treated equally (Marcus, 2015). In spite of its simple principles and goals, such as the "Me too Movement" against sexual harassment and sexual assault, there are many who argue that feminism has no relevance in today's society and that gender inequality exists but may be less pervasive. When looking objectively at the gender inequality issues that persist in our society, it is undeniable that women still face discrimination, especially regarding employment and objectification. While it is indisputable that women have advanced in society, there is still much progress to be made.

Throughout world history, gender has been correlated with economic discrimination, which suggests that discrimination will also transcend into the world of modern professional athletics. Professional sports are an important aspect of current American pop-culture. Many view professional sports as a means of enjoyable leisure activity and a time for fans to come together with a common interest. Even though sports indiscriminately reach the masses, where viewers are concerned, America fails to look at the economic discrimination among athletes regarding gender that prominently exists in professional sports today.

The topic of economic discrimination in professional sports has been examined previously, (Buysse, 2004; Hanson, 2012), so comparing the results among multiple sports to identify which sports exhibit the most gender inequality is not a difficult task. Substantial information (Kahn, 1991; Paserman, 2007) exists that relates to gender inequality in salary and prize money earned in professional sports, specifically tennis. Due to the popularity of professional tennis, in addition to the fact that there have been recent strides in reducing the sex pay gap in the sport, tennis has become an interesting case study to attempt to parse out the true discrimination that professional female athletes may face relative to their male counterparts.

Since there have been positive movements at a macro level for professional tennis in diminishing the sex pay gap, individuals may believe that the issue has been solved. However, Flake, Dufur, and Moore (2013) found that while prize money for men and women is equal in prestigious events such as the Grand Slams, which include Wimbledon, the US Open, Australian Open, and French Open, women's prize money is considerably lower in many of the less-publicized tournaments. This creates financial barriers for players who compete in their remaining tournaments for the season and for those that do not qualify for the Slams. The prize money earned by the female winners of the four tennis majors being equal to that of the male champions was not always the case. The US Open was the first major to offer equal pay in 1973, championed by Billie Jean King. Approximately 28 years later, the Australian Open granted men and women champions equal prize money too. The French Open and Wimbledon soon followed suit in 2006 and 2007, respectively.

A snapshot into the economic discrimination that Flake et al. (2013) exposed in his work showcases the many barriers that professional women tennis players face today, even though the media often portrays tennis as an equal sport. In examining the prize money won per tournament played by each athlete in 2018, roughly 70% of the world's top 100 men still earned more than women of the same ranking (WTA, 2018; ATP, 2018). Past male tennis athletes have spoken up and claimed that men earn the higher prize money since they attract more income and viewers; however, data suggest viewing figures are not based on gender but more so on the individual competing in the tournament. This trend was supported by factual evidence when, in 2010-2014, the women's US Open final drew a larger audience in America than the men's final. The reason for this is simple. Serena Williams, one of the most irrefutably popular athletes in any sport, competed in four of those US Open finals.

Prior to the distribution of equal prize money in the Grand Slams, Kahn (1991) discovered that in the Wimbledon tennis tournaments between the years of 1987 and 1990, there was an 11% pay gap between men and women. Similarly, in the French Open, this gap ranged from 10% to 26% over the period. These numbers are most intriguing because as mentioned previously, women's tennis matches draw at least as much revenue as the men's matches, which is typically the strongest argument in condoning the sex pay gap in professional sports holistically. The above findings and extensive research conducted prior to this analysis provide evidence of a clear gender-related pay gap in professional sports, specifically professional tennis. This information led the authors to conduct a data analysis between the top fifty ranked male and top fifty ranked female tennis players in the world between the years of 2011 and 2017.

Since there is history of gender inequality in professional tennis, and past research has uncovered the pay gap between men and women in professional tennis across the period of 1987-1990 (Kahn, 1991), the authors sought to extend these previous findings and update them to measure the evolution of gender inequality in professional tennis, mainly since the Grand Slam tournaments have distributed equal prize money for both men and women since the year 2007.

Since the objective of this chapter is to reveal the gender wage gap that remains present in professional tennis despite the media claiming equality in the sport has been achieved, the authors unveil the gender wage gap present in this industry by taking the mean salary earned by both male and female professionally ranked tennis players from their regression model and calculate the wage disparity that still exists today.

BACKGROUND

In order to have a more comprehensive understanding of feminism's relevance in today's society, it is important to trace the history of its development, which begins with the late nineteenth century. Looking at society as it exists today, it is difficult to fathom that women were once denied the right to vote, own capital, borrow or inherit money, have ownership over the money they earned, start divorce proceedings, maintain custody of children in the event of a divorce, seek education at the collegiate level, argue a case in court, or serve on a jury. As Judith Lorber explains in "Feminisms and Their Contributions to Gender Equality," "First wave feminism's goal was to get equal legal rights for women, especially the right to vote" (Lorber, 2010). While suffrage was the predominant goal for the first wave of feminism, women also made gains regarding economic independence, manifesting in rights for wages, property, and pursuit of higher education. The second wave of feminism, emerging in the 1970s and 1980s, witnessed a focus on "increasing women's legal rights, political representation, and entry into occupations and professions dominated by men" (Lorber, 2010). There was also a focus on ceasing sexual violence, pornography, sexual harassment, and objectification within the media. The third wave of feminism, emerging in the 1990s, focused on the pursuit of gender equality as a norm rather than a rarity.

Despite advances that have been made, women today still see unequal treatment in the workplace and in politics. While American women have advanced in educational attainment and intellectual achievements, they continue to make 81.8 cents for every dollar earned by a male (IWPR, 2020). Women also face employment discrimination because of the negative effects of maternity leave and the caretaker role that they assume within their households. This also limits the likelihood of career advancement or possibility of promotion within the workplace. In politics, gender inequality and sexism pervade as is evidenced when political pundits dwell on characteristics of likeability when ascertaining whether a female candidate will be successful in her political aspirations. In stark contrast to male political contenders, females cannot simply be the most "qualified" to win the election; they must also be "likeable." Therefore, it is not surprising that in the United States House of Representatives, women only occupy 102 out of the 435 seats, and in the United States Senate, women only occupy 25 of the 100 seats. It is rather jarring to consider that females make up more than half of the population, yet only 25% of the elected seats within the legislative branch of the US government are held by females. This is not proportional to the population they are to represent. Much of the sexism that women face within both the employment and political arenas is tied to their violation of societal gender expectations. Hence, if a woman is assertive or competitive rather than living up to society's expectations of warmth and kindness, people are uncomfortable, and the woman is deemed unlikeable (Cooper, 2013).

In considering the negative impacts of violation of societal gender expectations within both the workplace and politics, it might be reasonable to conclude that the unequal treatment of females within athletics could be tied to female athletes violating societal expectations of what women should and can be. Since women are thought of as the milder or gentler sex, in contrast to males, female athletes could seem to be disconcerting because athleticism relies not on mild manners but on strength, endurance, and drive. Perhaps because of this anomaly, those in athletic organizations feel as if they may take unfair advantage of their female athletic stars.

Objectification of women and girls is also a consequence of gender inequality today. Women face objectification not only in terms of sexual objectification but in the media's representation of women as well. As a consequence of sexual objectification, one in six women will fall victim to sexual violence. In the media, objectification of women results in the development of "mental health problems that disproportionately affect women" such as depression and eating disorders (Szymanski, 2011). Much of the objectification from society leads to internalization of objectification for women, so that women feel as if they are objects to be admired and assessed based on external appearance, which takes away some of their agency externally as well. Due to society's focus on female appearance and expectations, women may also face difficulties in advancement within their respective fields. These consequences across many represented outlets signify one simple fact, which is the principle that women in a variety of facets have historically faced obstacles in the surge to achieve equality with men.

LITERATURE REVIEW

Kahn (1991) sought to determine whether there was gender discrimination in professional sports using data from the years 1987-1990. To do so, he needed to find a sport that had the same events for men and women. Kahn (1991) used tennis, and more specifically, Wimbledon and the French Open, to determine if there was evidence of a gender gap in salaries earned through these tournaments. Kahn (1991) utilized the prize money that was won by both males and females alike as the dependent variables while also including year, length of matches, revenue, entertainment value, television ratings, rain delays, and audience differences for Saturday/Sunday views as the independent variables. By using regression of prize money, Kahn (1991) found that the total prize money awarded to men was approximately ten times compared to that of women during 1987-1990.

Buysse (2004) focused on how the traditional definitions of femininity and masculinity throughout society have persisted and are reflected in the world of sports. Using the NCAA Division I media guide cover photographs representing female and male sports teams in basketball, golf, gymnastics, tennis, and softball/baseball from the 1989-1990 and 1996-1997 academic years, Buysse (2004) gathered 307 photographs from the 1989-1990 academic year and 314 photographs from the 1996-1997 academic year. The dependent variable was media guides, media guide cover photograph, while the independent variables included true athleticism, posed athleticism, femininity, masculinity, sexual suggestiveness, student-athletes, movies and/or songs included, and the coded use of sports equipment. Using OLS regression, the author determined the extent to which the sexist depictions of women athletes occurred in the gendered images produced by intercollegiate athletic programs. Confirming the author's expectations, the analysis showed that women athletes were less likely to be portrayed in uniform, on the court, or in action in the media in 1990. In 1997, the gender difference in wearing uniforms had disappeared, but the other findings in 1990 were still present with the degree to which women appeared on the court decreasing. The hypothesis was accepted; the gender variable implied that female players' photographs were less likely to be athletic and sports-based than male players' photographs. Additionally, female players were more sexualized.

Hanson (2012) focused on how the coverage of women's sports lags men's and how the female athletes' femininity and sexuality are the main focus of coverage rather than their achievements on the court and field. Despite the fact that female athleticism challenges gender norms, female athletes are still depicted in a way that reaffirms their femininity as wives, mothers, or sex objects; in contrast, males are framed as athletes who are strong, courageous, and masculine. The Hanson (2012) research argued that while smaller prize money is the easiest quantifiable insufficiency to study, the monetary barrier for female professional tennis players is accompanied by endorsement hardships, lack of media coverage, and other prejudices such as objectification that is still embedded towards women's tennis.

In a different study, Paserman (2007) attempted to investigate whether men and women respond differently to competitive pressure in a real-world setting with large monetary rewards. To do this, she conducted a pooled cross-sectional analysis of the years 2005-2007. In this study, tennis player performance, measured as the total percentage of shots of a given type played by both players, was the dependent variable, while the following were independent variables: percentage of unforced errors, percentage winners, number of matches, number of sets, percentage of forced errors, percentage of first serve, percentage points won by server, and average player rank and rating. Paserman (2007) estimated the equation both with and without match fixed effects. To account for potential correlation in the error terms, standard errors were adjusted for clustering at the match level. In addition, the equations were estimated separately for both genders and then stacked and interacted. The results showed that performance measured by either unforced errors or winners deteriorates in the final set for both men and women. Women dropped, on average, 2.58%-2.72%, and men declined 1.32%-1.55% on average. These results demonstrate that men and women respond differently to competitive pressure in this type of atmosphere when large sums of money are on the line. Female tennis players commit more errors if the point being played is high in value. Men, on the other hand, seem to be unaffected by the significance of the given point.

Flake et al. (2013) hypothesized that much of the previous literature on female discrimination in sports has mainly been focused on media bias and objectification issues. Contrary to their peers, these authors sought to target gender discrimination in tennis using quantifiable measures such as the prize money earned by the athletes. Using the top 100 professionally ranked tennis players at the end of the 2009 season, they calculated the median prize money earned by the athletes and found evidence for a clear pay gap that still exists today, even in spite of the evolution of the equal prize money distribution in the Grand Slams in 2007. The statistically significant variables in their model included productivity in 2009 and differential payouts for middle and low-tier tournaments. The lesser publicized middle and low-tier tournaments are directly related to the professional tennis player pay gap because Flake et al. (2013) found that women's prize money is substantially less in these types of tournaments.

In a recent study, Wheaton and Thorpe (2018) evaluated the opportunities for women in more progressive gendered power relations such as actions sports. These action sports include skating and surfing, which are certainly outside the norm for women's participation in sports. Using an analysis of niche media, their studies revealed the different struggles and shortcomings women face in this type of sports culture along with the challenges that female athletes endure as far as establishing effective empowerment for women in these specific sports.

REGRESSION ANALYSIS

This paper attempts to reveal which variables play a significant role in determining the components of professional tennis players' salaries and whether there is an apparent gender wage gap in payouts to professional tennis athletes today. There is a multitude of reasons why people love the sport of tennis – whether it be following their favorite professional tennis player in the U.S. Open or playing it leisurely themselves. Tennis is a way to bring civilians together in a community sense, even if they may disagree on their favorite professional to watch at the end of the day. Even with the dedicated following professional tennis has garnered on a large scale, tennis is arguably the most prominent sport for studying gender inequality between the male and female professional athletes. Tennis has now become the most popular women's sport in regards to TV ratings and prize money earned by the athletes (Flake, 2013), and although four of the top five highest paid female athletes are tennis players, this excludes advertisements, which is another barrier female athletes face.

Tennis Rankings

Women and men professional tennis players can compete in 21 tournaments in a given season, with four being the Grand Slams that now award equal prize money to the male and female champions. However, in the remaining 17 tournaments, men have out-won women in terms of prize money by large degrees (Flake, 2013). The controversy stated above is what compelled the authors to conduct the present study in order to determine if men are continuing to out-earn women in professional tennis. The major contribution to literature that the researchers provide in the area of gender inequality in professional tennis is the significance of the Grand Slam tournaments awarding these equivalent prizes to the male and female winners. Additionally, the authors consider certain variables that have not been previously used in this type of analysis such as a country variable that determines inequality that athletes experience in different countries. Lastly, this paper helps extend previous findings of gender inequality, and as with the trend that has surfaced in modern day society with the gender-wage gap, it provides an updated lens to this issue in professional tennis.

To conduct this analysis, the authors collected data on the top fifty ranked men and top fifty ranked women tennis professionals worldwide between the years 2011 and 2017 from the Women's Tennis Association (WTA) and The Association of Tennis Professionals (ATP). The final sample size was n = 700. The data obtained from these organizations include the dependent variable, which is the real salary earned by the ranked professional tennis players, and the independent variables, such as the number of tournaments played, age, country, rank differentiation, gender, and WTA/ATP score.

The rankings are determined by an athlete's WTA or ATP score. According to the Women's Tennis Association, the basis for calculating a player's ranking is those tournaments that yield the highest ranking points during a rolling 52-week period, with the condition that they must include points from the Grand Slams, Premier Mandatory tournaments, and the WTA Championships. In addition, for Top 20 players, their best two results at Premier 5 tournaments also count. The WTA also distributes ranking points (for singles players only) who compete at the Summer Olympics. Points earned during Summer Olympics play will apply only to a player's overall ranking during that calendar year (WTA, 2018). In comparison, ATP rankings are based on calculating the total points for each player from the four

Grand Slams; the eight mandatory ATP World Tour Masters 1000 tournaments; the Barclays ATP World Tour Finals of the ranking period; and their best six results from all ATP World Tour 500, ATP World Tour 250, ATP Challenger Tour, and Futures tournaments (ATP, 2018).

Hypotheses

REALSAL, the dependent variable, is the prize money earned by each athlete in a given calendar year for the 2011-2017 time period, which is consistent with previous literature (Kahn, 1991). The base year for the salary is 2017.

Professional tennis players can make money through four different income sources: tournament prize money, endorsements, exhibitions, and bonuses. Since the basis of this research is to unveil the gender wage disparity that still exists today, even in light of the Grand Slams awarding equivalent rewards, prize money earned has been the primary benchmark for measuring gender inequality in professional tennis. Additionally, prize money is an objective source to measure earnings. This is in comparison to the other income avenues such as endorsements and bonuses. Past studies have shown that if a male and female athlete were to receive equal prize money, the top male athletes will still earn more due to better endorsement deals. These studies have shown that sponsors feel male athletes tend to be more marketable. This imbalance of endorsement deals expands the income gap between male and female athletes but is based on opportunistic factors. Using prize money alone to determine gender inequality in professional tennis eliminates various skewed biases that can occur in the income sources for tennis players (Perasso, 2017).

Table 1 presents the descriptive statistics for real salary attained by the top ranked professional male and female tennis players in the world. This table clearly demonstrates the presence of a wage gap based on the average prize money earned between the years 2011 and 2017. These values show almost a $350,000 deficit for women tennis players, which suggests a clear discrepancy in prize money earned by the athletes.

SCORE is the independent variable in the model representing the WTA (female) and ATP (male) scores given to each player. The researchers expected the sign to be positive for this variable because the scores that are awarded to each player determine the athlete's rank. In the ATP scoring, the higher the ATP was for a male athlete, the higher his salary. Nevertheless, this general trend held to be largely true with the WTA rankings, but there were exceptions. SCORE was included in the model because a player's score and ranking is one of the most important indicators in professional tennis to signify the success of a tennis player on an aggregated system (WTA, 2018; ATP, 2018).

Table 1. Variable descriptions and descriptive statistics

Variable	Description	Mean	Maximum	Minimum	Std. Dev.	Expected Signs
Female Salary	Prize money earned by a female professional tennis player in a calendar year.	1493571	12125936	76271.95	1616005	(-)
Male Salary	Prize money earned by a male professional tennis player in a calendar year.	1837468	14462739	108388	2243696	(+)
ATP Score	The basis for a male player's rank.	2322.34	15785	825	2338.149	(+)
WTA Score	The basis for a female player's rank.	2547.129	13260	697	1849.742	(+)
Male Age	The age of the male tennis players.	27.61	37	18	3.306073	(?)
Female Age	The age of a female tennis player.	25.61	37	17	3.71366	(?)
Number of tournaments played	The number of tournaments a male or female played in during a calendar year.	23.18	36	3	4.111331	(+)
Gender Dummy	The variable used to separate males and females.	0.50	1	0	.5003575	(-)
Rank Differentiation	How much a given player's ranked improved or worsened from the previous year.	5.542857	552	-39	30.3984	(+)
Country Dummy	The variable used to separate North American athletes and Non-NA Athletes.	.1114	1	0	.3148871	(-)
Year Dummy 2012-2017	The variables used to separate 2011 from the other years.	0.142	1	0	. 350177	(+)
Gender Wage Gap	The division of women's average yearly prize money by the male's average yearly prize money for years 2011-2017 and multiplying by 100.	(1493571/ 1837468) = .8128419107 (1 - .79005) = .1871581 (.21 * 100) = **18.72%** wage gap				

TOURN is the explanatory variable that signifies the number of tournaments played by the individual. This has been explored in previous literature (Flake 2013), so the expected sign was positive given it seems to account for the maximum opportunity to accumulate points and therefore higher prize money earned. RANKDIFF is the variable that indicates rank differentiation, which is calculated by taking an athlete's previous year rank and subtracting his or her current rank. The authors predicted that this variable's sign would be positive because it measured whether the athlete improved or deteriorated year over year. AGE held an ambiguous expected sign because the relationship with the dependent variable is not obvious in terms of accounting for the nuances of being young and arguably more athletic versus having more experience in professional tennis. GEN is a dummy variable for which females take on the value of 1, while males are represented by 0. COUNTRY is a dummy variable in which athletes from North America take on the value of 1, and non-North American athletes are represented by 0.

The WTA/ATP scores have different variables that factor into the formulas used to generate the values, so they are incomparable. The maximum WTA (female) score reached is 13260, while the maximum ATP (male) score is 15785. The mean age for male tennis players is approximately 27.61 years, whereas the mean age for females is 25.61 years. To adjust the data, the authors include dummies (YEAR_DUMMY) for the years 2012-2017. Each specific year dummy takes on a value of 1 during its specified year, while every other year has a value of 0. This technique excludes the year 2011 in order to avoid multicollinearity.

As shown in Table 1, the mean of the dependent variable, the prize money earned by professional tennis players, is lower for women at $1,493,571 in comparison to a mean of $1,837,468 for their male counterparts. The standard deviation for the women tennis players is 1,616,005 in the sample, whereas the men have a standard deviation of 2,243,696. Each gender has a sample size of 350. The above details in the descriptive statistics are noteworthy because we can see men out-earning women.

It is important to determine if there is a statistically significant difference in the sample means between the two groups. Thus, a t-test on the difference between the means of the prize money earned by men and women is conducted. The difference between the means is $343,897, and the t-value derived is roughly 2.33. Based on a critical value of 1.96 for 698 degrees of freedom, the null hypothesis that the sample means are equal is rejected at the 5% level.

Model

This analysis uses ordinary least squares (OLS) regression to explain professional tennis players' salaries among the top fifty ranked men and top fifty ranked women tennis players in the world. This model considers the independent variables mentioned in the above section to explain the dependent variable, which is prize money earned. By using this dependent variable, the researchers can calculate the gender wage gap. The researchers are consistent with the previous literature (Kahn, 1991) in assembling their econometric model, which is as follows in Model 1:

$$REALSAL = \beta_0 + \beta_1 SCORE + \beta_2 TOURN + \beta_3 RANKDIFF + \beta_4 AGE + \beta_5 GEN + \beta_6 COUNTRY + e_i \quad (1)$$

This study evaluates the same equation but adds year dummies as follows in Model 2:

$$REALSAL = \beta_0 + \beta_1 SCORE + \beta_2 AGE + \beta_3 GEN + \beta_4 YEAR\_DUMMY\_2012 + \beta_5 YEAR\_DUMMY\_2013 + \beta_6 YEAR\_DUMMY\_2014 + \beta_7 YEAR\_DUMMY\_2015 + \beta_8 YEAR\_DUMMY\_2016 + \beta_9 YEAR\_DUMMY\_2017 + \beta_{10} COUNTRY + e_i \quad (2)$$

where β_0 is the constant and the β's are the estimated coefficients of the independent variables.

Another important part of this analysis is to determine if there is a structural break in the sample between men and women. The Chow test for the sample size using gender interactive variables yields an F-statistic of 22.56 with a p-value of 0.0. Thus, the null hypothesis, that the regression coefficients across the two groups are equal, is rejected, and separate regressions are in order. Therefore, the following regression is run splitting the male and female samples in Models 3 and 4:

$$REALSAL = \beta_0 + \beta_1 SCORE + \beta_2 AGE + \beta_3 YEAR\_DUMMY\_2012 + \beta_4 YEAR\_DUMMY\_2013 + \beta_5 YEAR\_DUMMY\_2014 + \beta_6 YEAR\_DUMMY\_2015 + \beta_7 YEAR\_DUMMY\_2016 + \beta_8 YEAR\_DUMMY\_2017 + \beta_9 COUNTRY + e_i \quad (3,4)$$

Econometric Issues

The authors tested for heteroskedasticity using the White test because there was reason to believe the model might possess it based on insight gained from the previous literature (Paserman, 2007). The authors also wanted to ensure that they were not violating Classical Assumption V. The results showed that there was heteroskedasticity present in the model, so corrections were made using heteroskedasticity-consistent standard errors for the final results. Another issue this analysis encountered was multicollinearity due to the ATP/WTA variables being close in nature but encompassing many different variables over which the researchers had no control. This variable was the most significant variable in the model, which restricted the researchers from removing it from the equation.

RESULTS

The results of the first regression are shown in Table 2. The following variables are found to be statistically significant at the 1% level: WTA/ATP score, age, country, and gender. Along with being statistically significant, WTA/ATP score matches its expected sign of being positive. Age was expected to be ambiguous, and it holds a positive sign, showing the importance of having experience in professional tennis. Gender holds a negative sign, which indicates that there is indeed wage disparity in favor of the male tennis players. This is consistent with previous literature (Flake 2013). Country holds a positive sign, which indicates that there is a disparity in favor of North American athletes overall. The R-squared value is high at 0.8983, while the adjusted R-Squared holds a value of 0.8974. The size and closeness of these variables showcases that the model fits the data well.

Due to the data being pooled cross-sectional, the authors added year dummies for years 2012-2017. The results of this regression are shown in Table 2. The R-squared value in Model 2 is 0.9127, while the adjusted R-squared held a value of 0.9113. The model's t-statistics also changed in values, heightening their significance, especially for the WTA/ATP score and the gender dummy. The variables that held

Table 2. Overall model regression results

Variable	Model 1	Model 2	Model 3	Model 4
CONSTANT	826552.6***	-1169193***	-1879364***	-885030***
SCORE	865.9283 ***	875.933 ***	796.0308***	924.1918***
_OF_TOURNAMENTS_PLAYED	-8322.128			
AGE	30140.76 ***	21023.17***	32229.3***	11715.28*
RANK DIFFERENCIATION	732.7144			
GENDER_DUMMY	-504599.2***	-503496.4***		
COUNTRY_DUMMY	212159.2 ***	195745.1***	354635.2***	30165.04
YEAR_DUMMY_2012		100765.4	205891.3**	-20641.22
YEAR_DUMMY_2013		343046.1***	343269.6***	329582.28***
YEAR_DUMMY_2014		613675.6***	665758.8***	527772.4***
YEAR_DUMMY_2015		300691.3***	509417***	55758.18
YEAR_DUMMY_2016		618470.2***	733111.5***	481227.4***
YEAR_DUMMY_2017		638770***	876832.9***	376004***

*** variables are significant at the 1% level

** variables are significant at the 5% level

* variables are significant at the 10% level

Note: t-statistics are based on heteroskedasticity-consistent standard errors.

a statistical significance at the 1% level include WTA/ATP Score, gender dummy, country dummy, age, and year dummies 2013-2017. Though already statistically insignificant when included in both models, the signs on the rank differentiation and number of tournaments played variables also changed in the model when the authors included the year dummy variable for 2012-2017, which prompted the researchers to drop the variables for Model 2. Research indicates that the number of tournaments played may not be as significant to an athlete; instead, the caliber of tournaments played and won carries more weight. This conclusion is solidified factually since the WTA ranking calculations take the tournaments with various conditions that yield the highest-ranking points during the rolling 52-week period. This detail also holds true for the men's side in which case the ATP ranking points are awarded dependent on the prestige of the tournament reached (WTA, 2018; ATP, 2018).

Based upon the results of the Chow test and the justification to separate the male and female regressions, Model 3 and Model 4 were run. Model 3 indicates the regression for the female sample. The results of Model 3 are shown in Table 2. The R-squared value is 0.8855, while the adjusted R-squared value is 0.8824. When running the regression for just the female sample, all independent variables became statistically significant at some level. The variables that held a statistical significance at the 1% level include: WTA Score, gender dummy, country dummy, age, and year dummies 2013- 2017. The 2012-year dummy variable held a statistical significance at the 5% level. None of the signs changed in our model when the authors ran the regression for just the females, which shows consistency in the variables.

Similar to Model 3, the authors ran the same regression for just the male sample. Model 4 indicates the regression for the male sample. The results of Model 4 are also shown in Table 2. The R-squared value is 0.9378, while the adjusted R-squared value is 0.9361. When running the regression for just the male sample, various independent variables lost their statistical significance at some level. The variables that held a statistical significance at the 1% level include ATP Score and year dummies 2013, 2014, and 2016. The age variable held a statistical significance at the 10% level.

It is important to note the differences in Model 3 and Model 4 to determine how the coefficient estimates in this model differ for males and females. Based on the results, it is suggested that the ATP score is a stronger predictor of prize money for males (924.19) than the WTA score is for females (796.03). However, based on the results of the models, all other independent variables are stronger predictors when it comes to the female sample in predicting prize money earned. It is specifically significant to note the country dummy variable that is statistically significant for the female population at the 1% level, but not statistically significant for the male population. This indicates that there is a disparity in favor of North American female athletes, but the male athletes might not have the same discriminatory barrier. Another variance the split models reveal is the dissimilarity of age when it comes to predicting the prize money earned. For the females, age is statistically significant at the 1% level with a much larger coefficient estimate (32229.3) in comparison to the male sample, where age is statistically significant at the 10% level with a much lower coefficient estimate (11715.28).

SOLUTIONS AND RECOMMENDATIONS

By using real salary as the dependent variable, the authors are able to calculate the wage gap by dividing the women's average yearly prize money by the male's average yearly prize money for years 2011-2017 and multiplying by 100 to find the disparity. This calculation reveals a 19% pay gap in favor of professional male tennis players. Other research similarly demonstrated that in 2018, women working full-time, year round earned an average of 81.1 cents for every dollar earned by men working (i.e., the wage gap for the entire female population in the U.S. was 18.9% in 2018) (IWPR, 2019). Hence, the present study finds a virtually identical wage gap in professional tennis between 2011 and 2017. Furthermore, in previous literature, Flake et al. (2013) obtained a 20.5% pay gap in professional tennis in 2009, which is consistent with the above findings as well.

The solution is rather simple. With the fact that gender equality is a basic human right and professional sports are a major publicized platform, men and women collectively have the ability to create an environment where they are not only providing women in sports opportunities and resources but also promoting them in their involvement. With the heightened interest in participation at all levels in women's sports, not to mention the growing interest in viewership at a more professional level, sports need gender equality on all levels more than ever. Civilians can begin to transform the current climate in professional sports immediately by continuing to provide visibility, enhance research, demonstrate support, and promote best practices.

FUTURE RESEARCH DIRECTIONS

This study could be extended by expanding gender inequality research into the entire sports world. However, this type of further research may have problems due to variability in the structure between male and female professional sports, which mainly reflect average revenue and viewership differences. In order to extend this analysis into another sport, where the prize money earned by the professional athlete is the key dependent variable to be measured, careful consideration of that sports' market structure would be critical. Tennis has a fair means of measurement because of the nature of male and female athletes competing in the same tournaments throughout the year. Furthermore, women's tennis is the most popular women's professional sport in terms of TV viewership, and it arguably brings in as much revenue as men's tennis does (Flake, 2013). Accounting for these factors, golf would be the next recommended avenue for future research; its structure has similarities to tennis.

Additionally, soccer would provide another direction for investigating gender-related inequality in professional sports because the US Women's National soccer team filed a wage discrimination lawsuit in 2016. The US Women's National soccer team, ranked number 1 in 2019 in the FIFA Women's World Rankings, has won the World Cup three times and the Olympics four times. These accolades propel the women's team far beyond the success of the men's US National team, which has never won either tournament and even failed to qualify for the 2018 World Cup. In an analysis of the general comparison between the men and women's professional soccer players' earnings, top-tier female players earn roughly 38 percent of the compensation of a similarly positioned player on the men's team (Wamsley, 2019). However, direct compensation differences can be complicated to analyze since each team has its own collective bargaining agreement with US Soccer. In particular, with these relevant statistics and the lawsuit that was filed in 2016, the US Women's National soccer team reached a new collective bargaining agreement with US Soccer in 2017. Furthermore, the Equal Employment Opportunity Commission (EEOC) issued letters granting four plaintiffs, namely four of the original professional women's soccer players who were involved in the lawsuit, the right to sue in May of 2019 (Wamsley, 2019). This type of extension of gender inequality research into professional soccer would showcase the limitations that professional women face in sports not necessarily in comparison to their male peers in terms of viewership and revenue but more so in overall success within a sport on a global scale.

In addition, an analysis centered on gender inequality that measures the impacts of specific political and cultural factors on success and earnings for men and women professional athletes globally would be another stimulating extension of this type of research. In a study previously performed (Congdon-Hohman, 2011), it was found that economic and demographic factors affect men and women differently across the world of professional sports. More specifically, Latin heritage is prominent in men's determinants of success but not in that of women. Furthermore, Muslim religious affiliation reduces women's success but not men's in this field. Additionally, communist political systems improve women's success and earnings but reduce that of men (Congdon-Hohman, 2011).

A further extension of the current line of research would encompass the coaching gap that is present in women's sports, both collegiately and professionally. This is another recent example of discrimination in sports that has garnered a new spotlight. Title IX has been an area of progress for women's sports in terms of participation by athletes; however, it has had the reverse consequence in women's coaching. Prior to

1972, 90% of all head coaches in women's athletics at the college level were women, but in 2018, that number was approximately 43% (UMN, 2018). Hence, determining the factors that are most influential when hiring and firing decisions are made for head coaches in relation to gender is another potential layer to this type of research.

Lastly, an extension of this study would be to investigate the racial component of professional athletics. Though sports, in a historical sense, have provided powerful opportunities for African-Americans and individuals of other ethnicities, barriers remain that these athletes face on the big stage. Such a study must not only measure wage inequality in professional sports through gender as this research did but also unveil other aspects of discrimination based on an athlete's race.

CONCLUSION

By determining the factors that affect professional tennis players' prize money, the authors have concluded that there is evidence for men out-earning women in professional tennis. This is an obvious conclusion because it follows the trend of a gender-related wage disparity that civilization has seen throughout human history. This wage gap for the entire female population was found to be 18.9% in 2018 according to government data (IWPR, 2019), which shows alignment to the wage gap that this research exposed in professional tennis between 2011 and 2017. Similarly, previous research found that in 2009, a 20.5% pay gap in professional tennis existed, which is consistent with the findings of this analysis as well (Flake et al., 2013).

The variables that have a statistically significant impact include WTA/ATP score, age and the gender, country, and some year dummies. These explanatory variables play a large role in explaining professional tennis players' salaries. Even though professional tennis has attempted to diminish the wage gap between men and women by awarding equal prize money in the Slams since 2007, strong evidence remains that a gap continues to exist due to the less-publicized tournaments that the athletes compete in throughout a calendar year. Through the authors' regression analysis, strong evidence to stand behind this notion has been revealed.

Equality, in terms of prize money earned, is only one part of the equation in measuring inequality in professional sports. Progress in women's professional sports has seen a dramatic improvement throughout history, specifically in participation, opportunities, and media coverage. However, there are still prominent disparities that exist for women in all of these facets today. Underrepresentation of coverage and sexualization in the media represent two trends that have remained consistent in women's sports. Additionally, opportunities depict inequality in professional sports due to the multitude of men's leagues and teams in contrast to those for women. One most notable example is the MLB (Major League Baseball) versus the NPF (National

Pro Fastpitch). The MLB is comprised of 30 teams, while the NPF has a mere six teams in the league. Furthermore, the average salary for a NPF softball player is roughly $5,000 to $6,000 for a 48-game season running from June through August (NPF, 2019). The average salary of a professional baseball player in the MLB is about $3.4M per year in a 162-game season (MLB, 2019). The discrepancies for these figures show that MLB players make on average $21,000 per game in comparison to the NPF players who make about $115 per game played. These figures do not even scratch the surface for representing opportunities, or the lack thereof, for women in the world of professional sports.

Civil rights advancement in sports and society can take a substantial amount of time, endurance, and energy. The absence of opportunities and representation in the media compound to represent the hardships that modern-day-professional women must face in sports. While much progress has been made, gender discrimination for both individual and team sports should continue to be explored in the quest for equality.

REFERENCES

Buysse, J. A., & Embser-Herbert, M. S. (2004). Constructions of gender in sport. *Gender & Society*, *18*(1), 66–81. doi:10.1177/0891243203257914

Congdon-Hohman, J., & Matheson, V. A. (2011). International women's soccer and gender inequality: Revisited. *Handbook on the Economics of Women in Sports,* 345-364. doi:10.4337/9781849809399.00026

Cooper, M. (2014, August 7). *For women leaders, likability and success hardly go hand-in-hand*. Retrieved April 23, 2019, from https://hbr.org/2013/04/for-women-leaders-likability-a

Flake, C. R., Dufur, M. J., & Moore, E. L. (2013). Advantage men: The sex pay gap in professional tennis. *International Review for the Sociology of Sport*, *48*(3), 366–376. doi:10.1177/1012690212442166

Hanson, V. (2012). The inequality of sport: Women < men. *Undergraduate Review: A Journal of Undergraduate Student Research, 13*(5), 15-22.

Hegewisch, A., & Hartman, H. (2019). *Pay Equity & Discrimination*. Retrieved January 8, 2020, from http://www.iwpr.org/initiatives/pay-equity-and-discrimination

Kahn, L. M. (1991). Discrimination in professional sports: A survey of the literature. *Industrial & Labor Relations Review*, *44*(3), 395–418. doi:10.1177/001979399104400301

Lorber, J. (2005). *Gender inequality: Feminist theories and politics.* Roxbury Publishing Company.

Marcus, B. (2015, March 31). *True Feminism Is About Equality for Both Genders.* Retrieved April 25, 2019, from https://www.forbes.com/sites/bonniemarcus/2015/03/31/true-feminism-is-about-equality-for-both-genders/#72db11b2190d

MLBPlayers.com. (n.d.). Retrieved May 04, 2019, from https://www.mlbplayers.com/

Official Site of Men's Professional Tennis | ATP World Tour | Tennis. (n.d.). Retrieved April 19, 2018, from http://www.atpworldtour.com

Paserman, M. D. (2007, June). *Gender differences in performance in competitive environments: Evidence from professional tennis players.* CEPR Discussion Paper 6335.

Perasso, V. (2017, October 23). *100 Women: Is the gender pay gap in sport really closing?* Retrieved September 3, 2018, from https://www.bbc.com/news/world-41685042

Progress and Inequality: Women's Sports and the Gender Gap. (2018, January 3). Retrieved May 10, 2019, from https://cehdvision2020.umn.edu/blog/progress-inequality-womens-sports-gender-gap/

Sun, Q., Zheng, L., & Zheng, Y. (2013). Sexual objectification and women's self-objectification. *Xinli Kexue Jinzhan*, *21*(10), 1794–1802. doi:10.3724/SP.J.1042.2013.01794

Walton, J., & Wilson, G. L. (2019). *National Pro Fastpitch (NPF) is a growing professional sports platform for women in sport, specifically the sport of fastpitch softball.* Retrieved from https://profastpitch.com/

Wamsley, L. (2019, March 8). U.S. *Women's Soccer Team Sues U.S. Soccer For Gender Discrimination.* Retrieved April 25, 2019, from https://www.npr.org/2019/03/08/701522635/u-s-womens-soccer-team-sues-u-s-soccer-for-gender-discrimination

Wheaton, B., & Thorpe, H. (2018). Action Sports, the Olympic Games, and the Opportunities and Challenges for Gender Equity: The Cases of Surfing and Skateboarding. *Journal of Sport and Social Issues*, *42*(5), 315–342. doi:10.1177/0193723518781230

WTA. (n.d.). Retrieved April 24, 2018, from http://www.wtatennis.com

KEY TERMS AND DEFINITIONS

Agency: A thing or person that acts to produce a particular result.

Chow Test: Indicates if the regression coefficients are different for split data sets. Basically, it tests whether one regression line or two separate regression lines best fit two different groups in a data set.

Cross-Sectional: A type of data collected by observing many subjects (such as individuals, firms, countries, or regions) at the same point of time or without regard to differences in time.

Dependent Variable: A variable whose value depends on that of another.

Descriptive Statistics: Brief descriptive coefficients that summarize a given data set, which can be either a representation of the entire or a sample of a population.

Discrimination: The unjust or prejudicial treatment of different categories of people or things, especially on the grounds of race, age, or sex.

Dummy Variable: A numeric variable that represents categorical data such as gender, race, political affiliation, etc.

Heteroskedasticity: Refers to the circumstance in which the variability of a variable is unequal across the range of values of a second variable that predicts it.

Independent Variable: A variable whose variation does not depend on that of another.

Multicollinearity: A state of very high intercorrelations or inter-associations among the independent variables.

Regression: A measure of the relationship between the mean value of one variable (e.g., output) and corresponding values of other variables.

Statistical Significance: The claim that a result from data generated by testing or experimentation is not likely to occur randomly or by chance; instead, it is likely to be attributable to a specific cause.

t-Statistics: Used in a t-test when deciding to support or reject the null hypothesis.

Chapter 7
Socioeconomic Influences on Fertility Rate Fluctuations in Developed and Developing Economies

Kayla M. Good
Indiana University of Pennsylvania, USA

Anthony M. Maticic Jr.
https://orcid.org/0000-0002-3917-2817
Indiana University of Pennsylvania, USA

ABSTRACT

This study investigates what socioeconomic factors determine the varying fertility rates among developed and developing nations and the implications of this information. Social and economic variables are analyzed using a panel of 20 nations with annual data from 1991-2015 to determine the most sizable and significant variables that impact fertility rates. A one-way fixed effects model is utilized. This study includes an aggregate model as well as two models isolating the fertility rates of developed nations and of developing nations, in accordance with Chow-Test results. The results find that there is a divergence between the determinants of fertility rates, based upon the development level. It is clear from these results that fertility and population control issues are specific to the state of a nation's development; thus, blanket policies will not fully address the issue of excessive population growth.

DOI: 10.4018/978-1-7998-1093-3.ch007

INTRODUCTION

In the past century, the world's population has expanded greatly even though the number of births per woman has generally been stagnant or on the decline. This global population growth has led to overcrowding, depletion of resources, and social unrest. On the surface, the causes of such a large increase in population seem obvious: greater access to healthcare, longer lifespans, and higher birth rates. However, the population has been growing more rapidly in developing economies, such as those on the continents of Africa and Asia, in comparison to industrialized western nations. Population growth has become such an acute concern that the United Nations and World Bank devote much of their efforts to providing family planning services to the developing world that is struggling to support their growing populations ("World Population Plan of Action", 2018). At the same time, fertility rates have been declining or stagnating worldwide, with the greatest decrease occurring in developed economies, compared to a smaller decline in the developing world. The factors contributing to high fertility rates in underdeveloped economies is of great importance to the global community as it grapples with population managment.

In 1961, the worldwide average fertility rate was 5.01; in other words, each woman will give birth to about five children in her lifetime. In 2015, this rate was cut in half to approximately 2.45 children per woman. However, this aggregate measure does not adequately describe the story of reproductive behavior for developed economies in the same way that it does for developing economies. For example, data from 2015 show that in the Democratic Republic of the Congo, the fertility rate is still more than five births per woman, whereas in South Africa, the fertility rate is nearing only one birth per woman. The hypothesized cause of this disparity is socioeconomic differences between these two nations.

Understanding the factors that lead to lower fertility rates across diverse economies has the potential to encourage a sustainable level of population growth around the world without implementing severe one-child policies that have been used in nations like China. Therefore, this study will use a similar approach to Gries and Grundmann (2012), Lutz and Qiang (2002), and Gauthier and Hatzius (1997), which utilized fertility rates or childhood health levels as the dependent variables and designed panels using socioeconomic data from a sample of countries with several possible explanatory variables. The dataset also includes the most recently available data from 1991-2015, which sets it apart from previous research.

This chapter is examined from the perspective of researchers in an economically developed nation with low fertility rates in comparison to many countries in the models. The motivation for this research stemmed from interests in reproductive policies, the advertised necessity of immigration, and the apparent decline in the populations of developed countries compared to developing countries. The objectives of the chapter are to determine which socioeconomic variables exert the most influence on the change in fertility rate in economies at differing stages of development and economic output.

This paper attempts to determine which socioeconomic variables, health determinants, and country-specific population control policies contribute to the fertility rates in developed and developing nations. A literature review that explores previous studies regarding fertility rates in relation to historical data from the World Bank can be found in Section 2. Section 3 describes the panel dataset analyzed in this paper and includes justifications for the inclusion of each explanatory variable, as well as their respective expected signs according to the literature. Section 4 details the use of a one-way fixed effects model ordinary least squares regression estimation followed by an exploration of the econometric issues that were encountered and subsequently resolved. To conclude, an interpretation of the regression results can be found in Section 5 with conclusions, policy implications, and future avenues of research in Section 6.

LITERATURE REVIEW

Empirical Studies

Recently, multiple studies have studied economic development and trade in a comparative analysis. One common area of focus is the fertility rates in economically developed countries as compared to the rates in impoverished and developing countries. Gries and Grundmann (2014) empirically analyzed trade in relation to the fertility rates in both developed and developing nations. Their study hypothesized that an intensification of trade between wealthy and poor countries asymmetrically impacts demographic shifts and population growth in both countries. Gries and Grundmann's (2014) key prediction was based on their theory that gains from trade in industrialized economies will be invested in the improvement of human capital, whereas developing economies will invest toward increasing population growth. Using a panel of 100 countries over 38 years and a generalized methods of moment (GMM) system estimator, the study measured the effects of low-skill exports versus high-skill exports while using economic and demographic variables as controls. The results from Gries and Grundmann (2014) support the hypothesis that developed and developing countries react differently to shifts in economic variables, which they argue are generally harmful to economic development in poorer nations.

Similarly, Galor and Mountford (2006) argued that the expansion of international trade in the second phase of the industrial revolution played a key role in the varying demographic transitions across the world. The increase in global trade led to a greater specialization of industrial and skill-intensive goods, leading to a more pronounced emphasis on investing in the quality of human capital in industrial economies. As a result of this new focus, the researchers hypothesized that due to the weaker technology and mass production capabilities in developing economies, the population in poorer countries must grow at a faster rate than their industrialized peers in order to remain competitive. However, this growth will result in a lower income per capita in the developing world. Galor and Mountford (2006) analyzed their hypothesis by comparing theoretical economies. As in the modern world, one economy specialized in the production of industrial goods, while the other specialized in agricultural goods. Over time, the population growth rate diverged between the two economies, with the agricultural economy growing faster. Galor and Mountford (2006) theorized that this growth will eventually lead to a greater diversification of skill and consequently reduce the fertility rate to levels that are seen in the developed world.

A low fertility rate is cited as a key indicator of economic development and a strong indicator of consumerism (Maruyama & Yamamoto, 2010). Therefore, Maruyama and Yamamoto (2010) built a model which served to highlight the importance of consumerism in determining fertility rates. They suggest that more materialism in society coincides with declining fertility. Furthermore, the model demonstrated the idea that parents allocate their fixed time either to working or child-rearing, indicating a trade-off between nominal income and children. Maruyama and Yamamoto (2010) integrated the endogenous fertility model and the Grossman-Helpman-Romer (GHR) type of the variety expansion growth model. By using a simple model in which variety expansion reduces fertility rates, Maruyama and Yamamoto (2010) determined that innovative activities in the economy, which they described as an engine for economic growth, facilitate fertility decline. According to Maruyama and Yamamoto (2010), this innovation and increase in consumer choice is a primary driver of the already lowered fertility rates across the world, especially in developed nations. Maruyama and Yamamoto (2010) also suggested analyzing urbanization in countries closely because historically, urbanization and demographic transitions have been closely related.

Lutz and Qiang (2002) analyzed population growth using biological and economic approaches. Specifically, their study looked at population density, education, mortality rates, age, and life expectancy as important independent variables. Child labor, contraceptive availability, availability of healthcare, and a subjective variable measuring child-value were other key explanatory variables. By using time-series data from 1960-2000 from a sample of data composed of 187 countries, Lutz and Qiang (2002) built models that included many macroeconomic and socioeconomic variables. Lutz and Qiang (2002) utilized structural breaks every five years and found that many of the included explanatory variables were statistically significant actors in the decline of fertility rates and overall population growth across models. The results were robust, allowing Lutz and Qiang (2002) to conclude that demographic transitions have led to increased population growth and that fertility rates should level out across economies in the long run as populations become increasingly dense.

Ahn and Mira (2002) analyzed data from OECD countries regarding total fertility rates and labor market data to include female labor force participation rates from 1970 to 1995. Cross sectionally, fertility rates and female labor force participation had a significant negative correlation from the 1970s through the early 1980s. However, in the late 1980s, the correlation reversed to positive and significant. The sign reversal coincided with spiking unemployment rates in OECD countries in the early 1980s. The data from the 1980s are consistent with the neoclassical theory that fertility will increase alongside income, implying that children are a normal good. However, this theory is challenged by the modern reality that as a country's income and level of development increases, fertility rates tend to decline. Ahn and Mira (2002) point out that this more recent theory suggests that since raising children imposes a high time opportunity cost for women, higher female wages could be resulting in lower fertility rates.

Given the below-replacement fertility levels that are common among industrialized nations, Gauthier and Hatzius (1997) set out to discover if governmental policies that encourage families to have more children have had any effect on fertility rates; in essence, they aimed to learn if government intervention in family planning is effective and justified. Gauthier and Hatzius (1997) utilized a panel of 22 industrialized countries from 1970-1990 to investigate. As expected, the direct cost of childbearing has a negative influence on fertility rates, and longer maternity leaves positively affected fertility rates. They also found that incentives targeting first children were more effective in increasing fertility rates than incentives for the second or third child. However, these policies are quite expensive for governments to sustain, as first children occur more often than second or third children. Overall, Gauthier and Hatzius (1997) found a limited effect of 0.7 additional children per woman where governmental incentives for childbearing are 25% higher than average.

Murthi, Guio, and Dreze (1995) conducted a district-level analysis of child mortality, total fertility rates, and gender bias in India through a cross section of data from the 1981 census and consisting of 296 districts. India is demographically diverse as some districts' characteristics fall into the category of a middle-income economy and others of a developing economy. They focused especially on the influences of per capita income, male and female literacy, female labor force participation rates, level of urbanization, accessibility of healthcare, and other socioeconomic variables as data were available. They found female literacy and female labor force participation to have a negative and statistically significant effect on the fertility rate. Murthi et al. (1995) also noted that there may be a causal link between child mortality and fertility rates, wherein one will decline as the other does. Therefore, they suggest that directly promoting child health, female literacy, and female participation in the labor force may be more effective in managing population growth than indirectly promoting economic development.

DATA

Sample

This study utilizes annual data provided by the World Bank Group that were collected for the years 1991-2015 on an annual basis with 20 cross sectional units that include developed and developing nations. A full list of included nations can be found in Table 1. The total sample size is 500. Prior studies have used similar regressands and explanatory variables for datasets as early as 1960 but no more recent than 2000 (Gauthier & Hatzius, 1997; Ahn & Mira, 2002; Lutz & Qiang, 2002) with a sample of countries ranging from two hypothetical economies (Galor & Mountford, 2006) to 187 countries (Lutz & Qiang, 2002). This study includes a sample of 20 countries which were chosen based on their development status and the availability of data for key explanatory variables across the time period of interest. Data for many of what the literature identifies as key explanatory variables were unavailable prior to 1991 and were absent for countries believed to be of paramount importance to the validity of the study. It is important to note that female literacy rate, which was presented as a key variable in the literature and economic theory, was excluded due to a lack of recorded data on the indicator in developing countries. Thus, this variable was excluded due to its unavailability for most nations included in the panel. Despite being an imperfect measure, female labor force participation rate is used as a proxy for female education and literacy rate, assuming that nations with higher rates of females participating in the workforce would similarly have more opportunities for females to receive primary education.

Explanation of Variables and Expected Relationships to Fertility

The dependent variable in this study is the fertility rate (FERTILITY) which is defined as the average number of births per woman. The independent variables for this study have been divided into three main groups: economic variables, demographic variables, and health variables. Complete definitions, expected relationships to fertility, and sources for these explanatory variables are located in Table 2 of the Appendix.

Included in the economic variable grouping are Real Gross Domestic Product per capita (RGDP), exports of goods and services as a percent of gross domestic product (EXPORTS), female labor force participation (FEMLFP), and unemployment rate (UNEMPLOY). According to Maruyama and Yamamoto (2010), increasing levels of economic development have been linked to a decline in the fertility rate. Thus, this study predicts that RGDP will have an inverse relationship with the fertility rate, meaning that as individual income rises, fertility is expected to decline. FEMLFP is also expected to have an inverse relationship with the fertility rate as there is a time trade-off involved with child-rearing versus working. Parents must allocate their fixed time to either activity; thus, if more women are working, they will likely have fewer children due to time constraints (Maruyama & Yamamoto, 2010; Ahn & Mira, 2002; Murthi et al., 1995). Based on the diversity of results in prior research, this paper assigned an ambiguous expected sign to the unemployment variable (Ahn & Mira, 2002; Maruyama & Yamamoto, 2010). According to the literature, higher unemployment will have a negative effect on FERTILITY in developed nations (Ahn & Mira, 2002). This is likely because individuals in developed nations that are not working have access to family planning methods and are more able to opt to wait until they are financially stable to have children. Alternatively, higher unemployment may lead to higher FERTILITY in developing nations because of fewer time constraints and limited access to contraceptive methods.

The relationship between EXPORTS and FERTILITY is expected to differ between developed and developing nations and is thus given an ambiguous expected sign. According to Gries and Grundmann (2014), EXPORTS is expected to have an inverse relationship with FERTILITY in developed nations and a positive relationship in developing nations. They suggest that in developing nations that are experiencing higher levels of trade in labor-intensive goods, there will be similarly increased demand for laborers. This results in an increasing fertility rate in an attempt to produce workers to fulfill those demands. Alternatively, developed nations export mainly skill-intensive and technologically advanced goods, which emphasize the need for quality over quantity in human labor. This likely lowers FERTILITY as parents are more concerned with raising skilled children (Gries & Grundmann, 2014).

Included in the demographic variable group are population density (POP_DENS), the total population (POP_TOTAL), the percentage of the total population living in urban areas (URBAN), the percentage of the male population that falls between the ages of 15-64 (MAL_AGE), and the same age category for females (FEM_AGE). While population density is often overlooked in existing literature, it may be an important psychological determinant of the fertility rate. POP_DENS has been found to have a negative relationship with the fertility rate, indicating that an already crowded nation might experience lower fertility as its residents experience the effects of overcrowding in their daily lives (Lutz & Qiang, 2002). Theoretically, one can extrapolate these results to predict that POP_TOTAL will also have an inverse relationship with FERTILITY. The percentage of the population living in an urban setting (URBAN) is expected to have an inverse relationship with the fertility rate in accordance with findings by Murthi et al. (1995). The researchers found that a high percentage of the population living in urban areas is associated with a lower fertility rate, which coincides with the similar inverse relationship of population density cited by Lutz and Qiang (2002). MAL_AGE and FEM_AGE are expected to have a positive association with the fertility rate, given that if a nation has a large proportion of its population within the 15-64 age bracket, there will likely be more children.

The last group contains the health-related variables, including infant mortality rate, (INF_MORT), overall death rate (DEATH), and a dummy variable for the legality of abortion (ABORT). INF_MORT is expected to have a positive relationship with FERTILITY. If infants are likely to not survive their first years of life, parents may opt to have more children in hopes of having more survivals. On the other hand, parents living in developed nations with increased access to healthcare would experience a lower infant mortality rate and in turn reduce the number of births per woman since the probability of survival for each child is higher (Murthi et al., 1995; Lutz & Qiang, 2002). A decline in DEATH due to improved health conditions in a nation is expected to be followed by an eventual decline in fertility rate as the population ages. In the short term, the two can have an inverse relationship due to the adjustment period that occurs when conditions improve within a nation (Lutz & Qiang, 2002).

The use of a dummy variable allowed the legality of abortions to be quantified in the sample (ABORT). The ideal variable here would have been access to contraception; however, such data were available for very few countries. Thus, the legality of abortion is used to capture the effects of the availability some type of family planning method, even though this particular method is ethically controversial. For the abortion dummy variable, a value of 1 indicates that abortion is legal in most cases, and a value of 0 indicates that abortion is illegal except in cases where the mother's health is jeopardized or is illegal in all cases. This variable is hypothesized to have an inverse relationship with the fertility rate since increased access to safe abortions generally reduces the number of births per woman (Lutz & Qiang, 2002).

Descriptive Statistics

Table 3 presents a complete summary of the descriptive statistics for both the dependent and independent variables included in this study. In this sample, the highest fertility rate was 6.77 in the Democratic Republic of Congo in 1995, and the minimum FERTILITY was 1.07 in South Korea in 2005. Likewise, the lowest real GDP per capita (RGDP) in this sample was \$102.64 in the Democratic Republic of Congo in 1999, while the maximum RGDP belongs to Luxembourg in 2015 of \$114,446.80. The female labor force participation variable also has a wide disparity between maximum and minimum values with the highest rate at 51.32% in the Democratic Republic of Congo in 1991 and the lowest being 24.09% in India in 2012. EXPORTS range from 6.73% of GDP in Brazil to 222.70% of GDP in Luxembourg. Of the health-related variables observed, Indonesia has the highest infant mortality (INF_MORT) in the sample at 117.4 deaths per 1,000 births, whereas the lowest rate was in Japan with 2 deaths out of 1,000.

ECONOMETRIC MODEL

General Procedure/Methodology

This study uses a panel data and a one-way fixed effects model to analyze the determinants of variation in fertility rates among the 20 included nations and to control for unobserved heterogeneity. Hausman Test results dictated the use of a one-way fixed effects model as opposed to a random effects or pooled cross-sectional model. Cross-section weights (PCSE) were utilized to correct for heteroskedasticity, multicollinearity, and serial correlation. This approach is similar to Gauthier and Hatzius (1997) who used a panel of 22 industrialized countries spanning 20 years while incorporating a dummy variable for developed nations. Three versions of the model are included in this study. The first model is the aggregate model with both developed and developing economies. Models 2 and 3 specify determinants of fertility rates in developed nations and developing nations separately, as per the results of a Chow-Test.

MODEL SPECIFICATION

Model 1 included both developed and developing nations in the regression. Prior research included indicators related to specific economic, demographic, or health related variables, so the explanatory variables in this study were grouped in a similar manner (Murthi et al., 1995). The following is the equation used in the first model:

$$FERTILITY_{it} = \beta_1 + \beta_2 ECONOMIC_{it} + \beta_3 DEMOGRAPHIC_{it} + \beta_4 HEALTH_{it} + \alpha_i + \varepsilon_{it} \quad (1)$$

By examining the results of this model (Table 3), all the included variables show statistical significance with an overall adjusted R-Squared of 0.9943. However, the results do not differentiate the degree of impact that the included explanatory variables have in developed economies in comparison to developing economies. Maruyama and Yamamoto (2010) suggest that these two different economic circumstances could be substantially different due to variations in economic output. As a result, a Chow-Test was conducted to determine the existence of a structural break between developed and developing economies in relation to fertility rates. The test confirmed that a structural break was appropriate; therefore, separate estimations of the equation for developed and developing economies were created. Countries with a real GDP per capita of $12,000 or lower were classified as developing (World Bank, 2018). The resulting equations are specified using the same econometric techniques and explanatory variables, except only data for developed countries are included in Model 2, where the dependent variable is labeled as FERTILITY_DEV. Additionally, only data for developing countries are included in Model 3, where the dependent variable is labeled as FERTILITY_UNDEV as written below:

$$FERTILITY\_DEV_{it} = \beta_1 + \beta_2 ECONOMIC_{it} + \beta_3 DEMOGRAPHIC_{it} + \beta_4 HEALTH_{it} + \alpha_i + \varepsilon_{it} \quad (2)$$

$$FERTILITY\_UNDEV_{it} = \beta_1 + \beta_2 ECONOMIC_{it} + \beta_3 DEMOGRAPHIC_{it} + \beta_4 HEALTH_{it} + \alpha_{it} + \varepsilon_{it} \quad (3)$$

The structural break models allow for a more detailed analysis of the differing impacts that the explanatory variables have on the fertility rate in developed versus developing nations. In both Models 2 and 3, some variables lost significance in comparison to Model 1. In order to assure correct specification, F-tests were conducted for the ECONOMIC, DEMOGRAPHIC, and HEALTH groupings of explanatory variables. The results indicated a rejection of the null hypothesis in each instance, demonstrating joint significance of each grouping. As a result, the same independent variables are present in both Models 2 and 3.

RESULTS

Model 1

The results for all models can be found in Table 4. In Model 1, all independent variables are significant at the 1% level, and the overall fit of the model is high with an adjusted R-Squared of 0.9939. In the ECONOMIC group, RGDP, FEM_LFP, and UNEMPLOY are statistically significant with RGDP and UNEMPLOY having an unexpected relationship to fertility. RGDP has an unexpected positive sign and is statistically significant. The sample is different from prior literature, so the impacts of changes in RGDP over the past 25 years may be different than the previous 20 (Murthi et al., 1995). Due to variations in previous studies, we were not able to predict the relationship of EXPORTS to fertility. In this model, EXPORTS is inversely related to FERTILITY. The expectation for UNEMPLOY was also ambiguous, but it has a small and significant negative coefficient in Model 1. In the DEMOGRAPHIC group, all variables have their expected signs except for MAL_AGE and URBAN. The HEALTH group has significance and expected signs for all variables.

The multiple unexpected signs that are present in Model 1 are likely due to the fact that the data sample calls for structural break between the fertility rates of developed and developing nations. Thus, results from this model should be considered with caution. Models 2 and 3 evaluate the data with a structural break in place and thus provide more reliable and precise results.

Model 2

Model 2 is specified to include data from the developed nations in this study; thus, the sample size (N*T) is reduced to 275 as opposed to 500 in Model 1. This model has a lower adjusted R-Squared of 0.923. This lower overall fit is expected since restricting the dependent variable to developing nations reduces the level of variance in the data. In the ECONOMIC group of variables, EXPORTS, FEMLFP, and UNEMPLOY are significant at the 1% level. FEMLFP has an unexpected positive sign, although this can be explained in the context of the societal structure of many western developed nations. The improved access to healthcare and additional support from maternity benefits may lower the opportunity cost of having children, encourage working females to have children, and enable them to raise those children comfortably (Maruyama & Yamamoto, 2010; Ahn & Mira, 2002; Murthi et al., 1995). The unemployment variable was ambiguous, but Model 2 assigned it an inverse relationship with fertility. Following the same assumption that access to maternity benefits increases fertility, high levels of unemployment would logically decrease fertility in developed nations as those women may not have access to benefits or comprehensive health insurance. This would then increase the opportunity cost of having children and discourage high fertility.

EXPORTS is also negative in this model because many countries that have levels of service exports also have higher education levels, which corresponds to lower rates of fertility (Maruyama & Yamamoto, 2010). In the DEMOGRAPHIC group, only MAL_AGE has statistical significance as well as a negative sign. A higher percentage of males aged 18-64 is robust across models with a significant inverse impact on FERTILITY, which may point to a lack of women of childbearing age. The lack of significance in the other variables in this group may be due to the differing nature of developed and developing economies and their trends. In the HEALTH group, INF_MORT and DEATH are significant at the 1% level both demonstrating the expected relationships to fertility. ABORT is not significant in this model, presumably because abortion has been legalized in most of the developing countries for a large part of the 25-year sample. This could also be due to the plethora of other more commonly used methods of family planning, particularly preventative measures. The overall decrease in the explanatory power of this model could be due to diminishing returns to improved economic positions as well as a decreased marginal trade-off between childcare and work as a result of improved maternal benefits in developed nations.

Model 3

Model 3 uses the fertility rate in developing nations (FERTILTY_UNDEV) as the dependent variable. This model has the highest adjusted R-Squared of the three models in this study at 0.996. In this model, all explanatory variables are significant at the 1% level except for population density (POP_DENS) and the death rate (DEATH). In the grouping of economic variables (ECONOMIC), there is an unexpected positive sign on the real gross domestic product per capita (RGDP) coefficient, suggesting that fertility rates rise as individual productivity increases in the included developing nations. The unexpected positive sign on RGDP contradicts some prior research (Maruyama & Yamamoto, 2010). This deviation from literature could be explained by a significant difference in the sample used in this study as compared to previous literature and temporal variation. This finding insinuates that among developing nations, a higher RGDP results in more families feeling comfortable having children. Conversely, among already developed nations, increased individual productivity is associated with a lower fertility rate.

Female labor force participation (FEMLFP) behaves as expected in this model with a small, negative, and statistically significant coefficient. This finding indicates that in developing economies, increasing female labor force participation decreases the fertility rate. As a proxy for female education, this result also indicates that improving female access to education may also decrease fertility. The last variable in the ECONOMIC grouping, unemployment (UNEMPLOY), has a positive sign in this model, suggesting that the theory of decreased time constraints (more leisure time) and lower access to contraceptives may contribute to higher fertility during times of unemployment in developing nations.

In the DEMOGRAPHICS group, all variables are significant at the 1% level except population density. The population density variable may have lost the significance it carried in the pooled model due to the overall poorer living conditions in developing nations. This contrasts with the developed nations in Model 2 that have more variation in living conditions between urban and rural areas. In the HEALTH group, INF_MORT and ABORT are significant, but DEATH is not. The availability and legality of safe abortions in these nations is much less common than in developed nations. Model 3 finds that any availability significantly decreases the number of births per woman, a finding that is consistent with previous literature (Gauthier & Hatzius, 1997). As expected, high rates of infant mortality in the first year of life also have a significant positive impact on fertility rates in developing nations as women bear more children to increase the chances of having one survive.

CONCLUSION

The key finding of this study is that the most powerful determinants of fertility vary depending on the development status of a nation. In developed economies, the legality of abortion does not have a significant impact on fertility. Conversely, in developing economies, the legality of abortion has a strong statistical impact on decreasing the overall fertility rate. Likewise, among developed nations, an increase in real GDP per capita was found to have no significant effects on fertility rates, but among developing countries, increases in individual productivity actually correlated to increases in fertility rate. The diverging natures of the societies and economic conditions in the two classifications, according to the models in this study and in the literature, exert varying degrees of influence on the fertility rates (Galor & Mountford, 2006). Poor health conditions in developing economies are less indicative of higher fertility rates than in industrialized economies, due in part to the lower marginal differences between one developing cross section and the next. In developed nations, where fertility rates are already very low, independent demographic variables have little impact on fertility. In developing economies, demographic variables have a stronger influence on fertility rates, which are still much higher than in developed nations.

POLICY IMPLICATIONS AND RECOMMENDATIONS

The findings of this study could be used to better understand policy areas to target and to understand why the developing world is still experiencing rapid population growth despite the strains on resources. Developed nations have largely obtained sustainable fertility rates as they experience economic growth and move away from labor-intensive economies. However, developing countries maintain higher fertility rates which can put additional pressure on scarce familial resources and exacerbate poverty. Based upon the findings in Model 3, initiatives to provide alternative options for unplanned pregnancies, particularly increasing access to preventative measures, will likely reduce the number of births per woman in developing nations. Female education initiatives may also result in more women in the workforce, which could bring fertility to a sustainable level in the long-run.

Though the repercussions of fertility rate decline are not explicitly evaluated in this study's models, the consequences of both high and low fertility rates are mixed. In increasingly globalized societies, economies are competing for the best talent, technology, and laborers. For countries that are concerned about negative economic impacts from declining fertility and a lack of population replacement, their governments could incentivize the immigration from other countries. Such a policy would prevent the decline of the overall population level, particularly as aging populations pass away and young workers leave their home countries to work and live elsewhere.

FUTURE RESEARCH DIRECTIONS

To continue this research, incorporating more variables that directly relate to female education, which have been key indicators of fertility rate in prior studies, could be pursued if such data became available. Furthermore, integrating additional dummies for relevant policy and cultural variables, such as specific family planning initiatives, religion, and family dynamics, could reduce the possibility of omitted variable bias. Incorporating a lag on these variables may also capture longer-term effects of changes in those dynamics. Additional policy and cultural variables with lags were not included in this study due to constraints presented by data availability. In the future, such data may become available. Furthermore, incorporating additional countries or selecting different countries as data on socioeconomic factors becomes more readily available could also potentially improve results and grant additional explanatory power to the model.

Additionally, as the economy continues to integrate globally, the behavior of fertility rates will continue to change to match the evolving needs of world economies. Moreover, because the results of the models and literary review in this study indicated that the specialization of economies, in either exporting or importing activities, had a significant impact on the variation in fertility rates, a more connected worldwide economy could facilitate demographic shifts that may produce varying results. If this research were to be duplicated with a different sample or time period, supplemental insights into the nature of fertility rate variations around the globe could be gained.

ACKNOWLEDGMENT

This study was made possible by the guidance and mentoring of Dr. James J. Jozefowicz, Ph.D. of The Indiana University of Pennsylvania. His knowledge and expertise in the field of econometric techniques greatly advanced the ability of this paper to produce meaningful results. The authors also thank former student Paul Shaloka, a 2018 graduate of Indiana University of Pennsylvania and a current doctoral student at the University of Notre Dame, for providing useful insights that furthered the progress of this study.

REFERENCES

Ahn, N., & Mira, P. (2002). A note on the changing relationship between fertility and female employment rates in developed countries. *Journal of Population Economics*, *15*(4), 667–682. doi:10.1007001480100078

DataBank. (2017). *World development indicators*. The World Bank. Retrieved from https://databank.worldbank.org/data

Galor, O., & Mountford, A. (2006). Trade and the great divergence: The family connection. *The American Economic Review*, *96*(2), 299–303. doi:10.1257/000282806777212378

Gauthier, A. H., & Hatzius, J. (1997). Family benefits and fertility: An econometric analysis. *Population Studies, 51*(3), 295-306. Retrieved from http://www.jstor.org/stable/pdf/2952473.pdf?refreqid=excelsior%3A9ba38324047f0a9cb49af458d3727e50

Gries, T., & Grundmann, R. (2014). Trade and fertility in the developing world: The impact of trade and trade structure. *Journal of Population Economics*, *27*(4), 1165–1186. doi:10.100700148-014-0508-x

Lutz, W., & Qiang, R. (2002). Determinants of human population growth. *Philosophical Transactions of the Royal Society of London. Series B, Biological Sciences*, *357*(1425), 1197–1210. doi:10.1098/rstb.2002.1121 PMID:12396512

Maruyama, A., & Yamamoto, K. (2010). Variety expansion and fertility rates. *Journal of Population Economics*, *23*(1), 57–71. doi:10.100700148-008-0223-6

Murthi, M., Guio, A. C., & Dreze, J. (1995). Mortality, fertility, and gender bias in India: A district-level analysis. *Population and Development Review, 21*(4), 745-782. Retrieved from http://www.jstor.org/stable/pdf/2137773.pdf?refreqid=excelsior%3Ae57579fdfb96f33664d2e2ca0cee5d23

World Population Plan of Action. (2018). Retrieved from https://www.un.org/popin/icpd/conference/bkg/wppa.html

ADDITIONAL READING

Barro, R. J., & Becker, G. S. (1989). Fertility choice in a model of economic growth. *Econometrica, 57*(2), 481–501. doi:10.2307/1912563

Becker, G. S., Murphy, K. M., & Tamura, R. (1990). Human capital, fertility, and economic growth. *Journal of Political Economy, 98*(5, Part 2), S12–S37. doi:10.1086/261723

Doepke, M. (2004). Accounting for fertility decline during the transition to growth. *Journal of Economic Growth, 9*(3), 347–383. doi:10.1023/B:JOEG.0000038935.84627.e4

Freedman, R. (1979). Theories of fertility decline: A reappraisal. *Social Forces, 58*(1), 1–17. doi:10.2307/2577781

Lee, R., & Mason, A. (2010). Fertility, human capital, and economic growth over the demographic transition. *European Journal of Population/Revue européenne de Démographie, 26*(2), 159-182.

Lutz, W. (2006). Fertility rates and future population trends: Will Europe's birth rate recover or continue to decline? *International Journal of Andrology, 29*(1), 25–33. doi:10.1111/j.1365-2605.2005.00639.x PMID:16466521

Mathews, T. J., & Ventura, S. J. (1997). Birth and fertility rates by educational attainment: United States, 1994. *Monthly Vital Statistics Report, 45*(10).

Rindfuss, R. R., Morgan, S. P., & Offutt, K. (1996). Education and the changing age pattern of American fertility: 1963–1989. *Demography, 33*(3), 277–290. doi:10.2307/2061761 PMID:8875062

KEY TERMS AND DEFINITIONS

Chow-Test: An econometric test used to determine if there is a structural break in a dataset.

Cross-Sectional: Analyzes data at one point-in-time across multiple samples.

Developed Economies: Any nation with a real gross domestic product per capita greater than 12,000 USD.

Developing Economies: Any nation with real gross domestic product per capita of 12,500 USD or less.

Diversified Economy: An economy which has various means of producing output and whose economy would not be severely hampered by a decline in one specific industry.

Panel Data: Dataset that includes both a time series and cross-sectional element for variables.

Structural Break: A point in a dataset where there is a divergence or change in the behavior of the data in question.

APPENDIX

Table 1. Countries included in the sample

Developed Nations	Developing Nations
Canada Denmark France Germany Japan Luxembourg Netherlands South Korea Spain United Kingdom United States	Brazil China Democratic Republic of Congo Republic of Congo India Indonesia Mexico Russian Federation South Africa

Table 2. Definition of variables

Variable Name	Description	Expected Signs
Dependent Variable		
FERTILITY	Fertility rate per woman, obtained from *The World Bank Database.*	N/A
Independent Variables		
	Economic Variables	
RGDP	Real Gross Domestic Product per capita measured in current US dollars. Obtained from *The World Bank Database.*	-
EXPORTS	Exports of goods and services (% of GDP) obtained from *The World Bank Database*	?
FEMLFP	Female labor force participation as a % of total labor force obtained from *The World Bank Database.*	-
UNEMPLOY	Unemployment as a percent of labor force obtained from *The World Bank Database.*	?
	Demographic Variables	
POP_DENS	Population density (people per sq. km of land area) obtained from *The World Bank Database.*	-
POP_TOTAL	population, total number of people obtained from *The World Bank Database.*	-
MAL_AGE	Population ages 15-64, male (% of total male population). Obtained from *The World Bank Database.*	+
FEM_AGE	Population ages 15-64, female (% of total female population). Obtained from *The World Bank Database.*	+

continues on following page

Table 2. Continued

Variable Name	Description	Expected Signs
URBAN	Urban population - % of total population living in urban areas or city. Obtained from *The World Bank Database*.	-
	Health Variables	
INF_MORT	Infant mortality rate before 1 year per 1,000 live births obtained from *The World Bank Database*.	+
DEATH	Death rate, crude (per 1,000 people) obtained from *The World Bank Database.*	-
	Dummy	
ABORT	Dummy variable for the legality of abortion. If legal in most cases, 1, if illegal except for mother's health, 0. Information obtained from *various sources.*	-

Table 3. Descriptive statistics

Common Sample	Mean	Median	Maximum	Minimum	Std. Dev.
VARIABLE					
Dependent Variable					
FERTILITY	2.289	1.76	6.779	1.076	1.330361
Independent Variables					
RGDP	21850.59	16544.37	119225.4	102.644	21859.25
EXPORTS	36.538	27.228	222.703	6.730	31.982
FEMLFP	42.715	44.246	51.325	24.097	5.482
UNEMPLOY	7.834	6.05	27.1	1.5	5.441
POP_DENS	156.618	116.481	523.337	3.0979	153.050
POP_TOTAL	1.95E+08	62342853	1.37E+09	387000	3.43E+08
MAL_AGE	66.036	67.275	74.783	50.408	5.691
FEM_AGE	64.232	65.066	74.001	50.774	4.750
URBAN	69.045	76.221	93.498	25.778	17.79805
INF_MORT	21.984	6.9	117.4	2	26.327
DEATH	8.978	8.6	16.655	4.592	2.739
ABORT	0.666	1	1	0	0.472

Table 4. Summary of regression outputs for models 1, 2, and 3

	MODEL 1		MODEL 2		MODEL 3	
N x T	**500**		**275**		**225**	
VARIABLE						
Dependent Variable						
	FERTILITY		**FERTILITY_DEV**		**FERTILITY_UNDEV**	
	Coefficient	**Test Statistic**	**Coefficient**	**Test Statistic**	**Coefficient**	**Test Statistic**
Independent Variables						
RGDP	0.00000***	3.392	0.000	0.138	0.0000***	5.179
EXPORTS	-0.003***	-6.317	-0.003***	-6.884	-0.002***	-2.861
FEMLFP	-0.018***	-3.364	0.034***	9.891	-0.068***	-7.666
UNEMPLOY	-0.007***	-2.608	-0.011***	-7.324	0.009***	2.202
POP_DENS	-0.003***	-3.785	0.001	0.929	0.001	0.441
POP_TOTAL	-1040000000***	-2.579	0.000	0.299	-0.000***	-5.412
MAL_AGE	-0.058***	-3.999	-0.047***	-4.208	-0.319***	-6.629
FEM_AGE	0.048***	3.337	0.020	1.493	0.315***	6.426
URBAN	0.018***	6.468	-0.001	-0.300	0.011***	3.007
INF_MORT	0.019***	7.672	0.048***	5.355	0.011***	3.941
DEATH	-0.047**	-4.212	-0.035***	-2.684	-0.016	-1.142
ABORT	-0.209***	-6.474	-0.028	-0.954	-0.239***	-6.297
CONSTANT	3.505***	8.499	6.580***	4.134	6.580***	10.734
R-Squared	0.994		0.930		0.997	
Adjusted R-Squared	0.993		0.923		0.996	

Significance Levels: *** at 1%, ** at 5% * at 10%

Table 5. Model 1 - Developed and developing economies

Dependent Variable: FERTILITY Method: Panel Least Squares Sample: 1991-2015 Periods Included: 25 Cross-Sections Included: 20 Total Panel (balanced) observations: 500 Cross-section weights (PCSE) standard errors & covariance (d.f. corrected)				
Variable	**Coefficient**	**Std. Error**	**t-Statistic**	**Probability**
CONSTANT	3.505***	0.412	8.499	0.0000
RGDP	0.0000***	7.76E-07	3.391	0.0008
EXPORTS	-0.003***	0.000	-6.317	0.0000
FEMLFP	-0.018***	0.005	-3.364	0.0008
UNEMPLOY	-0.007***	0.002	-2.608	0.0094
POP_DENS	-0.003***	0.000	-3.784	0.0002
POP_TOTAL	-1040000000***	4.04E-10	-2.579	0.0102
MAL_AGE	-0.058***	0.014	-3.999	0.0001
FEM_AGE	0.048***	0.014	3.337	0.0009
URBAN	0.018***	0.002	6.467	0.0000
INF_MORT	0.019***	0.002	7.672	0.0000
DEATH	-0.047**	0.011	-4.211	0.0000
ABORT	-0.209***	.0.323	-6.474	0.0000
EFFECTS SPECIFICATION				
Cross-section Fixed (Dummy Variables)				
R-squared		0.994	Akaike Info Criterion	-1.637
Adjusted R-squared		0.993	Durbin-Watson Stat	0.313
F-statistic		2647.049	Schwarz Criterion	-1.367
Prob(F-statistic)		0.00000		

Significance Levels: *** at 1%, ** at 5% * at 10%

Table 6. Model 2 - developed economies

Dependent Variable: FERTILITY_DEV
Method: Panel Least Squares
Sample: 1991-2015, IF DEVELOPED=1
Periods Included: 25
Cross-Sections Included: 11
Total Panel (balanced) observations: 275
Cross-section weights (PCSE) standard errors & covariance (d.f. corrected)

Variable	Coefficient	Std. Error	t-Statistic	Probability
CONSTANT	6.580***	0.542	4.133	0.0000
RGDP	9.14E-08	6.63E-07	0.137	0.8905
EXPORTS	-0.003***	0.000	-6.884	0.0000
FEMLFP	0.034***	0.003	9.890	0.0000
UNEMPLOY	-0.011***	0.001	-7.323	0.0000
POP_DENS	0.001	0.001	0.928	0.3540
POP_TOTAL	2.57E-10	8.61E-10	0.298	0.7653
MAL_AGE	-0.047***	0.011	-4.208	0.0000
FEM_AGE	0.019	0.013	1.493	0.1367
URBAN	-0.001	0.003	-0.299	0.7645
INF_MORT	0.048***	0.009	5.355	0.0000
DEATH	-0.035***	0.013	-2.683	0.0078
EFFECTS SPECIFICATION				
Cross-section Fixed (Dummy Variables)				
R-squared		0.930	Akaike Info Criterion	-2.440
Adjusted R-squared		0.923	Durbin-Watson Stat	0.448
F-statistic		152.288	Schwarz Criterion	-2.319
Prob(F-statistic)		0.0000		

Significance Levels: *** at 1%, ** at 5% * at 10%

Table 7. Model 3 - developing economies

Dependent Variable: FERTILITY_UNDEV Method: Panel Least Squares Sample: 1991-2015, IF DEVELOPED=0 Periods Included: 25 Cross-Sections Included: 9 Total Panel (balanced) observations: 225 Cross-section weights (PCSE) standard errors & covariance (d.f. corrected)				
Variable	**Coefficient**	**Std. Error**	**t-Statistic**	**Probability**
CONSTANT	6.580***	0.613	10.733	0.0000
RGDP	0.000***	6.24E-06	5.178	0.0000
EXPORTS	-0.002***	0.000	-2.860	0.0047
FEMLFP	-0.068***	0.008	-7.665	0.0000
UNEMPLOY	0.009***	0.004	2.202	0.0288
POP_DENS	0.000	0.001	0.440	0.6598
POP_TOTAL	-0.000***	7.08E-10	-5.411	0.0000
MAL_AGE	-0.319***	0.048	-6.629	0.0000
FEM_AGE	0.315***	0.049	6.426	0.0000
URBAN	0.011***	0.003	3.007	0.0030
INF_MORT	0.011***	0.003	3.940	0.0001
DEATH	-0.015	0.013	-1.141	0.2548
ABORT	-0.239***	0.0379	-6.297	0.0000
EFFECTS SPECIFICATION				
Cross-section Fixed (Dummy Variables)				
R-squared		0.997	Akaike Info Criterion	-1.851
Adjusted R-squared		0.996	Durbin-Watson Stat	0.416
F-statistic		3468.944	Schwarz Criterion	-1.533
Prob(F-statistic)		0.0000		

Significance Levels: *** at 1%, ** at 5% * at 10%

Chapter 8
Categorical Dependent Variables Estimations With Some Empirical Applications

Alhassan Abdul-Wakeel Karakara
https://orcid.org/0000-0001-7378-1678
University of Cape Coast, Ghana

Evans S. Osabuohien
https://orcid.org/0000-0002-3258-8326
Covenant University, Nigeria

ABSTRACT

Microeconomic datasets are usually large, mainly survey data. These data are samples of hundreds of respondents or group of respondents (e.g., households). The distributions of such data are mostly not normal because some responses/variables are discrete. Handling such datasets poses some problems of summarizing/reporting the important features of the data in estimations. This study concentrates on how to handle categorical variables in estimation/reporting based on theoretical and empirical knacks. This study used Ghana Demographic and Health Survey data for 2014 for illustration and elaborates on how to interpret results of binary and multinomial outcome regressions. Comparison is made on the different binary models, and binary logit is found to be weighted over the other binary models. Multinomial logistic model is best handled when the odds of one outcome versus the other outcome are independent of other outcome alternatives as verified by the Independent of Irrelevant Alternatives (IIA). Conclusions and suggestions for handling categorical models are discussed in the study.

DOI: 10.4018/978-1-7998-1093-3.ch008

INTRODUCTION

Econometric data analyses deal mostly with finding the 'maxim' of a statement of hypothesis or preposition with a view to finding a causal relationship among variables. Some econometric models are conducted in order to estimate the characteristics of variables. That is, they are performed in order to determine if a change in one variable influences the other. Examples include analysis of supply and price of goods, consumption pattern of individuals or groups, the interest rate in the financial market, and personal savings. Also, econometric analysis develops economic ways of forecasting the behavior and or trend of economic variables to help in decision-making and policy planning processes.

Models used in econometric analysis give a numerical estimated result based on modelling the pattern of variables to help predict phenomenon in a giving situation. The potential uses of econometrics depend on the degree to which a model reflects the objective; availability, nature, and quality of the data; and techniques employed in the evaluation as well as data generating process (Verbeek, 2004). In some instances, econometric analysis makes it possible to use factual material in order to consolidate and verify theoretical hypotheses and models (Greene, 2003). The type of model used depends on the nature of the variables in estimation and the nature of the relationship among the variables (e.g., models may be stochastic or already determined, may be linear or nonlinear, continuous, or discrete).

The kind of econometric model or analysis adopted depends on, among other things; the nature of the data, the data generating process, and objective of the study. Investigating an aggregate issue like economic growth with the use of gross domestic products (GDP), gross investment, aggregate consumption, among other variables, for an extended period could best be analyzed with a time series analysis. Analyzing survey data with information for a group of respondents at a particular point in time could be performed with cross-sectional models. This depends on the nature of the data and the objective of the analysis. Also, studying the same respondents over a longer period at a successive interval of data gathering could be done with micro econometric panel analysis. Again, studying a group of countries or firms over a longer period is mostly done with panel analysis.

Of the aforementioned econometric ways of data analyses, time series is most often straightforward as its data may be highly balanced with no missing observations. Cross country panel data is also without missing data points or observations. Survey data, which is mainly used for cross-sectional analysis, contain problems of missing observations of interest, nonresponse to essential information from respondents, and categorical nature of the dependent variable. For this reason, many scholars find it to be challenging and uncomfortable dealing with survey data analysis. Therefore, this study examines the issue of categorical dependent variable analysis using empirical household survey data for illustration.

The remainder of the study is structured as follows. The second section looks at the methods and applications of categorical dependent variables as well as theoretical explanations. Section three follows with the presentation of empirical analysis of categorical dependent variable using household survey data. Section four concludes and suggests categorical data analysis.

CATEGORICAL DEPENDENT VARIABLES: METHODS AND APPLICATIONS

Binary Models

The main source of microeconomic data is surveys of individuals, group of individuals, households, ðrms, and data from government entities. The term 'microeconomic data' usually refers to survey data collected by sampling the relevant population of subjects from a whole population without any attempt to control the characteristics of the sampled data (Cameron & Trivedi, 2005). In binary outcome models, the dependent variable '*Y*' takes on one of two possible values. As part of its objectives, this chapter examines the determinants of household access to a computer. In this case, what are the factors that aid in a household acquiring and using a computer? Thus, either a household has a computer or not are the two possible outcomes (which is the case of a binary response model). In modelling this circumstance, either a household has a computer or not. Hence, we let:

$$y = \begin{cases} 1\, has\ a\ computer\left(with\ probability\ P\right) \\ 0\, has\ no\ computer\left(with\ probability\ 1-P\right) \end{cases}$$

The regression model is formed by modelling the probability ***P*** to depend on a regressor vector X (independent variables) and a K×1 parameter vector β (coefficients). There is no loss of generality in setting the values to 1 and 0 if all that is being modelled is ***P***, which determines the probability of the outcome. A maximum likelihood estimation is usually applied in this instance, which leads to parameter estimates (coefficients) given.

As an illustration, let P_i represent the probability of a household having access to a computer in the house such that the probability of not having a computer is given as $1- P_{i.}$ It can be observed that the outcome $Y=1$ will be the case if the household has a computer and Y=0 if the household does not have a computer. Then, we have the following model specification:

$$Pr\left(Yi = 1\right) = Pi \tag{1}$$

$$Pr\left(Yi = 0\right) = 1 - Pi \tag{2}$$

Where *Pr* is the probability; *Yi* is the outcome (having a computer or not). Then, the probability of a household having a computer is given as in equation 3, while the probability of not having a computer is represented in equation 4.

$$Pi = E\left(Y = 1 \mid X\right) = \frac{1}{1 + e^{\left(\beta_0 + \beta' Xi\right)}} \tag{3}$$

$$Pi = E\left(Y = 0 \mid X\right) = \frac{1}{1 + e^{-\left(\beta_0 + \beta' Xi\right)}} \tag{4}$$

Where: *X* is a vector of independent variables (that determines acquisition or access to a computer), and β is a vector of their respective coefficients.

When equations (3) and (4) are reformulated, in terms of the odds ratio of the probability of having a computer to not having a computer, we will have equation (5).

$$\frac{Pi}{1 - Pi} = \frac{1 + e^{\left(\beta_0 + \beta' Xi\right)}}{1 + e^{-\left(\beta_0 + \beta' Xi\right)}} \tag{5}$$

The expression $\frac{Pi}{1 - Pi}$ is simply the odds ratio in favor of having a computer in the house

For ease of expression and understanding, equation (3) through equation (5) is simplified in equation (6) as:

$$Pi = E\left(Y = 1 \mid X\right) = \frac{e^{\left(\beta_0 + \beta' Xi\right)}}{1 + e^{\left(\beta_0 + \beta' Xi\right)}} \tag{6}$$

The probability, therefore, of a household not having computer can be given as:

$$\left(1-Pi\right)=E\left(Y=0\mid X\right)=\frac{1}{1+e^{\left(\beta_0+\beta' Xi\right)}} \tag{7}$$

As observed in equations (6) and (7), P_i ranges from 0 to 1 and is non-linearly related not only to the regressors (independent variables) but also to the parameters, thereby causing some estimation problems if an Ordinary Least Squares (OLS) estimation technique is applied. An OLS regression of *Yi* on *Xi* ignores the discrete nature of the dependent variable and does not constrain predicted probabilities to be between zero and one. A more appropriate model will be a probabilistic model such as the logistic or probit models. In this case, the dependent variable (having a computer) has only two outcomes (having or not having), and hence, this is called a binary outcome model (binary logit or binary probit).

In a binary outcome model estimation and presentation of results, we may present descriptive statistics to provide a picture of the data distribution and generation process. Presenting descriptive statistics include the mean, standard deviation, and maximum as well as minimum values. In categorical variables, it will not be appropriate just to present the mean and standard deviation of the variables as such values will have no meaning. An example is a dummy variable of the gender of the respondent, where 0 represents male, and 1 represents female; the estimation process will add the 0, 1, and strike the average figure as the mean of the variable gender of respondent, which will have no meaning. Thus, it will be good for one to present the percentage of males over females or females over males as this will provide a better picture of the distribution of the data.

Multinomial Models

Multinomial models consider several possible outcomes for a dependent variable, usually mutually exclusive. For example, the use of a type of cooking fuel by a household (electricity, LPG, wood, or charcoal) and the use of different transport mode to a destination (car, bus, bicycle or foot) all have mutually exclusive modes. Mutually exclusive, in this case, means choosing one of the outcomes. In multinomial models, statistical inference is often straightforward, and the data must have multinomial distribution, while the estimation is by maximum likelihood. Multinomial models also usually have different functional forms for the probabilities of the multinomial distribution. Most often, a distinction is made between multinomial models where regressors (independent variables) vary across alternatives for a given individual and models where regressors are constant across alternatives. In the household's choice of cooking fuel, the cost will vary between alternatives, but the age and gender of the respondent will be constant across alternatives.

The conditional or multinomial logit model is the simplest form of multinomial models; however, it is thought to be too restrictive (Cameron & Trivedi, 2005). For instance, in our household's choice of fuel type for cooking, multinomial logit will estimate the results as a multinomial outcome from household choice where the choice is not ordered. However, a household may choose a particular fuel type based on the utility it gains from such fuel type. Thus, in this case, unordered outcomes, which are less restrictive models, can be obtained using the random utility model. Different speciðcations of the random components lead to different functional forms for choice probabilities and hence to different multinomial models (Cameron & Trivedi, 2005). Such different circumstances often lead to different models such as ordered logit, ordered probit, and to Tobit models.

For the second objective of the paper, the authors modelled the determinants of household fuel choice for cooking using the GHDS household survey data and multinomial logistic in theoretical or empirical modelling. These determinants modelled are socioeconomic characteristics of the household (age of household head, the gender of household head, wealth status of the household, where a household stays – rural/urban, educational level of household head, size of household members and marital status of household head). In the data, all the regressors or some of the regressors may be alternative invariant, meaning that *X* does not vary across alternatives of the dependent variable. Some of our regressors, such as wealth status, do not vary across the different alternative fuel types; hence, multinomial logit is best for this analysis (Wooldridge, 2002).

Let P_i represent the probability of a household using a particular fuel alternative, say wood, such that the probability of not using wood is given as $1- P_i$. We cannot observe P_i as '*Y*' is a latent variable. However, we can observe the outcome *Y=1* if the household chooses alternative *j*, say wood and *Y=0* if he does not, then there is this model specification as depicted in equation (8):

From a linear model of

$$Y_i = \beta_1 + \beta_2 X_i + \varepsilon_i \tag{8}$$

We can look at a case of multinomial, where the dependent variable has mutually exclusive choices or modes as in equation (9).

$$P_r\left(Y_i = j \mid x\right) = \frac{\exp^{\left[X'_{ij}\beta\right]}}{1 + \exp^{\left[X'_{ij}\beta\right]} + \ldots + \exp^{\left[X'_{ij}\beta\right]}}; j = 1, 2, \ldots J \tag{9}$$

Equation (9) is summed, as shown in equation (10).

$$P_r\left(Y_i = j \mid x\right) = \frac{\exp^{\left[X\beta_j\right]}}{1+\sum_{h=1}^{J}\exp^{\left[X\beta_h\right]}}; j = 1,2,\ldots J \tag{10}$$

A positive β coefficient implies that households attach positive utility to the corresponding characteristic. The probability of not choosing wood as fuel among the other alternatives is given in equation (11).

$$P_r\left(Y_i = 0 \mid x\right) = \frac{1}{1+\sum_{h=1}^{J}\exp^{\left[X\beta_h\right]}}; j = 1,2,\ldots J \tag{11}$$

Where: X is a vector of independent variables, and β is a vector of their respective coefficients. As noted from equations (9) and (10), P_r ranges from 0 to 1 and is non-linearly related not only to the regressors but also to the parameters, thereby causing some estimation problems if ordinary least squares (OLS) estimation technique is to be applied.

It is possible, however, to reformulate these equations in terms of the odds ratio of the probability of household using wood as its fuel to the probability of the household not using wood but say charcoal. Assuming the use of wood is the alternative one and charcoal is alternative two, then the probability ratio (odds ratio) is given in equation (12) as:

$$\left[\frac{P\left(Y_i = 2\right)}{P\left(Y_i = 1\right)}\right] = \exp^{\left[X_{i2}^{'}\beta\right]} \tag{12}$$

Taking the natural logarithms of the equation (12), our multinomial logit model shows that the log of the odds ratio, L, is not only linear in X but also in the parameters; *L* is called the logit and hence the name logit model for models like (13) and (14).

$$Ln\left[\frac{P\left(Y_i = 2\right)}{P\left(Y_i = 1\right)}\right] = Ln\left[\exp^{\left(X\beta_2\right)}\right] = X\beta_2 \tag{13}$$

$$\frac{\partial}{\partial Xk} Ln\left[\frac{P\left(Y_i = 2\right)}{P\left(Y_i = 1\right)}\right] = \frac{\partial}{\partial Xh}\left(X\beta_2\right) = X\beta_1 \tag{14}$$

In general, the marginal effect at representative values (MER) is

$$Ln\left[\frac{P_j\left(X\beta\right)}{P_h\left(X\beta\right)}\right] = X\left(\beta_j - \beta_h\right) \tag{15}$$

Thus, it is these MER values that are estimated and interpreted for intuitiveness and policy archiving.

Empirical Illustration

The study utilized the Ghana Demographic and Health Survey data (GDHS VI) for 2014 to illustrate some empirical estimation of categorical dependent variables. The GDHS data is a two-stage sample design. The first stage was the selection of sample points (clusters) known as enumeration areas (EAs). In total, 427 sample points were selected with 216 in urban and 211 in rural areas. The second stage was the systematic sampling of households from the sampling points with households to be included in the survey that were randomly selected from these lists. Thirty (30) households were selected from each sample point, for a total sample size of 12,831 households. Three questionnaires were used for the 2014 GDHS: The Household Questionnaire, the Female's Questionnaire, and the Male's Questionnaire. A total of 12,831 households were selected for the sample, of which 12,010 were contacted for interview and 11,835 were successfully interviewed, yielding a response rate of 99%.

The data captured household access to cooking fuels as well as ICTs (television, telephone, computer, and radio). The data also capture lots of information about the health outcomes and demography of households. This study utilized information on household access to cooking fuels and ICTs (computer) for empirical illustration.

Binary Outcomes

Binary outcomes estimations are usually conducted by maximum likelihood estimations since the distribution of the data is deðned by the Bernoulli model. If the probability of one category occurring is represented by p, then the probability of the other outcome not occurring must be $(1-p)$. For regression applications, the probability p will vary across individuals as a function of regressors. The two standard binary outcome models, the logit and the probit models, specify different functional forms for this probability as a function of regressors.

In estimating a dummy dependent variable, it can be conducted in at least three ways: the linear probability model (LPM), the logistic regression model (LOGIT), and the probit model. The LPM is the simplest to use of these models. For instance, if we want to analyze whether a household has access to a computer or not, it can be modelled as:

y_i =1 if a household has a computer
y_i = 0 if a household does not have computer

Suppose we want to regress Yi on Xi, then the LPM will be:

$$Y_i = \beta_1 + \beta_2 X_i + \varepsilon_i \tag{16}$$

LPM has some limitations. The error term violates the assumption of normality, the model suffers from heteroscedasticity, and there is always the possibility of the estimated probability lying outside the 0 – 1 bounds. Because Y_i has only two possible outcomes (0 or 1), the error term, for a given value of x_i, has two possible outcomes as well. It implies that the variance of the error term is not constant but depends on the explanatory variable(s) in the model. The error also depends on the model parameters β (Verbeek, 2004). If we carry out an OLS regression of *Yi* on *Xi*, the model will do away with the discrete nature of the dependent variable, and this does not constrain the predicted probabilities of such regression to be between zero and one (Cameron & Trivedi, 2005).

Even if the outlined problems above are resolved, the LPM is not a very attractive model logically in that it assumes the conditional probabilities increase linearly with the values of the explanatory variables. Therefore, what is generally needed is the probability model that has an S-shaped feature of the Cumulative Distribution Function (CDF). However, logit and probit models translate the values of the independent variables (Xi), which may range from -∞ to +∞ into a probability for which ranges from "0" to "1" and compel the disturbance terms to be homoscedastic (Greene, 2003). In practice, the logistic and the normal cumulative distribution functions are chosen, the former giving rise to the logit and the latter to the probit.

The probit and logistic distributions are very similar and close to each other. In practice, the logit and probit models tend to yield remarkably similar results. In most cases, the only real difference between them is the way in which the elements of the coefficients are scaled. This difference in scaling occurs because of the variance of the distribution for which the logit function in the cumulative distribution function can be shown to be $\Pi^2/3$. In contrast, that of the standard normal distribution is unity (Davidson, MacKinnon & Others, 1993). The logit estimates, therefore, tend to be larger than probit estimates, although usually by a factor less than $\Pi^2/3$. Thus, using one or the other will lead to the same result (Maddala, 1991). These two distribution functions are very similar if we correct for this difference in scaling; the logistic distribution has slightly heavier tails. Accordingly, the probit and logit models typically yield very similar results in empirical work (Verbeek, 2004). Logit models arise if the error is a logistic distribution, and probit models arise if the error is a standard normal distribution. The command in STATA is "logit Y_i X_i" for the logit model and "probit Y_i X_i" for the probit model where Y_i is the dependent variable, while X_i is a set of independent variables.

DESCRIPTIVE STATISTICS AND DISTRIBUTION OF DATA

This study runs the three different binary outcome models (LPM, Logit, & Probit) using household survey data from Ghana to illustrate this with the empirical result. The data report whether the household has access to a computer. Households that report 'yes' are given '0,' and households reporting 'no' are given '1'. The response of households is binary - either it has a computer in the household or not. However, the descriptive statistics and distribution of the data are captured in Table 1. It is germane to report the descriptive statistics and distribution of variables in categorical dependent variable estimations. It is so because the descriptive statistics give a picture and distribution of the variables. It also allows us to picture the data-generating process, and finally, descriptive statistics could help us explain why an unexpected result is found upon running a regression.

In estimating the summary statistics or distribution of such data, we need to differentiate dummy variables from continuous variables. This is because dummies are in categories, and there is the need to present them in percentages and continuous variables in mean figures as this gives a straightforward interpretation and accurate picture of the descriptive. In Table 1, 11.86% of the households have a computer in the house in comparison to 88.14% of the households that have no computer at home. Also, the percentage of male-headed households is 67.66% in comparison to 32.34% for female-headed households. Households from rural settings comprised 49.82% of the total households in the survey. Also, a household where the head is married comprised 63.01% of the total households, which shows that most of the heads of the household are married.

In Table 1, as little as 28.3% of the heads of the household have no formal education, while the majority (71.7%) have at least primary education. The richer and richest households comprise 36.56% of the total households, while the remaining 63.44% are either middle-level household, poorer, or poorest households. The age of household heads and the size of household members are continuous variables, and therefore, the mean age of the household head is 44.9 years, and the mean of household size is 3.71. Thus, in presenting the descriptive statistics and distribution of

Table 1. Descriptive statistics and distribution of variables

Variable	Measurement	Response	Percent	Obs.
Access to computer	Household has a computer	Yes No	11.86 88.14	1,403 10,423
Gender of household head	The gender type of household head	Male Female	67.66 32.34	8,002 3,824
Age of household head	The age of household head, measured in years	Age	*44.90	11,826
Size of household	The number of household members	Household members	*3.71	11,826
Residence of household	The place where household stays (rural/ urban)	Rural Urban	49.82 50.18	5,892 5,934
Education	Educational level of household head	No education Primary Secondary Higher	28.30 14.05 47.27 10.38	3,347 1,662 5,590 1,227
Marital status	Marital status of the household head	Never Married Married Widowed Divorced Other	14.83 63.01 11.52 10.61 0.03	1,754 7,451 1,362 1,255 4
Wealth status	Poorest Poorer Middle Richer Richest	Poorest Poorer Middle Richer Richest	21.21 20.45 21.77 19.33 17.23	2,508 2,419 2,575 2,286 2,038

Note: *=represents mean figures
Source: The Authors

variables of categorical variable estimation, it is good to present them in percentages if the variables are in discrete form and mean figures if the variables are continuous.

Table 2 reports the regression results of the binary outcome models (logit, probit, & LPM). The results show marginal effects at representative values (MER). The MER are values that are marginal changes for continuous variables and discrete changes for dummy variables. To interpret the coefficients of categorical dependent variables is usually in terms of marginal effects on the odds ratio rather than on the probability. That is, the function $\frac{P}{\left(1-P\right)}$ measures the probability that $y=1$ relative to the probability that $y=0$ and is called the odds ratio or relative risk. Consider a college student grade, where $y=1$ denotes passing (possible with distinction) and $y=0$ denotes not passing at all, and regressors include a measure of how the student carries on his/her studies and attends lectures. An odds ratio of 3 means that the odds of passing are three times as failing. For the logit model, the log-odds ratio is

Table 2. Marginal effects at representative values (MER) for binary outcome regressions (Dependent variable is Household have access to computer)

Explanatory Variables	Logit	Probit	LPM (OLS)
Gender of household head (Female)	-0.036*** (0.005)	-0.038*** (0.005)	-0.05*** (0.01)
Age of household head	-0.001*** (0.0002)	-0.001*** (0.000)	-0.0002 (0.00)
Size of household	0.0073*** (0.001)	0.0075*** (0.001)	0.006*** (0.001)
Residence of household (Urban)	0.0413*** (0.01)	0.037*** (0.01)	0.040*** (0.007)
Educational level of household head	0.0554*** (0.004)	0.050*** (0.003)	0.0488*** (0.003)
Marital status of household head	0.022*** (0.01)	0.023*** (0.01)	0.034*** (0.01)
Wealth status of household			
Poorest Base category			
Poorer	0.0044** (0.002)	0.004*** (0.002)	-0.0002 (0.01)
Middle	0.0241*** (0.004)	0.025*** (0.004)	0.0343*** (0.01)
Richer	0.071*** (0.01)	0.078*** (0.01)	0.11*** (0.01)
Richest	0.284*** (0.031)	0.316*** (0.03)	0.41*** (0.01)
Pseudo R^2	0.3515	0.3458	0.2641
Prob>Chi^2	0.0000	0.0000	0.0000
Log Likelihood	-2793.2126	-2817.8433	423.93
Observations	11,826	11,826	11,826

Notes: LPM is linear probability model (OLS: ordinary least squares).
The standard errors are within brackets; ***, **,* denote significant at 1%, 5% and 10% level, respectively.
Source: The Authors

linear in the regressors. With probit, unlike the logit model, the weight varies across observations.

All the socioeconomic variables are significant in determining household access to a computer as shown by the probability Chi^2 of the models estimated. To interpret these results, households that stay in urban areas are approximately 4% more likely to acquire computers compared to their rural counterparts. Just like the age of the household head, the probability of acquiring a computer reduces by 0.1% in the logit and probit models. Comparing use of the variable age of household head, the

OLS estimation gives a direct estimate of -0.0002. Although the slope coefficients necessarily differ across the models, from Table 2, the t-statistics are similar, and are all very high. The log-likelihood for the probit model is 24.63 higher than that for the logit, favoring the probit model since both models use the same number of parameters. In OLS, we assume that Pr [Yi =1|Xi] = $\beta_1 + \beta_2$Xi is linear in Xi, whereas the nonlinear functions for logit and probit are substantially equivalent.

Choosing Logit Over Probit

Logit and probit models often give similar estimation results, but most scholars prefer logit over probit for some reasons. In theory, which model we should go by depends on the data-generating process (dgp) which is generally unknown. In categorical variables, there is no problem in the specification of the distribution as a (0, 1) variable distribution is the Bernoulli. Specifying the functional form for the parameters of the model is where there is a problem. If the dgp has a function like $P=\Lambda(X^1\beta)$, then a logit model should be used, and if the dgp has a function like $P=\theta(X^1\beta)$, the probit model is preferable (Cameron & Trivedi, 2005). The logit model has a relatively simple form for first-order conditions and asymptotic distribution (Berkson, 1951). The interpretation of coefficients in terms of the log odds ratio is also one of the features of logit that is attractive over probit. Also, in the logit model, there is an analysis of the discriminant, which is one of the advantages it has over the probit model. In the discriminant analysis, both Y and X are random variables (i.e., X is observed, but Y is not observed, and thus, given X, we will determine whether Y is 0 or 1). The probit model analysis a latent normal random variable and extends to Tobit models. Thus, for this and other reasons, some scholars like to use the probit model.

In empirical studies, either model (logit or probit) can be used as there is little difference between them. The difference observed is mostly in their predicted probabilities. The difference is most significant in the tails where the probabilities are close to 0 or 1.

Multinomial Outcomes

Luce first proposed multinomial outcomes in 1957 (Cameron & Trivedi, 2005). This model differs according to whether regressors vary across alternatives. Multinomial models are usually estimated by maximum likelihood. Thus, to the extent that models are nested, we can use the standard likelihood ratio test. When models are non-nested, we can use variant Akaike information criteria based on the fitted log-likelihood with degrees of freedom adjustable for the number of parameters (Cameron & Trivedi, 2005). Table 3 reports the multinomial logistic regression result. The result is the marginal effect at representative values (MER), which is run after the regression command. MER considers the odds ratio; the coefficients are shown as marginal changes in the probability of households having access to the fuels for continuous variables and the discrete change in the probability for dummy variables. Multinomial logit is used for this analysis because it best fit the data. The dependent variable (choice of cooking fuel type) is not ordered for us to use ordered logit. The choice of LPG is not lower than electricity as an option or higher than wood as fuel. The respondents were asked to mention the fuel that they use most but not to grade or to order the fuel type. Also, the choice of the fuel type is not conditional for us to use conditional logit.

In interpreting the results from the regression, take, for instance, the age of household head. If the age increases by one year, the probability of the household adopting and using wood as their main fuel increases by 0.1%, and the probability of using LPG will reduce by 0.1%. One thing that should be noted in interpreting these results is that some variables are continuous, while other variables are dummies. For a dummy variable such as wealth of the household, the poorest category is set as the base upon which the other categories are compared. In the Table, if a household is the richest home, it is 57.4% more likely to use LPG as its source of fuel compared to a household which is the poorest home. If the size of a household increases by an individual, it reduces the probability of such a household using LPG as fuel to cook by 1.4% and increases the probability of using wood by 1.2%. A large household calls for more cooking than a small household, and it will be cost-effective to use wood over LPG for extensive cooking. Also, if a household is from an urban area, it has a 6.1% more chance to use LPG for cooking than a household from rural settings. Perhaps, urban homes have greater access to LPG than rural homes.

Post-Estimation Tests Results

In multinomial model estimation, to be sure of our modelling and estimation as well as the distribution of the data, we can run a series of post estimation tests. These tests include goodness of fit, the test of the coefficient of independent variables (jointly or individually), the test of two independent variables that have combined effect equal to zero, test for combining outcome categories, and test of independence of irrelevant alternative (IIA). Using empirical household survey data for Ghana, these tests are illustrated herein.

The Goodness of Fit Test

A goodness-of-ðt measure is a summary statistic indicating the accuracy with which the model approximates the observed data such as the R^2 measure in the linear

Table 3. Marginal effects at representative values (MER) for cooking

Explanatory Variable	Electricity	LPG / Natural Gas	Charcoal	Wood	Kerosene	Others
Gender of Household Head (Female)	-0.003*** (0.001)	-0.0103** (0.01)	0.021** (0.01)	-0.01 (0.01)	-0.002** (0.001)	0.003 (0.004)
Age of Household Head	-0.00004* (0.000)	-0.001*** (0.0002)	0.0003 (0.00)	0.001*** (0.000)	0.0001 (0.000)	0.000 (0.000)
Size of Household	-0.0002 (0.000)	-0.0143*** (0.0014)	0.003 (0.002)	0.012*** (0.002)	-0.00001 (0.000)	0.0002 (0.000)
Residence (Urban)	-0.0005 (0.001)	0.061*** (0.006)	-0.169*** (0.011)	0.11*** (0.01)	-0.003 (0.002)	0.0021 (0.003)
Educational level of Household Head (Primary)	0.0004* (0.000)	0.041*** (0.003)	-0.036*** (0.006)	-0.004 (0.004)	0.000 (0.001)	-0.0013 (0.001)
Marital Status of Household Head (Married)	0.001 (0.000)	-0.007 (0.006)	0.027** (0.011)	-0.024*** (0.01)	0.002 (0.001)	0.001 (0.003)
Wealth Status of Household						
Poorest	Base category					
Poorer	-0.0002 (0.000)	0.002 (0.002)	0.152*** (0.016)	-0.118*** (0.019)	0.0003 (0.002)	-0.036*** (0.012)
Middle	0.0004 (0.000)	0.024*** (0.003)	0.552*** (0.015)	-0.533*** (0.019)	-0.0022 (0.002)	-0.041*** (0.013)
Richer	0.0011** (0.001)	0.133*** (0.01)	0.676*** (0.02)	-0.768*** (0.018)	-0.001 (0.002)	-0.041*** (0.013)
Richest	0.0041** (0.002)	0.574*** (0.02)	0.29*** (0.024)	-0.826*** (0.085)	0.001 (0.003)	-0.042*** (0.013)
Pseudo R^2 0.4539						
Prob>Chi^2 0.0000						
Log Likelihood -7085.276						
Observations 11,362						

Note: The standard errors are within brackets; ***, **,* denote significant at 1, 5 and 10% levels, respectively.

Source: The Authors

regression model. There are several ways of testing the goodness-of-fit of the model. The model fit implies whether the model specified fits the distribution and nature of the data available. One way to check model fitness is log-likelihood chi-square in the estimated result. The log-likelihood chi-square is an omnibus test to determine if the model is statistically significant. It is two times the difference between the log-likelihood of the current model and the log-likelihood of the intercept-only model. A Pseudo R-square is slightly different from the log-likelihood, but it also captures the same thing in that it is the proportion of change in terms of likelihood.

Another commonly used test of model fit is the Pearson or Hosmer and Lemeshow's goodness-of-fit test. The Hosmer and Lemeshow's goodness-of-fit test will establish that the predicted frequency and observed frequency match closely, and that the closer they match, the better the fit. The Hosmer-Lemeshow goodness-of-fit statistic is computed as the Pearson chi-square from the contingency table of observed frequencies and expected frequencies. Similar to a test of association of a two-way table, a good fit, as measured by Hosmer and Lemeshow's test, will yield a significant P-value to indicate that the model fits the data. Apart from the Hosmer-Lemeshow test, the McFadden R^2 is also a test for the goodness-of-fit of a model (McFadden, 1974).

When the dependent variable is qualitative, accuracy can be judged either in terms of the ðt between the calculated probabilities and observed response frequencies or in terms of the model's ability to forecast observed responses. Contrary to the linear regression model, there is no single measure for the goodness of ðt in binary choice models, and a variety of measures exist. Usually, goodness-of-ðt is relatively low for discrete choice models (Verbeek, 2004). This study uses the Hosmer-Lemeshow goodness-of-fit statistic to test the goodness of fit of the model. This is performed by running the regression '*mlogit Y Xi*' where Y is the dependent variable and Xi is the set of explanatory variables. After the regression, we need to type the command, '*quietly fitstat, saving (Mod1)*' as the first model of interest, then estimate another model by dropping one or some of the explanatory variables, and finally, run the regression. After which, we type the fit base test command '*fitstat, using (Mod1)*'.

Table 4. Fit base test of model specification

	Current	**Saved**	**Difference**
Model	Mlogit	Mlogit	
Observations	11362	11362	0
Log-Likelihood – intercept only	-12973.796	-12973.796	0.000
Log-Likelihood – model	-7309.755	-7165.900	-143.855
BIC'	-11001.251	-11288.961	287.710

Source: The Authors'

The test of goodness of fit results from the Hosmer-Lemeshow gave a Prob>chi2 value of 0.004 for household access to fuels. These Prob>chi^2 values are evidence that the null hypothesis stating that the model is not of good fit is rejected and concludes that the models are reasonably fit well (is of good fit). We run the fit base test (fitstat) to ascertain the specification and fit of our multinomial logit for cooking. The result is shown in Table 4. Specifically, it shows that the difference of 287.710 in BIC' of our full model, and the reduced model provides robust support for our model that it is correctly specified and of fit. The regression *fitstat* results are captured in the appendix.

Hypothesis Testing of Coefficients of Independent Variables

In the multinomial logit model, we can test for the effect of the explanatory variables as being zero or otherwise. If we have Z dependent categories, there are Z-1 non-redundant coefficients associated with each independent variable Xk. For our model of logistic of fuel consumption, there are six coefficients associated with a variable say the educational level of household head (EduHH). The hypothesis that Xk does not affect the dependent variable can be written as

$$Ho: Bk, 1/b= \dots =Bk, z/b=0 \quad (17)$$

Where '*b*' is set as the base category, since Bk, b/b is necessarily zero; the hypothesis imposes constraints on Z-1 parameters. This hypothesis can be tested either using Wald or LR tests. We used the Wald test in this study since both tests yield almost similar results (Long & Freese 2001). In the Wald test, after running the regression in STATA, we need to type '*test Xi*' where Xi is the independent variable to be tested. Moreover, in the LR test, the command is '*lrtest Xi*' after running the regression.

To test the hypothesis that socioeconomic variables are not determinants of the household choice of fuels for domestic use such as cooking, the Wald test for explanatory variables is run. The result is shown in Table 5. The null hypothesis for the Wald test is that all the coefficients associated with the variables are zero. On Table 5, the probability chi-squared values for each of our explanatory variable is highly significant (at 0.01% level). It is evidence for us to reject the null hypothesis that all coefficients associated with the variables are zero and therefore conclude that the coefficients associated (effect of each variable on the dependent variable) with each of our explanatory is not zero. In other words, the socioeconomic variables are determinants of the household choice of a particular fuel for cooking.

Test of Two Independent Variables have Combined Effect Equal Zero

The study investigated whether educational levels of household heads and wealth status have combined effect equal zero and the size of household as well as residence

Table 5. Hypothesis test for explanatory variables results

Explanatory Variable	chi2	df	P>chi2
Gender of household head	35.334	5	0.000
Age of household head	102.758	5	0.000
Size of household	137.942	5	0.000
Residence of household (urban/rural)	313.292	5	0.000
Educational level of household head	135.596	5	0.000
Marital status of household head	15.514	5	0.008
Wealth status of household	2561.962	5	0.000

Note: Wald tests for independent variables; Ho: All coefficients associated with the given variable(s) are 0.
Source: The Authors

nature have combined effect being zero. In other words, the two variables may be correlating in determining our dependent variable. Our interest is motivated by our assumption that most rural households are made up of large sizes as an extended family system is prevalent in those areas. Also, we assume that wealth status corresponds to educational level. A more educated household head is likely to be wealthier than his counterparts who are less educated or have no education.

We tested for the combined effect of the educational level of household head and wealth status of household in one aspect and the size of household and residence nature of the household in another aspect to determine if the combined effect of the educational level of household head and wealth status is zero[1]. The combined effect of the size of household and residence nature of household is zero. After running the regression in STATA, we need to run the test, "*mlogtest, lr set* $(X_1\ X_2)$" where lr is likelihood ratio, X_1 is the education of household head, and X_2 is wealth status of the household.

The result from the test showed that the combined effect of the educational level of household head and wealth status of household had a chi-squared value of 6308.525, degrees of freedom as 10, and a probability chi-squared of 0.000 which is highly significant at less than the 1% level. The probability chi-square value is evidence to reject the null hypothesis that the combined effect of the educational level of household head and wealth status of household is zero. For the test of the combined effect of the size of household and residence nature of the household, the chi-square value is 459.762 with degrees of freedom as 10—the probability of the chi-square value of 0.000, which is also highly significant. Thus, evidence to reject the null hypothesis and conclude that the combined effect of these variables is not statistically equal to zero.

Test for Combining Outcome Categories

This study tested for the combination of outcome categories to determine if a pair of any two outcomes are indistinguishable. That is, if none of the independent variables significantly affect the odds of outcome *m* versus *n*, we say that *m* and *n* are indistinguishable for the variables in the model (Anderson, 1984, as cited in Long & Freese, 2001). Outcome *m* and *n* being indistinguishable corresponds to the hypothesis:

$$Ho: \beta_{1,m/n} = \beta_{2,m/n} = \ldots = \beta_{k,m/n} = 0 \quad (18)$$

This can be tested either by the Wald test or LR test. If two outcomes are indistinguishable for the variables in the model, we can then obtain more efficient estimates by combining them. The study used mlogtest command in Stata to test for indistinguishability of categories. The command is run after the regression, and the command is "mlogtest, combine"[2].

The Wald test for combining categories was run. The test is to determine if the two categories are similar and hence should be combined. It is somehow similar to the IIA test. The null hypothesis for this test is all coefficients except intercepts associated with a given pair of outcomes are zero (i.e., categories can be collapsed). Each category is compared to the other, say electricity to LPG/Natural gas or electricity to kerosene. We found that the Prob>chi^2 values are highly significant (0.000). Thus, we can reject the hypothesis that the various outcomes are indistinguishable and can be collapsed. The exception is the kerosene to charcoal category, which has the Prob>chi^2 value of 0.246, which we cannot reject the null. Statistically, the number of households using charcoal (3,546) is large and that of kerosene (21) is very insignificant; thus, combining them would lead to suppressing the effect of kerosene in the analysis. Besides, the data captured a questionnaire that asked households to mention the primary fuel used for cooking; thus, those who use kerosene reported kerosene as their primary fuel. Hence, this category cannot be combined with charcoal users as shown in Table 6.

Independent of Irrelevant Alternatives (IIA)

For both the multinomial logit model and the conditional logit model, there is a strong assumption known as the independence from irrelevant alternatives (IIA) where the odds do not depend on other available outcomes. In this sense, these alternative outcomes are "irrelevant." In other words, adding or deleting outcomes does not affect the odds among the remaining outcomes. This point is often made

Table 6. Test for combining categories

Categories Tested	Chi2	df	Prob>Chi2
Electricity – LPG/ gas	46.220	7	0.000
Electricity – kerosene	75.569	7	0.000
Electricity – charcoal	178.934	7	0.000
Electricity – wood	523.481	7	0.000
Electricity – others	403.342	7	0.000
LPG/Natural gas – kerosene	111.070	7	0.000
LPG/Natural gas – charcoal	1455.687	7	0.000
LPG/Natural gas – wood	3372.369	7	0.000
LPG/Natural gas – others	737.483	7	0.000
Kerosene – charcoal	9.092	7	0.246
Kerosene – wood	61.87	7	0.000
Kerosene – others	103.245	7	0.000
Charcoal – wood	2501.032	7	0.000
Charcoal – others	275.720	7	0.000
Wood – others	50.144	7	0.000

Note: Wald test for combining outcome categories

Ho: All coefficients except intercepts associated with a given pair of outcomes are zero (i.e. categories can be collapsed)

Source: The Authors

with the red bus/blue bus example. Suppose that we have the choice of a red bus or a car to get to work, and the odds of taking a red bus compared to a car are 1:1. IIA implies that the odds will remain 1:1 between these two alternatives even if a new blue bus company comes to town that is identical to the red bus company except for the color of the bus (Long & Freese, 2001).

There are two tests of the IIA assumption. Hausman and McFadden (1984) proposed a Hausman type test and likelihood ratio test that was improved by Small and Hsiao. For both the Hausman and the Small-Hsiao tests, multiple tests of IIA are possible (Long & Freese, 2001). The Hausman test of IIA involves the following steps:

1. Estimate the full model with all Z outcomes included, with estimates in β_F.
2. Estimate a restricted model by eliminating one or more outcome categories with estimates in β_R.
3. Let β∗ F be a subset of β_F after eliminating coefðcients not estimated in the restricted model.

The test statistic is:

$$H = \left(\beta_R - \beta_F\right)' \left[Var\left(\beta_R\right) - Var\left(\beta_F\right)\right]' \left(\beta_R - \beta_F\right) \tag{19}$$

Where H, is asymptotically distributed as chi-squared with degrees of freedom equal to the rows in βR if IIA is true. Signiðcant values of H indicate that the IIA assumption has been violated. The Hausman test of IIA can be computed with mlogtest command in Stata. This study goes by testing for the Hausman IIA and not the Small-Hsiao test since the Small-Hsiao test requires randomly dividing the data into subsamples (Long & Freese 2001). Our test of IIA, as shown in Table 7, indicates that all outcome categories are for the null hypothesis and that the odds of one outcome versus the other outcome are independent of other outcomes alternatives. The chi2 values are negative, which is found to be common (Long & Freese, 2001). Hausman and McFadden (1984) noted this possibility and concluded that a negative result is evidence that IIA has not been violated.

Table 7. IIA test results

Omitted	chi2	df	P>chi2	Evidence
Electricity	-348.148	15	1.000	for Ho
LPG/Natural gas	-366.007	23	1.000	for Ho
Kerosene	-336.538	22	1.000	for Ho
Charcoal	-337.953	16	1.000	for Ho
Wood	-544.496	16	1.000	for Ho
Others	-321.322	15	1.000	for Ho

Note: Hausman tests of IIA assumption
Ho: Odds (Outcome-J vs Outcome-K) are independent of other alternatives.
Source: The Authors

CONCLUSION

The chapter set out to look at estimation and modelling of categorical dependent variables. Using household survey data, we conducted an empirical illustration of binary categorical models (namely logit, probit, & LPM) and multinomial models (multinomial logit). The study found that the binary logit model is most preferred to the other binary models. The interpretation of coefficients in terms of their log odds ratio is attractive for the logit over probit. Also, in the logit model, there is an analysis of the discriminant, which is one of the advantages it has over the probit model.

The multinomial logit model was run, and a series of post estimation tests conducted. In the test, all the different tests yielded positive to the use of multinomial logit. It was observed that to use multinomial logit, the alternatives should be clearly defined and that they can be distinguished. The IIA test and the test for combining outcome categories all proved that multinomial logit is suited for the data chosen and the objectives of the analysis. Thus, doing categorical dependent variable estimation requires that we go through the data thoroughly, possible attempt to understand the data-generating process, and ensuring all the variables of interest have the required observations. Dummy variables should be identified and treated as such. After multinomial logit estimation, we can look at post estimation tests, especially the IIA test and the test for combining outcome categories.

ACKNOWLEDGMENT

This study is a product of the African Finance and Economic Association (AFEA)'s Mentorship Program; thus, the authors appreciate the useful ideas received from the platform. The second author acknowledges the Alexander von Humboldt Foundation [Ref: 3.4-1147508-NGA-GF-P] for supporting his visiting research fellowship at Faculty of Management and Economics, Witten/Herdecke University, Witten, Germany. In addition, the support of Covenant University Centre for Centre for Innovation, Research and Discoveries (CUCRID) while finalizing this chapter, is appreciated.

REFERENCES

Cameron, A. C., & Trivedi, P. K. (2005). Microeconometrics: Methods and Applications. Cambridge University Press. doi:10.1017/CBO9780511811241

Davidson, R., & Mackinnon, J. G. (1993). *Estimation inference in Econometrics*. Retrieved from http://www.jstor.org/stable/pdf/2171733.pdf

Greene, H. W. (2003). *Econometric Analysis* (5th ed.). Prentice-Hall.

Hausman, J. A., & McFadden, D. L. (1984). 'A Speciðcation Test for the Multinomial Logit Model. *Econometrica*, *52*(5), 1219–1240. doi:10.2307/1910997

Long, J. S., & Freese, J. (2001). Stata Press Publication: Vol. A. *Regression Models for Categorical Dependent Variables Using Stata*. Stata Corporation.

Maddala, G. S. (1991). A perspective on the use of limited-dependent and qualitative variables Models in accounting research. *The Accounting Review*, *66*(4), 788–807.

McFadden, D. (1974). Conditional Logit Analysis of Qualitative Choice Behavior. In P. Zarembka (Ed.), *Economic Theory and Mathematical Economics*. Academic Press.

Verbeek, M. (2004). *A guide to modern Econometrics* (2nd ed.). John Wiley & Sons Inc.

Wooldridge, J. M. (2002). *Econometric Analysis of Cross-Section and Panel Data*. MIT Press.

ADDITIONAL READING

Cosslett, S. R. (1981). Efficient Estimation of Discrete-Choice Models. In C. F. Manski & D. McFadden (Eds.), *Structural Analysis of Discrete Data with Econometric Applications* (pp. 51–111). MIT Press.

Cragg, J. (1971). Some Statistical Models for Limited Dependent Variables with Applications to the Demand for Durable Goods. *Econometrica*, *39*(5), 829–844. doi:10.2307/1909582

Davidson, R., & MacKinnon, J. G. (1984). Convenient Speciðcation Tests for Logit and Probit Models. *Journal of Econometrics*, *24*(3), 241–262. doi:10.1016/0304-4076(84)90001-0

Estrella, A. (1998). A New Measure of Fit for Equations with Dichotomous Dependent Variables. *Journal of Business & Economic Statistics*, *16*, 198–205.

Gregory, A. W., & Veall, M. R. (1985). On Formulating Wald Tests for Nonlinear Restrictions. *Econometrica*, *53*(6), 1465–1468. doi:10.2307/1913221

Karakara, A. A., & Osabuohien, E. (2019). Households' ICT Access and Bank Patronage in West Africa: Empirical Insights from Burkina Faso and Ghana. *Technology in Society*, *56*, 116–125. doi:10.1016/j.techsoc.2018.09.010

McFadden, D. L. (1984). Econometric Analysis of Qualitative Response Models. In Z. Griliches & M. D. Intriligator (Eds.), *Handbook of Econometrics* (Vol. 2, pp. 1395–1457). North-Holland. doi:10.1016/S1573-4412(84)02016-X

Osabuohien, E., Efobi, U., Odebiyi, J., Fayomi, F., & Salami, A. (2019). Bilateral Trade Performance in West Africa: Gravity Model Estimation. *African Development Review*, *31*(1), 1–14. doi:10.1111/1467-8268.12359

Osabuohien, E., Efobi, U. R., Herrmann, R., & Gitau, C. M. (2019). Female Labor Outcomes and Large-scale Agricultural Land Investments: Macro-Micro Evidence from Tanzania. *Land Use Policy*, *82*, 716–728. doi:10.1016/j.landusepol.2019.01.005

KEY TERMS AND DEFINITIONS

Binary Models: Models that have a categorical dependent variable that take on two outcome possibilities. For example, in a model of having access to a mobile phone or not, there is only two possible outcomes, whether an individual has a mobile phone or not. Binary models include binary logit and binary probit.

Categorical Outcome Variable: These are dependent variables that have mutually exclusive outcomes. That is, the choice of one outcome means non-use of the other outcome. An example is a household that may choose to use charcoal, LPG, or electricity for cooking but not the use of two of these categories at a time.

Linear Probability Model (LPM): LPM s a probability model that allows the independent variables (Xi) to assume negative infinite and positive infinite values. It is because the estimated probabilities lie outside the 0 – 1 bounds. The LPM does away with the discrete nature of the dependent variable, and the error term violates the assumption of normality.

Logit: Logit is a categorical dependent variable model (probability model) that translates the values of the independent variables (Xi), which ranges from negative infinity to positive infinite, into a probability to range from '0' to '1' and compel the disturbance term to be homoscedastic and thus becomes logistically distributed.

Multinomial Models: Multinomial models have categorical dependent variables that take on more than two outcome possibilities. An example is a choice of cooking fuel type by a household where a household may choose electricity, LPG, charcoal, or wood. The categories should be mutually exclusive for the model to be the best fit.

Probability: This is the likelihood of an event happening. Of which the likelihood of the event not happening is the opposite of it happening. The sum of the likelihood of an event happening or not happening should be equal to one. For instance, the likelihood of an individual having a mobile phone is 70%, it means that such individual has 70% of likely owning a mobile phone, and the likelihood of not having a mobile phone will be 30%. Thus, probability models deal with a phenomenon that is of a chance of happening based on specific characteristics (independent variables).

Probit: Just like the logit, probit also translates the values of the independent variables to range '0' to '1' and uses the standard normal distribution function. Thus, the error term is standard normal distribution. Probit has almost similar results as logit.

ENDNOTES

1 The results are not presented but available upon request.

2 If the mlogtest is not in STATA, then we can install it.

APPENDIX

Figure 1. Fit Base Test of Model Specification

Measures of Fit for mlogit of TCfuel_new

	Current	Saved	Difference
Model:	mlogit	mlogit	
N:	11362	11362	0
Log-Lik Intercept Only:	-12973.796	-12973.796	0.000
Log-Lik Full Model:	-7309.755	-7165.900	-143.855
D:	14619.509(11314)	14331.799(11314)	287.710(0)
LR:	11328.082(35)	11615.792(35)	287.710(0)
Prob > LR:	0.000	0.000	.
McFadden's R2:	0.437	0.448	-0.011
McFadden's Adj R2:	0.433	0.444	-0.011
Maximum Likelihood R2:	0.631	0.640	-0.009
Cragg & Uhler's R2:	0.703	0.713	-0.010
Count R2:	0.202	0.202	0.000
Adj Count R2:	0.000	0.000	0.000
AIC:	1.295	1.270	0.025
AIC*n:	14715.509	14427.799	287.710
BIC:	-91030.959	-91318.669	287.710
BIC':	-11001.251	-11288.961	287.710

Difference of 287.710 in BIC' provides very strong support for saved model.

Note: p-value for difference in LR is only valid if models are nested.

Chapter 9
Financial Determinants Affecting Leasing Policies:
Empirical Evidence From the Airline Industry

Kasım Kiracı
https://orcid.org/0000-0002-2061-171X
Iskenderun Technical University, Turkey

ABSTRACT

Airline companies have started to develop strategies to increase their market share and expand their network structure with the effect of globalization. In this process, one of the most important sources of airline companies to achieve competitive advantage is aircraft. Airline companies have to increase the number of aircraft in the fleet to expand their network structure. On the other hand, the high price of aircraft has led airline companies to adopt new financing strategies. Leasing is one of the financing methods used frequently by airline companies recently. Therefore, this study focuses on the leasing policies of airline companies. In this study, it is aimed to reveal the factors affecting the leasing policies of airline companies. In this context, 26 airlines operating in the period 2000-2017 were analyzed empirically. Panel data analysis was used as the method in the study. The empirical findings of the study indicate that return on assets, asset structure, tangibility, leverage ratio, and liquidity affects the leasing policies of airline companies.

DOI: 10.4018/978-1-7998-1093-3.ch009

INTRODUCTION

Since the deregulation act went into effect in the US in 1978, the air transport market has become liberalized, and the competition between airlines has significantly increased (Fu et al., 2010). In this process, the network structure of airline companies has been globalized, and airlines have started to offer flights to new destinations, which has increased the needs of airlines and their need for resources to buy aircraft. It is difficult for the airline companies to finance the aircraft investments that require large cash outflows and capital investments by using their equity capital. Therefore, airline companies have turned to alternative financing methods to reduce the risks and costs associated with aircraft acquisition. One financing method frequently used by airline companies for aircraft operations is financial leasing.

Financial leasing is an agreement on the right of airline companies to obtain aircraft usage rights for a certain period instead of buying the aircraft they need (Vasigh et al., 2015). Thanks to financial leasing, airline companies have the opportunity to strengthen their financial statements, reduce capital costs, and reduce market risk. From a historical point of view, the number of aircraft acquired by the airline companies through financial leasing has increased significantly, which makes examining their financial leasing activities crucial.

In this study, the financial factors affecting the rental/operating lease expense of airline companies are examined. The main objective of the study is to empirically examine the financial factors that determine the leasing activities of airline companies in the context of airline companies. The remainder of our study is designed as follows. The second section discusses the importance of leasing for airline companies, while the third section reviews the literature related to leasing. The fourth section focuses on the research design, the description of variables and the data set, and the presentation of the empirical models. The last section discusses the main findings.

AIRCRAFT LEASING IN THE AIRLINE INDUSTRY

A lease is an agreement between the lessee and the lessor for a specified period. In this agreement, the ownership of the asset is given to the lessor, and the right to use is given to the tenant (lessee). The lessee pays the lessor periodically for the asset he or she leases. The most important leasing asset in air transport is the aircraft. Therefore, in the air transport industry, airline companies rent the aircraft they need, and in return, the lessee makes payments to the lessor under the specified conditions.

Businesses resort to leasing to make their financial statements appear stronger to investors and lenders, to use more foreign resources by reducing their cost of capital, and to benefit more from the tax shield effect. In this way, companies can make various investments such as machinery, equipment, or aircraft, requiring large cash outflows by using off-balance sheet financing methods (Öztürk, 2016, p. 2). Airline companies also use leasing to obtain aircraft that require large capital investments. Although considered as a type of financing, leasing plays a distinct role in the capital structure of businesses. The following table shows the position and status of Operating Lease and Financial Lease in corporate liabilities.

Table 1 presents the characteristics of corporate liabilities for businesses. Accordingly, in the event of financial distress or bankruptcy of enterprises, the lessor has the priority right. The main reason for this is that the lessor holds the legal ownership of the asset subject to leasing and the right to withdraw it (if the entity is in default). The tenant (lessee) usually retains the right to use the asset in question. In addition, it is observed that economic ownership varies according to the type of leasing for the assets subject to leasing. For example, while economic ownership is possible in financial leasing, this is not the case for operating leasing. In addition, there are some differences between operating leasing and financial leasing in terms of tax shields. All payments made in the operating leasing may be shown as an expense. Whereas depreciation amortization is not an issue in operating leases, all assets obtained via other sources depreciate.

Table 1. Characteristics of corporate liabilities

Types of Corporate Liabilities	**Operating Lease**	**Financial Lease**	**Secured Debt**	**Ordinary Debt**	**Subordinated Debt**	**Preferred Stock**	**Common stock**
Priority of claim	Highest ←---→ Lowest						
Can default trigger bankruptcy	*Yes*					*No*	
Control rights	Right to use the asset		Rights limited to covenants in contract			Rights limited to covenants and voting rights of stockholder	Rights limited to voting rights
Legal ownership	*No*		*Yes*				
Economic ownership	*No*	*Yes*					
Tax shields: Cash flows	Full lease payment deductible	Interest part lease payment deductible	Interest payment deductible			Dividend not deductible	
Depreciation	No depreciation	Asset financed by financial lease, debt or equity is depreciated by economic owner					

Source: Barclay and Smith, 1995, p. 900; Lückerath-Rovers, 2007, p. 31

Elements of Leasing

Leasing agreements involve the transfer of the right to use the asset to another party for a certain period. There are three main elements in the leasing contract. These elements include lease, lessor, and lessee. In the following part of the study, the information will be given about these three main elements of the leasing contract.

Lease

In terms of the air transport industry, the lease is used to agree with the aircraft leasing company and the company (airline) that wants to rent a plane. In other words, it is referred to as an agreement between the company that owns the aircraft and wants to rent the aircraft and the airline company which is willing to use the aircraft for a certain time and is willing to pay for it. Here, the leasing company, which owns the aircraft, wants to rent this plane to another company and generate income. The company, which wants to rent a plane, is willing to make periodic payments to the lessor for the rented aircraft and aims to generate revenue by performing operations with the aircraft it hires.

Lessor

Lessor transfers the right of use of the aircraft to a lessee (airline company) for a certain amount of time. In the airline industry, there are many companies operating in the aircraft leasing industry. These companies are leasing their assets (airplanes) to airlines for a certain amount of time and a certain period. Therefore, it is possible to define aircraft leasing companies as a lessor. On the other hand, some airlines rent their airplanes to other airlines for a certain time. Therefore, the right to use the aircraft to the lessee (airline) for a certain price and duration of the transfer is called lessor.

Lessee

Lessee, under the leasing agreement with lessor, are the companies that have an agreement to obtain the right to use an asset. Airline companies lease the aircraft they need from the lessor to use them in the operations for a specific period. Here, the transfer of the right to use the aircraft is in question. Airline companies make agreements with leasing companies to obtain the right to use aircraft for a certain time for a specific use price. In this way, airline companies have the opportunity to continue their activities without having to buy aircraft, which is one of the most important costs.

Types of Leases

Many types of leasing have emerged depending on the needs of the lessee and the lessor. What matters here are the characteristics of the leasing agreement that is drawn up and what specific rights the lessee and the lessor are entitled by it. In the literature, leasing activities are generally placed in two main categories: operating leases and finance leases. Our study will focus on these two types of leases.

Operating Lease

Operational leasing is the rental of an asset in return for rent payments for a shorter period of the economic life of the property, provided that the ownership of the property remains with the lessor. In operational leasing, since all types of maintenance, repair, and insurance expenses are to be paid by the lessee, it is also referred to as "service lease" or "maintenance lease."

According to the Generally Accepted Accounting Principles (GAAP), to classify the lease as the true operating lease, the contract term between the leasing company and the lessee must be less than 75% of the remaining useful life of the asset. To exemplify operating leases through aircraft rentals, let us assume that the operational use of an aircraft is 12 years. In this case, the actual operating lease agreement period should be less than 9 years. In the air transport industry, the duration of operating leases for aircraft leases usually ranges from 2 to 7 years. With the expiry of the contract period, the airline company returns the aircraft to the lessor. The aircraft owner may use one of the options of renting, selling, or scrapping the aircraft at the end of the contract. In air transport, aircraft engines are one of the most valuable parts of aircraft, and engine replacement is possible in the same type of aircraft, which typically leads to the inclusion of multiple leasing companies in the aircraft leasing agreements and making various leasing arrangements regarding aircraft engines (Vasigh et al., 2015, p. 528).

One important feature of operating lease agreements is that the lessee is given the option to cancel the contract. In this option, the lessee has the right to cancel the lease before the end of the contract period. Depending on the content of the leasing agreement, the lessee can be subject to a monetary penalty if he/she cancels the contract. However, the contract cancellation option may provide significant advantages to the lessee. In terms of air transportation, airline companies may use the cancellation option in times of crisis (September 11, SARS, Global Financial Crisis etc.), which may adversely affect the sector. It can be argued that the option of canceling the contract in times of crisis gives an advantage to airlines.

Finance Lease

In financial leasing, the lessee obtains more than just the right to use the leased asset in return for periodic payments. In these agreements, the asset chosen by the lessee is purchased by the lessor and left to the use of the lessee. Also, at the end of the lease period, the ownership of the asset is transferred to the lessee at no charge or with a nominal price (Öztuğran, 1995, p. 4). Unlike operating leases in these agreements, all expenses related to the maintenance, repair, and insurance of the asset are covered by the lessee. Therefore, the risk and benefit related to the use of the asset in this type of leasing are transferred to the lessee.

For airlines, financial leasing is a type of financing that can be used when long-term financing is too costly. This is because the lease period is usually long in financial leasing. In leasing agreements, the lease term must be equal to at least 75% of the economic life of the asset subject to leasing. Therefore, airlines that want to use aircraft longer than 75% of their economic life may prefer to lease financially. In addition, the sum of the discounted leasing payments and interest payments in the financial leasing should be higher than 90% of the market value of the asset.

To illustrate financial leasing in terms of the airline industry, let us assume that the market price of an Airbus A321 type aircraft is $120 million, and its useful life is 20 years. For the agreement made by the airline to be considered financial leasing, the lease term must be at least 15 years, or the present value of the discounted lease payments must be $108 million.

Other Leasing Strategies

When the cost structure of airline companies is examined, it is seen that the operational costs of airlines are high. In this process, airline companies have developed modern leasing strategies to control their costs. Airline companies have also developed new types of leasing to meet changing passenger demand and reduce costs in meeting seasonal passenger demand. Airline companies are widely using two types of leasing, wet and Sale and Leaseback, in order to reduce the cost of buying new aircraft and keep costs under control.

Wet Lease

Wet Lease means that an aircraft will be rented together with the cabin crew. In this type of lease, the airline company leases the aircraft with the cabin and flight crew. Additionally, the lessor undertakes the maintenance costs and insurance costs of the aircraft. Therefore, in a wet lease, the airline leases the aircraft together with all the requirements for the operation of the aircraft. The lessee meets the costs associated with operating costs such as fuel, navigation, and ground handling of the aircraft.

Wet lease agreements are for the purpose of meeting the short-term passenger demand increase for airline companies. This increase in demand is usually experienced in the summer period, but there are also increases in demand outside of this period. In particular, haj pilgrimage flights, such as flights in the changing periods of the year can be shown as an example. In addition, seasonal differences in the northern and southern hemisphere and temporary demand increases due to international organizations (world cup etc.) may increase wet lease agreements. Therefore, in wet lease agreements, short-term increase in demand for air transport due to various reasons appears to be effective. In wet lease applications, the duration of the wet lease contract may be extended if the increase in demand for the airline is longer than expected or becomes permanent.

In wet lease agreements, maintenance and insurance costs are covered by the lessor. Therefore, this agreement is also referred to as the ACMI (aircraft, crew, maintenance, and insurance) lease agreement. In these leasing agreements, even if there is a the paint sheme and logo of the lessor (leasing company), a temporary sticker can be used to show the name of the lessee (airline) name on the fuselage (Morrell, 2007, p. 204).

Although wet lease practices are significantly similar to other types of leasing, the important point here is that the aircraft is seen in the fleet of the lessor. For example, Qatar Airways has leased an aircraft in its fleet to Turkish Airlines with a wet lease agreement. Here, the cabin crew as well as the aircraft are leased. Qatar Airways meets the maintenance and insurance costs of the aircraft it leased. In addition, the aircraft is operated by Qatar Airways' air operator certificate (AOC). Therefore, this aircraft is not officially available in the fleet of Turkish Airlines. In this lease type, lessor provides aircraft to the airline company as well as some operational support services. If the rental agreement is designed to provide only part of the lessor's operational support services, this agreement is also referred to as to "damp lease" contract. Such agreements fall between wet lease and dry lease (Morrell, 2007, p.204). For example, if a airline company uses its own cabin crew in its operations in order to better communicate with the passengers it serves and the leasing agreement prepared accordingly, it can be said that there is "a dumping lease" contract.

Airline companies make wet lease agreements in order to meet the temporary demand increases. Airline companies make wet lease agreements, especially when new aircraft purchases, certification, necessary permits, and personnel training are costly. In this way, temporary passenger demand is met, and the responsibility to cover long-term costs is eliminated. In addition, airline companies are also engaged in wet lease agreements to overcome legal restrictions. With the wet lease application, it can be said that airlines significantly reduce their costs, meet temporary passenger demand, and overcome legal restrictions.

Sale and Leaseback

Airline companies can use sale and leaseback agreements in order to overcome cash flow problems or to use aircraft in their fleets in new investments. In such agreements, the airline sells its aircraft in its fleet to another company (leasing company) in order to lease it back. In this way, the airline company continues its operations and meets its cash needs. Airline companies use this leasing method to meet capital adequacy for new investments or new aircraft purchases. In addition, the airline companies use this method in order to maintain the current value of the aircraft in case they expect the market price of existing aircraft in their fleets to decrease significantly (Morrell, 2007, p. 204).

Sale and leaseback agreements do not have a standard legal or legal form as in the case of leasing agreements. Despite this, it is possible to say that almost all leaseback contracts have a similar structure. For airline companies, sale and leaseback agreements are used when free cash flows are required. In this way, the current aircraft activities continue to generate revenue, and the cash flow needed is provided. Leasing companies have the advantage of acquiring assets without effort and finding customers to lease their assets. In addition, leasing companies aim to generate revenue from the lease payments and the value at the end of the aircraft lease (Vasigh et al., 2015, p. 535). Therefore, it can be said that there is a positive situation for both the airline company and the leasing company.

Advantages and Disadvantages of Leasing for Airlines

Leasing has some advantages over other financing options. With these advantages, companies prefer operating or financial leasing rather than short-term or long-term liabilities. The reasons for the companies to make leasing agreements instead of borrowing are that such agreements reduce the costs and have a more useful structure. Thomson (2003, p. 100) lists the main reasons for opting for leasing instead of the non-leasing debt under four headings, which are risk-sharing reasons, tax-savings reasons, borrowing-related reasons, and other financial/transactional reasons.

In terms of air transport, leasing offers some advantages and disadvantages for airline companies. According to Morrell (2007, p. 197-198), the advantages of leasing for the airline industry are as follows:

- Volume discounts for aircraft purchases can be passed on to the airline.

- Leasing agreements ensure the protection of the working capital and credit capacity of airline companies.
- Financing is ensured without any deposit or prepayment (the aircraft manufacturers are paid in advance 33% of the cost of airplane purchases and 15% of the cost of bank loans.)
- In the short-term leasing contracts, the risk of aircraft obsolescence is taken by the lessor.
- The aircraft can be acquired without any prior experience in aircraft purchase/trading.
- Financing related to financial leasing can be excluded from the balance sheet.

In addition to the advantages of aircraft rental in air transportation, there are some disadvantages. Morrell (2007, p. 198) outlines these disadvantages as follows:

- It is more expensive to acquire an airplane by leasing it than to obtain a loan to purchase it.
- The income from the final sale of the aircraft is given to the lessor who holds the legal ownership of the aircraft.
- Aircraft purchases have higher leverage than equity.
- In the case of short-term leasing contracts, the specifications and configuration of the purchased aircraft may not be tailor-made for the airline's order.

Current Status of Aircraft Leasing in the Airline Industry

Airline companies need new airplanes to expand their activities and make flights to new destinations. However, it is not common for airlines to purchase aircraft using only their funding sources. The main reason for this is that aircraft costs are prohibitively high. Airline companies generally prefer long-term borrowing or aircraft leasing options to acquire aircraft (Kiracı, 2018, p. 35). After the 1980s, airlines' leasing of aircraft to be used in their operations has rapidly increased. The ratio of the planes rented was around 4% in the total aircraft fleet in the 1980s. This ratio gradually increased, reaching 28% in 2004. The number of airlines with rented aircraft in the whole or part of their fleet has also significantly increased over the years. In 1986, 59% of the airline companies had a rental aircraft in some or all of their fleet, while in 1999, this rate increased to 85% (Morrell, 2007, p. 196).

Table 1 shows the total number of leased aircraft (operating leases) from 1990 to 2015. Accordingly, the share of aircraft leased by airline companies in total aircraft was 24.7% in 2000. This ratio increased to 35.7% in 2010 and 39.4% in 2015. This situation shows that the number of aircraft leasing activities has significantly increased over the years.

Figure 1.
Source: Philip, 2016

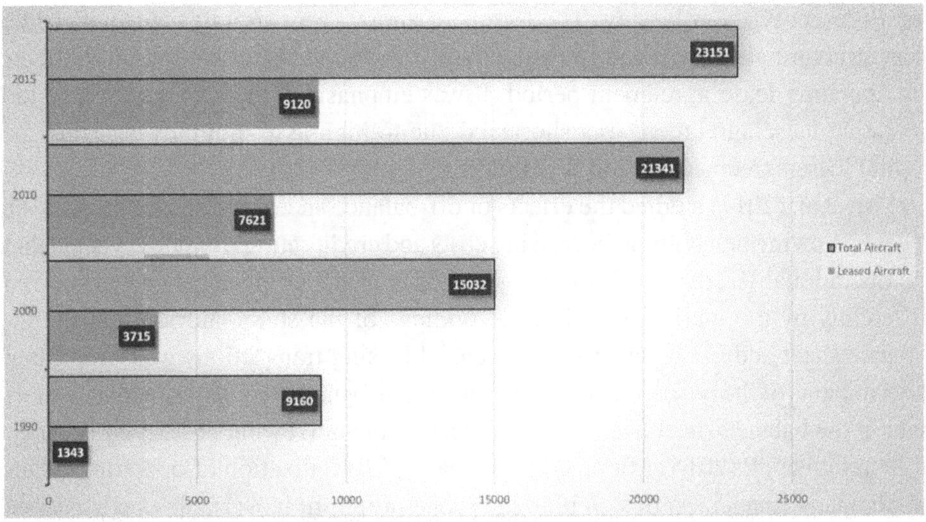

BACKGROUND

Leasing is one of the methods that is frequently used by airline companies to acquire airplanes. In this way, airline companies have the opportunity to obtain the aircraft they need to fly to new destinations, gain competitive advantage, and expand their flight networks. The related research literature reveals many studies that have been conducted on the development, importance, and impact of leasing for airline companies. In the following section, studies on leasing activities in air transport will be discussed.

Bourjade et al. (2017) discussed the relationship between leasing and profitability. In the study, the data of 73 airline companies operating in different regions of the world from 1996 through 2011 were empirically analyzed. The results of the study showed that leasing had a nonmonotonic effect on airway profitability. Also, the results of the study showed that the effect of leasing on airline operational profitability is stronger than the traditional business model in airlines with a low-cost business model.

Erickson and Trevino (1994) examined the effect of short and long-term leasing on the airline industry based on the Pecking Order theory. In the study which examined the period of 1985-1990, a relationship was established between leasing activities and the Pecking Order theory. The empirical results obtained in the study showed that the variables of profitability and growth rate affected leasing. The study also indicated that financial leasing is used as a substitute for debt and is more frequently used by companies with high credit risk. Gavazza (2010) examined the factors affecting the duration of operating and capital lease agreements, which are two different types of leasing. The factors of aircraft age, aircraft type, and airline fleet structure were included in the study, which found that asset liquidity affects the operating lease agreement period. It was emphasized that the duration of the operating lease agreement was shortened due to high asset liquidity and that the capital lease agreement period was longer.

Lim et al. (2017) studied the effects of off-balance sheet leasing and on-balance sheet borrowing behavior on borrowing costs and credit ratings, which revealed that the operational leasing and borrowing activities of the companies were perceived differently by the market. Besides, the findings of the study showed that the in-balance sheet and off-balance sheet financial leasing transactions were important determinants of the borrowing costs. The results also indicated that the balance sheet debt in the balance sheet had a greater effect on the borrowing costs than leasing.

Nuryani et al. (2015) examined the impact of capitalization of operating leases on company financial ratios. Within the scope of the study, variables such as asset quality, asset size, and growth opportunities were included in the analysis. In total, 343 companies listed in the Indonesia Stock Exchange (IDX) were reviewed from 2008 to 2011. The results of the study revealed that the variables of asset structure of the companies, growth opportunities, and firm size affect the leasing policies.

Richardson et al. (2014) analyzed the effect of leasing agreements between airports and airline companies on airport performance. Oum et al. (2000) examined the relationship between operating leases and capacity management from the perspective of airline companies and found that in the periods when demand for air transport is uncertain or cyclical, the operating lease provides flexibility in capacity management for airline companies.

AN EMPIRICAL APPLICATION ON THE AIRLINE INDUSTRY

This study examines the financial determinants of leasing activities in two parts: (1) the description and discussion of the variables used in the study and (2) the presentation of the empirical findings.

Variables and The Model

Focusing on the financial variables shaping the leasing practices of airline companies, the present study used the rental/operating lease expense variable as the dependent variable. The variables used within the scope of the study include return on assets,

Table 2. Definitions of variables

	Acronym	Variables	Variable Description
Dependent variables	LEXP	Lease expense	Rental/operating lease expense / total assets
	LLEPX	Lease expense	Log (rental/operating lease expense)
	LEXP2	Lease expense	Rental/operating lease expense / operating expenses
Independent variables	ROA	Return on assets	Pretax income / total assets
	ROS	Return on sales	EBIT / total sales
	SIZE	Firm size	Log (total assets)
	TANG	Tangibility	Property, plant & equip / total assets
	LEV1	Leverage ratio-1	Short term debt / total assets
	LEV2	Leverage ratio-2	Long term debt / total assets
	LIQ	Liquidity	Current assets / current liabilities

return on sales, firm size, tangibility, leverage ratio, and liquidity. Detailed information about the variables used in the study is given in the table below.

Literature was used to determine the variables in Table 2. Thus, return on assets and return on sales variables were used as indicators of airline company profitability. The natural logarithm of total assets was taken as an indicator of company size. The size of assets is quite important for airline companies. The ratio of property, plant, and equipment to total assets was used in the measurement of the asset structure in airlines. The ratio of short and long-term debt to total assets was used for the measurement of the airlines' leverage degree. The last variable used in the study is related to the liquidity ratio of airline companies. To measure this, the ratio of current assets to current liabilities was used.

Model 1:

$$LEXP_{it} = \beta_0 + \beta_1 ROA_{it} + \beta_2 ROS_{it} + \beta_3 TANG_{it} + \beta_4 LEV1_{it} + \beta_5 LEV2_{it} + \beta_6 LIQ_{it} + \varepsilon_{it}$$

Model 2:

$$LLEXP_{it} = \beta_0 + \beta_1 ROA_{it} + \beta_2 ROS_{it} + \beta_3 TANG_{it} + \beta_4 LEV1_{it} + \beta_5 LEV2_{it} + \beta_6 LIQ_{it} + \varepsilon_{it}$$

Model 3:

$$LEXP2_{it} = \beta_0 + \beta_1 ROA_{it} + \beta_2 ROS_{it} + \beta_3 TANG_{it} + \beta_4 LEV1_{it} + \beta_5 LEV2_{it} + \beta_6 LIQ_{it} + \varepsilon_{it}$$

In the study, three different models were created. In the first model (Model 1), the ratio of rental/operating lease expense to total assets is used as the dependent variable. In the second model (Model 2), the natural logarithm of rental/operating lease expense is used as the dependent variable. In the third model, the ratio of rental/operating lease expense to operating expenses is used as the dependent variable. The independent variables used in the model consist of the return on assets, return on sales, firmness, tangibility, leverage ratio, and liquidity as previously explained in detail.

Data Set and Methodology

This study aimed to reveal the factors affecting the leasing practices of airlines operating in various global markets. In this context, the financial data of 26 airlines are measured as continuous variables for the period of 2000-2017. The data used in the study were obtained from the Thomson Reuters Eicon database. The list of airlines included in the study is as follows:

Table 3. The list of airlines included in the analysis

ID	Airline	ID	Airline
1	AEROFLOT	14	FINNAIR
2	AIR CHINA	15	GOL LINHAS AEREAS
3	AIR FRANCE – KLM	16	HAINAN AIRLINES
4	AIR NEW ZEALAND	17	HAWAIIAN HOLDINGS
5	ALASKA AIR	18	JETBLUE AIRWAYS
6	AMERICAN AIRLINES	19	KOREAN AIRLINES
7	ASIANA AIRLINES	20	QANTAS AIRWAYS
8	CATHAY PACIFIC AIR	21	RYANAIR
9	CHINA EASTERN AIRLINES	22	SINGAPORE AIRLINES
10	CHINA SOUTHERN AIR	23	SKYWEST
11	DELTA AIRLINES	24	SOUTHWEST AIRLINES
12	DEUTSCHE LUFTHANSA	25	THAI AIRWAYS
13	EASYJET	26	UNITED CONTINENTAL

Measuring economic relationships based on cross-sectional data that include time-dimension and the panel data models created by using panel data are called "panel data analysis" (Tatoglu, 2016, p. 4). Panel data equations created with the help of panel data models using time data that identify both economic (Tataoğlu, 2016, p. 4) and financial relations are called *panel data analysis*. In the panel data equations, there are cases where the number of horizontal section units *(N)* is greater (N > T) than the number of periods *(T)*. Here, the cross-sectional units can be a country or a company. The number of periods (T) is annual, quarterly, or monthly data. In the panel data equation, *i* is the horizontal section units (*i=1,...,N*), t is the change over time (*t=1,...,N*), *Y* is the dependent variable, *X* is the independent variable(s), where $Y_{it} = \alpha_{it} + \beta_{it} X_{it} + \varepsilon_{it}$. Here, ε_{it} shows the unexplained part of the model (i.e., the error terms) (Kiraci & Aydin, 2018, p. 232; Tataoglu, 2016, p. 4).

The panel data model in which the dependent variable is denoted by Y and the independent variables by X are as follows (Erol H., 2007, s. 33).

$$Y_{it} = \alpha_{it} + \beta_{it} X_{it} + \varepsilon_{it} \quad (1)$$

Here,

i= 1,2,…,N units of horizontal section,
t= 1,2,…,T time period,
Y_{it}= *t* the value of the *i*'th unit of the dependent variable,
X_{it}= *t* the value of the *i*'th unit of the independent variable,
ε_{it}= error term with zero mean and constant variance, and
β= shows the linear slope coefficient.

In the panel data analysis, analyses should be performed on whether the series have horizontal cross-sectional dependence. Based on the analysis of the cross-sectional dependence in the series, whether the first-generation or second-generation unit root tests will be applied is decided. After the stability test of the series, by noting whether the model coefficients vary by the unit and/or time, the tests should be conducted to determine which model (classical, fixed effects, or random effects) to choose. After determining the appropriate model, variance and autocorrelation tests should be performed on the determined model. In the final stage of the analyses, it is necessary to obtain more robust standard errors than those in the pre-test results.

Empirical Findings

The descriptive statistics of the model, the pre-test results, and the results of the analysis will be presented in the following section.

Table 4 shows the descriptive statistics of the dependent and independent variables used in the study. The standard deviations of the independent variables used for leasing are relatively high. This is because the number of leasing aircraft in the fleet of the airlines is different from each other. The independent variables used in the study are in line with the expectation. We used a total of 468 observations in the study.

Table 5 shows the correlation matrix information for the independent variables of the study. The problem of multicollinearity occurs when the correlation between the independent variables is greater than 0.80. If the correlation between the independent variables was above 0.80, some variables would have been omitted. The correlation is above 0.80 which indicates that the variables move together. A closer look at the data in the table reveals that the correlation coefficient between the variables is significantly lower than the critical value of 0.80.

Table 4. Descriptive statistics for variables

	LEXP	LLEXP	LEXP2	ROA	ROS	SIZE	TANG	LEV1	LEV2	LIQ
Mean	0.3323	5.3366	0.0914	-0.0218	0.0645	6.8932	0.7238	0.0867	0.2939	0.9531
Maximum	96.617	6.5638	14.926	0.9022	1.2225	7.7190	56.943	0.3896	0.7707	4.4115
Minimum	0.0003	2.8887	0.0010	-19.719	-1.1908	2.9355	0.0000	0.0000	0.0000	0.1100
Std. Dev.	4.7954	0.6166	0.6886	0.9254	0.1218	0.5564	2.6082	0.0826	0.1313	0.6065
Skewness	18.401	-1.0261	21.436	-20.715	-0.9023	-1.8580	21.468	1.3716	-0.0575	2.3237
Kurtosis	357.05	4.2638	462.31	440.58	43.806	11.427	463.25	4.0811	2.8823	10.450
Jarque-Bera	24708	113.26	41497	37672	32533	1654	41666	169.54	0.5279	1503
Probability	0.0000	0.0000	0.0000	0.0000	0.0000	0.0000	0.0000	0.0000	0.7680	0.0000
Observations	468	468	468	468	468	468	468	468	468	468

Table 5. Correlation table of the independent variables

	ROA	ROS	SIZE	TANG	LEV1	LEV2	LIQ
ROA	1						
ROS	0.16589	1					
SIZE	0.35104	-0.05476	1				
TANG	-0.11657	-0.03441	-0.26738	1			
LEV1	0.03848	-0.03105	-0.01876	-0.03682	1		
LEV2	0.09384	-0.06163	0.16514	-0.08652	0.41867	1	
LIQ	0.08898	0.24482	-0.29209	-0.02688	-0.47362	-0.20276	1

In the panel data analysis, a cross-sectional dependence test is used to examine if all the units in the series are equally affected by a certain shock. Table 6 shows the results of the cross-sectional dependency test results for the variables used in the study. Accordingly, the hypothesis H_0 which is established as, "*there is no cross-sectional dependency*", is accepted for the LEXP, ROA, ROS, TANG, and LEV2 variables. It is rejected for the other variables. This shows that in the unit root test, the LEXP, ROA, ROS, TANG, and LEV2 variables should be applied to the first-generation unit root tests, and the other variables should be applied the second-generation unit root tests.

Table 6. Cross-sectional dependence test results

Variables	CDLM Adj. (PUY, 2013)	
	Stat	Prob.
LEXP	0.387	0.3490
LLEPX	4.284	0.0000
LEXP2	4.087	0.0000
ROA	0.587	0.2790
ROS	0.298	0.3830
SIZE	2.874	0.0020
TANG	-0.563	0.7130
LEV1	3.444	0.0000
LEV2	-0.42	0.6630
LIQ	3.598	0.0000

Table 7 shows the results of the first-generation panel unit root tests. The variables to be included in the analysis must be stationary. Otherwise, model prediction results may be inaccurate. Unit root testing is required not only in panel data analysis but also in time series analysis. So, we analyzed whether the variables are stationary. The variables included in the analysis are all stationary at the level values.

Table 8 shows the results of the second generation panel unit root tests. CADF panel unit root test results show that SIZE and LEV1 variables are stationary at the level. Other variables became stationary after the first differences were taken.

After the cross-sectional dependence and stability tests, the appropriate model from among the classical model, the fixed-effects model, and the random-effects model should be determined. In this context, to test the validity of the classical model against the fixed effects model, the F-test, and the Breusch-Pagan LM test was used. Additionally, in order to test the suitability of the classical model against the model of random effects, the Hausman test was used to choose between the fixed-effects and random-effects models. These test results are given in Table 9. As the table

Table 7. First-generation panel unit root tests

Variables	Model	LLC -t testi		IPS -W testi		ADF - Fisher	
		Stat	Prob.	Stat	Prob.	Stat	Prob.
LEXP	Constant	-126.77	0.0000	-26.387	0.0000	87.792	0.0014
	Constant and Trend	-86.582	0.0000	-17.979	0.0000	118.29	0.0000
ROA	Constant	-6.7899	0.0000	-6.8108	0.0000	141.22	0.0000
	Constant and Trend	-8.2028	0.0000	-7.1074	0.0000	138.84	0.0000
ROS	Constant	-7.8234	0.0000	-7.1227	0.0000	148.54	0.0000
	Constant and Trend	-9.7109	0.0000	-8.4601	0.0000	162.99	0.0000
TANG	Constant	-3.7543	0.0001	-4.2911	0.0000	104.21	0.0000
	Constant and Trend	-0.8832	0.1886	-2.2015	0.0138	84.894	0.0027
LEV2	Constant	-4.5747	0.0000	-4.8996	0.0000	119.21	0.0000
	Constant and Trend	-2.4765	0.0066	-5.4752	0.0000	117.19	0.0000

Table 8. Second generation panel unit root tests

CADF Panel Birim Kök					
Variables		Stat	1%	5%	10%
LLEPX	Sabit	-2.095***	-2.32	-2.15	-2.07
	Sabit ve Trend	-2.325	-2.82	-2.67	-2.58
ΔLLEPX	Sabit	-2.704*	-2.32	-2.15	-2.07
	Sabit ve Trend	-2.968*	-2.82	-2.67	-2.58
LEXP2	Sabit	-1.543	-2.32	-2.15	-2.07
	Sabit ve Trend	-1.971	-2.82	-2.67	-2.58
ΔLEXP2	Sabit	-2.666*	-2.32	-2.15	-2.07
	Sabit ve Trend	-3.035*	-2.82	-2.67	-2.58
SIZE	Sabit	-2.165**	-2.32	-2.15	-2.07
	Sabit ve Trend	-2.918*	-2.82	-2.67	-2.58
LEV1	Sabit	-2.461*	-2.32	-2.15	-2.07
	Sabit ve Trend	-2.801**	-2.82	-2.67	-2.58
LIQ	Sabit	-2.325*	-2.32	-2.15	-2.07
	Sabit ve Trend	-2.207	-2.82	-2.67	-2.58
ΔLIQ	Sabit	-2.839*	-2.32	-2.15	-2.07
	Sabit ve Trend	-2.875*	-2.82	-2.67	-2.58

Table 9. Tests for identification of appropriate model

	F testi		LM Testi		Hausman	
	Stat.	**Prob.**	**Stat.**	**Prob.**	**Stat.**	**Prob.**
Model 1	13.0162	0.0000	433.2518	0.0000	-2.94	0.0000
Model 2	0.67147	0.8850	3.177487	0.0747	5.85	0.5571
Model 3	0.94233	0.5459	0.397096	0.5286	-	-

suggests, the fixed-effects model is considered appropriate for Model 1, random effects appropriate for Model 2, and the pooled model appropriate for Model 3.

After determining the appropriate models, heteroscedasticity and autocorrelation should be examined in the model. Table 10 shows the variance and autocorrelation test results for the fixed effects, random effects, and pooled models. The test results indicate a variance and autocorrelation problem in the models. Several corrections were applied to eliminate the variance and autocorrelation problems in the model estimation and to obtain robust standard errors.

In models predicted by the Fixed Effects Model (FEM), Random Effects Model (REM), and Pooled estimator, Arellano (1987), Froot (1989), Rogers (1993), and Driscoll-Kraay developed a predictor that does not change the parameter estimates in the case of changing variance and autocorrelation problem but allows the obtainment of robust standard errors. The models created within this framework are re-estimated by the estimator developed by Arellano (1987), Froot (1989), Rogers (1993), Driscoll-Kraay (Parlakyıldız, 2015, p. 8). Table 11 shows the estimation results for the REM estimator under the presence of changing variance and autocorrelation. Following the study, the model results will be included.

Table 10. Tests for deviations of assumptions

		Modified Wald		**Durbin Watson**	**Baltagi–Wu**
Model 1		Stat.	Prob.	Stat.	Stat.
		3069.540	0.0000	1.1614	1.2821
	Test	**Stat.**	**Prob.**	**Durbin Watson**	**Baltagi–Wu**
Model 2	W0	3.052	0.0000	Stat.	Stat.
	W50	2.472	0.0001	2.4424	2.4982
	W10	2.628	0.0000		
		White Test		**Wooldridge test**	
Model 3		Stat.	Prob.	Stat.	Prob.
		90.170	0.0000	77201.8420	0.0000

Table 11 shows the model estimation results of the LEXP variable Rental/ operating lease expense to total assets used as the dependent variable. The analysis results show that return on assets and leverage variables have a negative effect on the LEXP. Also, the effect of return on sales, tangibility, and leverage ratio-2 variables on rental/operating lease expense is positive. The impact of liquidity on the rental/ operating lease expense was determined as positive.

Table 11. Regression with Driscoll-Kraay standard errors (Model 1)

Dependent Variable: LEXP						
Variable	**Coef.**	**Std. Err.**	**t**	**Prob.**	**[95% Conf. Interval]**	
ROA	-4.91980	0.0112067	-439.1	0.0000	-4.94288	-4.89672
ROS	3.87529	0.2084060	18.59	0.0000	3.44607	4.30451
SIZE	0.01797	0.0750569	0.24	0.8130	-0.13661	0.17255
TANG	0.44951	0.0027236	165.1	0.0000	0.44390	0.45512
LEV1	-0.22332	0.2218294	-1.01	0.3240	-0.68018	0.23355
LEV2	-0.53952	0.0920012	-5.86	0.0000	-0.72900	-0.35004
LIQ	0.07685	0.0307173	2.50	0.0190	0.01358	0.14011
_cons	-0.29232	0.5102157	-0.57	0.5720	-1.34313	0.75849
Number of obs = 442			F(7, 25) = 3126792.4			
Number of groups = 26			Prob > F = 0.0000			

Table 12 shows the model prediction results of LLEXP (rental/operating lease expense) as a dependent variable. The analysis findings show that return on assets has a positive effect on rental/operating lease expense. The findings also show that the effect of a firm variable on rental/operating lease expense is negative.

Table 13 shows the model estimation results of LEXP2 (Rental / operating lease expense / operating expenses) as a dependent variable. The analysis results show that the Tangibility variable has a positive effect on rental/operating lease expense.

CONCLUSION

The competition between the airline companies has increased considerably due to the increased regulation and globalization in the airline industry. In this process, airline companies have begun to apply several methods to strengthen their fleet structures and purchase new aircraft. One of the financing methods used by airline companies for aircraft acquisition is aircraft leasing. Therefore, it is very important

Table 12. Random-effects GLS regression (Model 2)

Dependent Variable: dllexp						
Değişken	**Coef.**	**Std. Err.**	**t**	**Prob.**	**[95% Conf. Interval]**	
ROA	0.019777	0.006804	2.91	0.0040	0.006441	0.033113
ROS	0.000179	0.057754	0.00	0.9980	-0.113017	0.113374
SIZE	-0.058400	0.024116	-2.42	0.0150	-0.105667	-0.011133
TANG	-0.002131	0.001807	-1.18	0.2380	-0.005672	0.001410
LEV1	-0.035486	0.130398	-0.27	0.7860	-0.291062	0.220090
LEV2	-0.061172	0.088817	-0.69	0.4910	-0.235250	0.112906
dliq	0.019424	0.021352	0.91	0.3630	-0.022425	0.061273
_cons	0.462434	0.188470	2.45	0.0140	0.093040	0.831829
Number of obs = 442			Wald chi2(7) = 652.77			
Number of groups = 26			Prob > chi2 = 0.0000			

Table 13. Regression with Driscoll-Kraay standard errors (Model 3)

Dependent Variable: dlexp2						
Değişken	**Coef.**	**Std. Err.**	**t**	**Prob.**	**[95% Conf. Interval]**	
ROA	-0.055814	0.033569	-1.66	0.1090	-0.124951	0.013322
ROS	0.163431	0.120177	1.36	0.1860	-0.084078	0.410939
SIZE	0.133442	0.145190	0.92	0.3670	-0.165583	0.432467
TANG	0.265683	0.010917	24.34	0.0000	0.243198	0.288167
LEV1	0.115164	0.216140	0.53	0.5990	-0.329985	0.560313
LEV2	0.183542	0.222493	0.82	0.4170	-0.274692	0.641776
dliq	-0.042801	0.047791	-0.90	0.3790	-0.141230	0.055627
_cons	-1.193943	1.123010	-1.06	0.2980	-3.506825	1.118940
Number of obs = 442			F(7, 25) = 66796.81			
Number of groups = 26			Prob > F = 0.0000			

to identify the financial factors affecting the rental/operating lease expenses of airline companies. In the current study, the financial factors affecting the rental/operating lease expense activities of airline companies were empirically investigated by using the financial data of 26 airlines operating in different markets around the world. Panel data analysis was applied to the airline companies whose financial data were available from 2000 to 2017. Within the scope of the study, three different research models were created, and rental/operating lease expense was used as a dependent variable in the models. The independent variables used in the study were returns on assets, return on sales, firm size, tangibility, leverage ratio, and liquidity.

Empirical analysis results show that return on assets, return on sales, Tangibility, Leverage ratio-2 and Liquidity variables for Model 1 have a significant effect on rental/operating lease expense. Accordingly, return on assets has a negative effect on the rental/operating lease expense. Therefore, the increase in return on assets seems to reduce the rental/operating lease expense. Besides, the findings suggest that the return on sales, tangibility and liquidity variables of airlines have a positive effect on the rental/operating lease expense. This shows that the positive increase in the return on sales of airlines increased rental/operating lease expense. Therefore, the increase in revenues due to sales in airline companies increases rental/operating lease expense. Model 1 findings also show that the tangibility and liquidity variables have a positive effect on the rental/operating lease expense. This situation shows that the increase in fixed assets and liquidity ratios of airlines increases rental/operating lease expense. The first model findings show that there is a relationship between leverage level and rental / operating lease expense. Accordingly, the increase in the long-term debt ratio of airline companies negatively affects rental / operating lease expense. Therefore, it is possible to say that the rental / operating lease expense of airlines with long-term debt ratio is lower.

The results of the second model show that the return on assets and firm size variables of airlines have a significant effect on rental / operating lease expense. Accordingly, the increase in return on assets of airlines increases rental / operating lease expense. Therefore, it is seen that the rental / operating lease expense in the airlines with high return on assets is increasing. The findings also show a negative relationship between firm size and rental / operating lease expense. In other words, the results show that airlines with high total assets have a lower rental / operating lease expense. The results of the third model indicate that there is a relationship between the asset structure of airlines and rental / operating lease expense. Accordingly, the asset structure of airlines increases rental / operating lease expense. Therefore, it is seen that airlines with asset structure which have high property, plant, & equip have high rental/operating lease expense.

In this study, financial factors affecting the rental / operating lease expense of airlines are examined, and it is seen that some financial ratios affect rental / operating lease expense. There are very few studies in the literature that affect rental / operating lease expense. Therefore, this study is expected to contribute to the literature. In the further studies, considering the markets in which the airlines operate can contribute to the literature. In addition, apart from the financial factors affecting rental / operating lease expense, the inclusion of operational factors in the model is expected to contribute significantly to the literature.

REFERENCES

Barclay, M. J., & Smith, C. W. Jr. (1995). The priority structure of corporate liabilities. *The Journal of Finance*, *50*(3), 889–917. doi:10.1111/j.1540-6261.1995.tb04041.x

Bourjade, S., Huc, R., & Muller-Vibes, C. (2017). Leasing and profitability: Empirical evidence from the airline industry. *Transportation Research Part A, Policy and Practice*, *97*, 30–46. doi:10.1016/j.tra.2017.01.001

Erickson, S. M., & Trevino, R. (1994). A pecking order approach to leasing: The airline industry case. *Journal of Financial and Strategic Decisions*, *7*(3), 71–81.

Fu, X., Oum, T. H., & Zhang, A. (2010). Air transport liberalization and its impacts on airline competition and air passenger traffic. *Transportation Journal*, 24–41.

Gavazza, A. (2010). Asset liquidity and financial contracts: Evidence from aircraft leases. *Journal of Financial Economics*, *95*(1), 62–84. doi:10.1016/j.jfineco.2009.01.004

Kiracı, K., & Aydin, N. (2018). Factors that Determine the Capital Structure: An Empirical Study on Low-cost Airlines. *Scientific Annals of Economics and Business*, *65*(3), 227–246. doi:10.2478aeb-2018-0018

Lim, S. C., Mann, S. C., & Mihov, V. T. (2017). Do operating leases expand credit capacity? Evidence from borrowing costs and credit ratings. *Journal of Corporate Finance*, *42*, 100–114. doi:10.1016/j.jcorpfin.2016.10.015

Lückerath-Rovers, M. (2006). *Operating lease disclosure: an empirical investigation*. Erasmus Universiteit Rotterdam.

Morrell, P. S. (2013). *Airline finance*. Ashgate Publishing, Ltd.

Nuryani, N., Heng, T. T., & Juliesta, N. (2015). Capitalization of Operating Lease and Its Impact on Firm's Financial Ratios. *Procedia: Social and Behavioral Sciences*, *211*, 268–276. doi:10.1016/j.sbspro.2015.11.034

Oum, T. H., Zhang, A., & Zhang, Y. (2000). Optimal demand for operating lease of aircraft. *Transportation Research Part B: Methodological*, *34*(1), 17–29. doi:10.1016/S0191-2615(99)00010-7

Öztuğran, A. O. (1995). *Leasing uçak finansmanı ve hava taşımacılığında leasing uygulamaları* (Unpublished MS thesis). Istanbul University.

Öztürk, C. (2016). UFRS 16 Kiralama işlemleri standardının eski UMS 17 standardı ile karşılaştırılması ve Almanya ve Türkiye'de hisse senetleri halka açık olan hava yolu şirketlerinin finansal durumuna etkisi. *Muhasebe Bilim Dünyası Dergisi, 18*(1), 1–50.

Philip, A. (2016), *Ownership Of Aircraft - Lease Versus Buy*. Director –Marketing, Airline Economic Analysis. Retrieved from https://www.iata.org/whatwedo/workgroups/Documents/ACC-2016-GVA/ACC2016_Alex_PHILIP.pdf

Richardson, C., Budd, L., & Pitfield, D. (2014). The impact of airline lease agreements on the financial performance of US hub airports. *Journal of Air Transport Management, 40*, 1–15. doi:10.1016/j.jairtraman.2014.04.004

Thomson, S. J. (2003). *The role of leasing in UK corporate financing decisions, accounting treatment and market impact* (Unpublished PhD thesis). University of Stirling.

Vasigh, B., Fleming, K., & Humphreys, B. (2014). *Foundations of airline finance: Methodology and practice*. Routledge. doi:10.4324/9781315813769

Yerdelen Tatoğlu, F. Y. (2012). *Panel veri ekonometris: stata uygulamalı*. Beta Basım Yayın.

ADDITIONAL READING

Desai, P., & Purohit, D. (1998). Leasing and selling: Optimal marketing strategies for a durable goods firm. *Management Science, 44*(11-part-2), S19-S34.

Grenadier, S. R. (1996). Leasing and credit risk. *Journal of Financial Economics, 42*(3), 333–364. doi:10.1016/0304-405X(96)00882-3

Johnson, J. P., & Waldman, M. (2003). Leasing, lemons, and buybacks. *The RAND Journal of Economics, 34*(2), 247–265. doi:10.2307/1593716

Krishnan, V. S., & Moyer, R. C. (1994). Bankruptcy costs and the financial leasing decision. *Financial Management, 23*(2), 31–42. doi:10.2307/3665737

Lewellen, W. G., Long, M. S., & McConnell, J. J. (1976). Asset leasing in competitive capital markets. *The Journal of Finance, 31*(3), 787–798. doi:10.1111/j.1540-6261.1976.tb01923.x

Miller, M. H., & Upton, C. W. (1976). Leasing, buying, and the cost of capital services. *The Journal of Finance, 31*(3), 761–786. doi:10.1111/j.1540-6261.1976.tb01922.x

Smith, C. W. Jr, & Wakeman, L. M. (1985). Determinants of corporate leasing policy. *The Journal of Finance*, *40*(3), 895–908. doi:10.1111/j.1540-6261.1985.tb05016.x

Yan, A. (2006). Leasing and debt financing: Substitutes or complements? *Journal of Financial and Quantitative Analysis*, *41*(3), 709–731. doi:10.1017/S0022109000002593

KEY TERMS AND DEFINITIONS

Aircraft: Vehicle can fly with or without an engine.

Airline: A company that operates services for carrying passengers and/or goods by aircraft.

Assets: Something valuable belonging to airline company that can be used for the payment of debts.

Empirical: Based on theory.

Financial Analysis: The study about financial information of the companies in order to understand their costs, debt, profits, cash flow, leasing policies, etc.

Leasing: Make a legal agreement in order to use aircraft for an agreed period of time.

Panel Data: Longitudinal data/cross-sectional time series data.

Chapter 10
Does Regional Variation in Startup Concentration Predict Employment Growth in Rural Areas of Ohio, Pennsylvania, and West Virginia?

Yaya Sissoko
Indiana University of Pennsylvania, USA

Brian W. Sloboda
https://orcid.org/0000-0003-0007-1725
University of Phoenix, USA

ABSTRACT

Measures of entrepreneurship, such as average establishment size and the prevalence of start-ups, correlate strongly with employment growth across and within urban areas. Is it possible for entrepreneurship to occur outside of urban areas and be active in rural areas such as Ohio, Pennsylvania, and West Virginia? There are causal links of entrepreneurial finance to industry or city growth but little link of the evidence of entrepreneurship outside of urban areas overall. This chapter examines the regional variation in startup concentration used to predict employment in the rural areas of Pennsylvania, Ohio, and West Virginia by metropolitan statistical area (MSA)/micropolitan areas for the year 2017. The authors find significant differences in new firm formation rates from industrial regions to technologically progressive regions using the generalized linear models (GLM). Variations in firm birth rates are explained by industrial size, population growth, the number of startups, human capital variables, and establishments.

DOI: 10.4018/978-1-7998-1093-3.ch010

INTRODUCTION

As the authors have driven through the rural areas of Ohio, Pennsylvania, and West Virginia, we often drive through areas that do not appear to be economically vibrant with limited employment opportunities and other limitations in economic opportunities. Anecdotally, there could be limited economic vibrancy, but is this true? Is it possible for entrepreneurship to occur outside of urban areas and be active in rural areas such as Ohio, Pennsylvania, and West Virginia? These three states share borders and have some similarities. We provide tables in the Appendix supporting the choice of the three states outlined in this chapter for population density. The tables include the following data in these three states: population repartition, per capita income, earnings per job, the poverty rates, educational achievement, and the unemployment and employment rates.

Can growth be predicted by industry sector, entrepreneurial behavior, regional resource munificence, or any other characteristic? In fact, the neoclassical growth theory did not explain either technological change or entrepreneurial activity because scale economies operate at the plant level, and in the traditional Solow model, economic growth relied on capital investment in larger plants (Solow, 1956). Despite these investments in capital investment in large plans, this capital accumulation can only explain a small amount of the variation in economic growth across regions (Ciccone & Hall, 1996). Since the advent of the Solow growth model, recent theories of economic growth have espoused the role of externalities in generating regional economic growth. There are causal links of entrepreneurial finance to industry or city growth (e.g., Samila and Sorenson, (2011)) but little link of the evidence of entrepreneurship outside of urban areas overall.

Using data from the Quarterly Workforce Indicators (QWI) from the Longitudinal Employer Household Data (LEHD) from the Census Bureau that tracks all employers in the whole U.S. private sector economy, we examine the impact of these externalities, as measured by entrepreneurial activity, on employment growth. We examine the relationship between startup concentration of firms and overall employment growth in Pennsylvania, Ohio, and West Virginia for the year 2017 and determine if entrepreneurship occurs in these rural areas of Ohio, Pennsylvania, and West Virginia. These states were selected for the analysis because of the rural nature of these states and to determine what level of economic activity occurs to promote economic development.

The remainder of this chapter is organized into four main sections. In the next section, we explore the relationships between regional economic growth and entrepreneurship. Section 3 discusses the data sources used in this empirical analysis and the methodology of the generalized linear model (GLM) to examine the relationships between employment and other variables in each of these areas in 2017. In section 4, we analyze the empirical results of employment in the rural areas of Ohio, Pennsylvania, and West Virginia. In the final section, we provide conclusions and policy implications.

EXISTING RESEARCH

It is well understood that startups create most new jobs in the United States' economy, and these jobs promote regional economic development (Haltiwanger, Jarmin, & Miranda, 2013). Schumpeter (1911, 1947) originally posited that startups are recognized as playing an important role in driving growth through innovation. In fact, startups create new jobs because they are sources of innovation that are good investment opportunities and create employment.

It has been argued that urban success depends upon a city's level of entrepreneurship or that entrepreneurship is mainly relegated to urban areas. This claim was famously made in Chinitz's (1961) comparison of New York and Pittsburgh and invoked by Saxenian (1994) to show the contrasts of regional performance of Boston and Silicon Valley. Glaeser, Kerr, and Ponzetto (2010) also document the strength of this relationship when modelling entrepreneurship through start-up employment shares. Similar conclusions are also reached by Delgado, Porter, and Stern (2010) as well as Gennaioli et al. (2012).

One measure of the process of change in economic activity that leads to regional economic development is the rate at which new firms are being established or what we call the firm birth rate. Presumably a relatively high regional rate of firm births indicates a process of resources concentrating within that region, while a relatively low rate of firm births indicates slower economic activity. A plausible implication is that localities would want to do more to attract and support startups. There is significant regional variation in new firm formation, and a set of regional determinants to explain this variation were noted (Reynolds, 1994; Armington & Acs, 2002; Acs & Mueller, 2008; Gennaioli et al., 2012). That is, there are regional variations that occur in the concentration of startups, so not all regions will have the same experiences with startups and their impacts on employment growth. More importantly, the effects of the startups on regional employment often have time lags. Fritsch and Mueller (2004) analyzed the impact of new business formation on regional employment, and they identified time lags using an Almon lag model. From their analysis, it was found that new firms can produce a positive and a negative effect on employment that impacts regional economic development. Also, their empirical results conclude that the peak of the positive impact of new businesses on regional development occurs eight years after formation. Significant regional variation heterogeneity exists in the new firm formation. Some of these differences in the formation of new firms can be attributed to the various measures of unemployment, population density, industrial restructuring, and availability of financing (Audretsch & Fritsch, 1994; Davidson, Lindmark, & Olofsson, 1994; Guesnier, 1994; Keebler & Walker, 1994: Gennaioli et al., 2012; Delgado, Porter, & Stern, 2010). More importantly, a change in the United States' economy has been accompanied by a regional shift in economic activity away from traditional industrial regions to new regional agglomerations of high technology that are stimulating entrepreneurial activity and leading to the formation of new firms as well as industrial clustering (Acs, Carlsson, & Karlsson, 1999; Stough, 2015; Stough, 2016).

In some regional economies, growth may be attributed to the application of technology that drives regional economic growth. That is, the availability of new technologies continues to develop and enables entrepreneurs to form new companies that have translated the associated research and technology possibilities into new marketable products as well as services in regional economies (Stough et al., 2013; Stough, 2016). That is, these companies do not need to exist in urban areas, and the technology enables them to operate elsewhere with ease and efficiency. Because of the availability of technology, many regions around the world are investing in technology development and related innovation as well as entrepreneurship policies to enable regional economic growth that results in industrial clustering (Stough, 2015). The development of these industrial clusters is promising, but some regions have been successful at this effort while other regions have not been as successful. Stough (2015) also provides evidence that entrepreneurship levels rise as clusters pass through the early development stages and decline as cluster maturity and decline set in. That is, entrepreneurship may be an important factor for cluster resiliency and regeneration. The goal of these industrial clusters is to learn more about how regions can build economic ecosystems that can support relevant technology and promote economic growth. The latter is crucial in the knowledge-based economies, and a greater emphasis is needed for how this knowledge-based economy contributes to regional economic growth.

Entrepreneurial activity enables the startups to hire employees, resulting in subsequent decreases in unemployment (Pfeiffer & Reize, 2000; Glaeser, Kerr, & Ponzetto, 2010). Entrepreneurs enter markets with new products, services, or improved production services (Acs & Audretsch, 2003). More importantly, Glaeser, Kerr, and Ponzetto (2010) determine that clusters of entrepreneurship exist, but they are unable to explain why they exist where they do. That is, why do they exist in urban areas but not elsewhere? A notable feature of entrepreneurial activity is that it also increases productivity by increasing competition (Nickell, 1996; Nickell, Nicolitsas, & Dryden, 1997; Sauka, 2008). That is, entrepreneurial activity directly affects the performance of the firms which can increase the productivity in the economy because these investments by entrepreneurs often create new jobs, intensify competition, and can increase productivity with the introduction of the new technologies as well as enhanced work practices.

The existence of regional entrepreneurship also varies from region to region throughout a country or is not homogenous throughout the country (Andersson & Koster, 2011; Carlsson, 2016; Fritsch & Wyrwich, 2017; Huggins & Thompson, 2014). A regional culture that is not static enables the presence of successful, innovative entrepreneurs to enable others to engage in entrepreneurship (Malecki & Spigel, 2017; Feldman, 2014). That is, the local culture is not some exogenous phenomenon which can be implemented by policy. A local culture is formed through social interactions via the actions of the ingenuities of the entrepreneurs and others in the private sector in the regional economies (Isenberg, 2010). As a result, regional entrepreneurship cultures are informal institutions that may include a high density of role model entrepreneurs who provide "a local abundance of information and knowledge about the practice of entrepreneurship" (Andersson & Henrekson, 2015, p. 171). Public–private governance would be a typical relationship that occurs in entrepreneurial ecosystems (Acs et al., 2017).

In brief, the general theme from the empirical literature is that most of the studies have found a positive relationship between entrepreneurship and job creation. In addition to this positive relationship, there are regional variations or heterogeneity (e.g., urban and rural areas) in the development of entrepreneurial activity. More importantly, past empirical evidence confirms that the source of innovations via entrepreneurship provides good investment opportunities that create employment on a regional level. As noted in the existing literature, the role of entrepreneurship in promoting technology and cluster related economic growth is important, and this is a new area that has little understanding. The latter becomes a new gap in regional economic growth and entrepreneurship literature. As the knowledge-based economies continue to grow, a greater understanding of the relationship between industrial clustering and entrepreneurship is needed.

DATA SOURCES AND THE EMPIRICAL METHODOLOGY

Data Sources

The Quarterly Workforce Indicators (QWI) within the Longitudinal Employer–Household Dynamics (LEHD) is the data source used in this analysis. The LEHD data were created through a partnership between the Census Bureau and U.S. states to provide local labor market information and to improve the Census Bureau's economic and demographic data programs. The LEHD data are comprised of different administrative sources, primarily Unemployment Insurance (UI) earnings data and the Quarterly Census of Employment and Wages (QCEW), as well as censuses and surveys. Firm and worker information are combined to create job level quarterly earnings history data, data on where workers live and work, and data on firm characteristics such as industry.

Descriptive Analysis Startup Concentration and Overall Employment Growth

We examined regional variation of employment in Pennsylvania, Ohio, and West Virginia by looking at the concentration of startup employment. More specifically, we looked at whether or not these MSAs with the highest concentration of startup employment in 2002 experienced high employment growth. We selected the year 2002 as the starting point of the analysis because this was the first year of economic growth after the national recession of 2001 (March 2001- November 2001). Table 1 summarizes the MSAs that showed high concentration of startups that could have correlated with economic growth of the metropolitan statistical areas/micropolitan areas.

Employment in these MSAs grew from 2,179,840 in 2002 to 2,401,290 in 2017, and the percentage of growth is 10.2%, which means that employment in these 15 MSAs of Pennsylvania grew by 10.2% from 2002 through 2017. To give this preceding estimate context, we compared this figure to the total employment for Pennsylvania, and employment in Pennsylvania increased from 4,202,408 in 2002 to 4,596,089 in 2017. Thus, employment in Pennsylvania grew by 9.37% from 2002 to 2017, meaning that employment in these MSA/micropolitan areas with the highest concentration of startup firms in 2002 grew faster than the overall employment growth in Pennsylvania, or 10.2% versus 9.37%.

Now, we examined the regional variation in West Virginia by looking at the concentration of startup employment. As with Pennsylvania, we looked at whether or not these MSAs with the highest concentration of startup employment in 2017 also experienced high employment growth. Table 2 summarized the results from West Virginia.

Employment in these MSAs of West Virginia grew from 275,564 in 2002 to 286,231 in 2017, and the percentage growth is 2.10%, which means that employment in these MSAs of West Virginia grew by 3.9% from 2002 through 2017. To give this preceding estimate context, we compared this to the total employment for West Virginia, and employment in West Virginia increased from 473,299 in 2002 to 483,253 in 2017. Thus, employment in West Virginia grew by 2.10% from 2002 to 2017, meaning that employment in these MSAs with the highest concentration of startup firms in 2017 grew faster than the overall employment growth in West Virginia, or 2.10% is less than 3.9%.

Table 1. Startup concentrations and employment by metropolitan statistical area/ micropolitan areas in Pennsylvania, 2017

MSA/Micropolitan Area	Employment-- All Firm Ages	Employment--The Number of Firms Startup (0-1 Years)	The Share of Firms Startup (0-1 Years)
Gettysburg, PA	25990	990	3.81%
Sayre, PA	17727	671	3.79%
New York-Newark-Jersey City, NY-NJ-PA (PA part)	7180	263	3.66%
New Castle, PA	21702	785	3.62%
Lancaster, PA	203568	6707	3.29%
East Stroudsburg, PA	37644	1160	3.08%
State College, PA	38603	1110	2.88%
Philadelphia-Camden-Wilmington, PA-NJ-DE-MD (PA part)	1607717	43754	2.72%
Erie, PA	96637	2516	2.60%
St. Marys, PA	12584	327	2.60%
Bradford, PA	11646	289	2.48%
Scranton--Wilkes-Barre--Hazleton, PA	199288	4810	2.41%
Altoona, PA	45676	1090	2.39%
Williamsport, PA	39026	922	2.36%
Youngstown-Warren-Boardman, OH-PA (PA part)	36302	812	2.24%

Finally, we examined the regional variation in Ohio by looking at the concentration of startup employment. As with Pennsylvania and West Virginia, we looked at whether or not these MSAs in Ohio with the highest concentration of startup employment in 2002 also experienced high employment growth. Table 3 summarized the results from Ohio.

Employment in these MSAs of Ohio declined from 354,257 in 2002 to 330,256 in 2017, and the percentage decline is 6.7%, which means that employment in these MSAs of Ohio declined by 6.7% from 2002 through 2017. To give this preceding estimate context, we compared this to the total employment for Ohio, and employment in Ohio increased from 3,9750,38 in 2002 to 4,091,685 in 2017. Thus, employment in Ohio increased by 2.93% from 2002 to 2017, meaning that employment in these MSAs with the highest concentration of startup firms declined faster than the overall employment increase in Ohio.

Table 2. Startup concentrations and economic growth by metropolitan statistical area/micropolitan areas in West Virginia, 2017

MSA of West Virginia	Employment-- All Firm Ages	Employment--The Number of Firms Startup (0-1 Years)	The Share of Firms Startup (0-1 Years)
Winchester, VA-WV (WV part)	2,297	102	4.44%
Weirton-Steubenville, WV-OH (WV part)	13,922	422	3.03%
Fairmont, WV	12,648	379	3.00%
Beckley, WV	31,572	910	2.88%
Morgantown, WV	45,660	1,272	2.79%
Washington-Arlington-Alexandria, DC-VA-MD-WV (WV part)	10,602	294	2.77%
Charleston, WV	79,569	2,129	2.68%
Point Pleasant, WV-OH (WV part)	3,789	93	2.45%
Hagerstown-Martinsburg, MD-WV (WV part)	23,020	551	2.39%
Huntington-Ashland, WV-KY-OH (WV part)	63,152	1,431	2.27%

Note: We used ten for West Virginia because the number of MSAs/Micropolitan areas is smaller.

EMPIRICAL METHODOLOGY

Description of the Variables

The *y* variable or the dependent variable for this analysis will use the number of employed in the startup firms with respect to the size of the labor force (measured in thousands) as suggested by Carree and Thurik (2010). The labor market approach implicitly assumes that the entrepreneur starting a new business is in the same labor market that the new establishment operates.

Once we identified the *y* variable, we estimated a regression *n* model where the dependent variable is the number employed at startups divided by the labor force (in thousands) which is almost consistent with the approach used by Carree and Thurik (2010), Davidsson et al. (1994), and Acs and Armington (2000), and others. Table 4 summarizes the regressors used in the analysis.

Table 3. Startup concentrations and economic growth by metropolitan statistical area/micropolitan areas in Ohio, 2017

MSA of Ohio	Employment-- All Firm Ages	Employment-- The Number of Firms Startup (0-1 Years)	The Share of Firms Startup (0-1 Years)
Norwalk, OH	16418	935	5.69%
Point Pleasant, WV-OH (OH part)	7901	383	4.85%
Jackson, OH	7381	315	4.27%
Port Clinton, OH	9065	294	3.24%
Ashland, OH	13871	444	3.20%
Huntington-Ashland, WV-KY-OH (OH part)	8222	247	3.00%
Weirton-Steubenville, WV-OH (OH part)	14807	409	2.76%
Wheeling, WV-OH (OH part)	15725	424	2.70%
Washington Court House, OH	8238	218	2.65%
Mount Vernon, OH	14715	384	2.61%
Mansfield, OH	36709	926	2.52%
Chillicothe, OH	18728	454	2.42%
Youngstown-Warren-Boardman, OH-PA (OH part)	126187	3037	2.41%
Van Wert, OH	8363	200	2.39%
Zanesville, OH	24216	571	2.36%

The Empirical Methodology Using Generalized Linear Models (GLM)

The empirical specification for this model is given in equation (1):

$$\begin{aligned} Emp = \beta_0 + \beta_1 * Unem + \beta_2 * Share + \beta_3 * Industry + \beta_4 * EST \\ + \beta_5 * Pop + \beta_6 * HS + \beta_7 * BA + \beta_8 * DWV + \beta_9 * DOH + \varepsilon_i \end{aligned} \tag{1}$$

where Emp is employment, Unem is the unemployment rate, share is the share of the proprietorship, Industry is the industry size, EST is the size of the establishment, Pop is the population growth between 2017 and 2018, HS is the share of adults with less than a high school education, BA is the share of adults with a bachelor's degree or higher, DWV is a binary variable for West Virginia, and DOH is the binary variable for Ohio. Finally, ε_i is the residual term which follows a white noise process $\varepsilon_i \sim N(0,\sigma^2)$.

Table 4. Description of the regressors

Regressor	Description	Source	Expectation of Sign
Establishment Size (EST)	A proxy for the structure of industry in the region. It is measured as 2017 employment divided by the number of establishments in 2017 in the MSA.	Employment Data were obtained from the Bureau of Labor Statistics. Establishment data were obtained from the U.S. Census Bureau, Statistics of U.S. Businesses.	It should be negatively related to regional birth rate since larger average establishment size indicates greater dominance by large firms.
Industry Size (Industry)	The number of establishments in the MSAs in 2017 divided by the MSA's 2017 population.	Establishment data were obtained from the U.S. Census Bureau, Statistics of U.S. Businesses. The population data by MSA were obtained from the Census Bureau.	This regressor will measure the following: The greater the number of establishments relative to the population, the more spillovers that can occur within the MSA. We expect the sign to be positive.
Population Growth (Pop)	Measures the average annual rate of increase in the MSA in a previous period. This was calculated by taking the two-year change from the ratio of the 2018 population divided by the 2017 population and using a square root of this ratio to calculate the annual change ratio.	The population data by MSA for 2018 and 2017 were obtained from the Census Bureau.	We would expect this to be positive because a larger population will, in general, lead to more employment.
Unemployment Rate (Unem)	This is the average number of unemployed in 2017 divided by the 2017 labor force.	Bureau of Labor Statistics	We expect the sign to be negative because as the unemployment increases, it reduces employment opportunities.
Share of Proprietors (Share)	Measures the number of proprietors in 2017 divided by the 2017 labor force. Proprietors are members of the labor force who are also business owners.	Bureau of Labor Statistics	The coefficient on the share of proprietors in the region is negative, because the share of proprietors is negatively correlated with employment.
Share of Adults with Less than High School Education (HS)	This is defined as the number of adults without a high school degree in 2017 divided by the number of adults in the labor force.	The number of adults in the labor force is from the Bureau of Labor Statistics. The number employed without a high school degree is obtained from the Quarterly Workforce Indicators (QWI) from the Census Bureau.	The lack of a high school degree should be a good proxy for the proportion of unskilled and semi-skilled labor and should be negatively related to the dependent variable.
Share of Adults with A College and Graduate/Professional Education (BA)	This is defined as the number of adults with college degrees in 2017 divided by the total number of adults.	The number of adults in the labor force is from the Bureau of Labor Statistics The number employed without a high school degree is obtained from the Quarterly Workforce Indicators (QWI) from the Census Bureau.	This would be a proxy measure of both technical skills needed in the economy, and we expect it to be positive.

In this regression specification, the cross-section will reveal interstate (across) variation, but this type of specification would be problematic because of the omitted variable bias problem. Consequently, this regression specification will focus on intrastate (within) variation, which will be estimated by use of the fixed effects regression. The fixed effects will be captured by the binary variables for Ohio and West Virginia. When doing a fixed effect regression, we omit one of the states, which is Pennsylvania. By including the fixed effects (group dummies), we are controlling for the average differences across the states in any observable or unobservable predictors. That is, the fixed effects coefficients soak up all the across group action, and the coefficient of each key predictor tells us the average (i.e., the common slope averaged across groups). What remains is the within group action (which is what we are interested in), and the problem of omitted variable bias is greatly reduced. Also, there is no binary variable for the time variable because there is no trend in the data.

Generalized linear models (GLM) were first defined by Nelder and Wedderburn (1972). GLM is an extension of traditional linear models that allows the mean of a population to depend on a linear predictor through a nonlinear link function and allows the response probability distribution to be any member of statistical distributions. In fact, many statistical models are GLM, and these models include classical linear models with normal errors, logistic and probit models for binary data, and log-linear models for multinomial data. More importantly, other statistical models can be formulated as GLM by the selection of an appropriate link function and response probability distribution.

Recall that a traditional linear model or the standard OLS model is given as $y_i = x_i^{'}\beta + \varepsilon_i$. where y_i is the dependent variable for the ith observation. The quantity x_i is a column vector of regressors for observation i, that is known from the experimental setting and is considered to be fixed or non-random. The vector of unknown coefficients β is estimated by a least squares fit to the data y. These unknown coefficients are assumed to be independent, normal random variables with a zero mean and a constant variance. The expected value of y_i, is $\mu_i = x_i^{'}\beta$. Applying the traditional linear model would not be appropriate because of the following reasons:

1. It may not be reasonable to assume that data are normally distributed. As an example, this assumption would not be appropriate for count data.
2. If the mean of the data is naturally restricted to a range of values, the traditional linear model may not be appropriate since the linear predictor $x_i^{'}\beta$ can take on any value.

3. It may not be realistic to assume that the variance of the data is constant for all observations. For example, it is not unusual to observe data where the variance increases with the mean of the data.

GLM extends the traditional linear model and would be more applicable to a wider range of data analysis problems. GLM works by providing a mapping of the theoretical portion of the model (the right hand side of the model) to the sample space of the outcome (the left hand side of the model). The latter is performed via a link function. The following components are used to estimate a GLM model:

a. The linear component is defined just as it is for traditional linear models $\varphi_i = x_i^{'}\beta$
b. A monotonic differentiable link function g describes how the expected value of y_i is related to the linear predictor φ_i: $g\left(\mu_i\right) = x_i^{'}\beta$
c. The response variables y_i are independent for i = 1, 2, and have a probability distribution from an exponential family.

In summary, we generalize E(Yi) ° $\mu_i = X_i\beta$ by allowing the expected value of Y to vary with Xβ according to a function to its link function g(). As in the standard OLS models, GLM can be summarized through statistics such as parameter estimates, their standard errors, and goodness-of-fit statistics. As such, one can also make statistical inference about the parameters using confidence intervals and hypothesis tests. In GLM, the inference procedures are usually based on asymptotic considerations because the exact distribution theory is not available or is not even practical for all GLM.

Empirical Results

Before the estimation of equation (1), the correlations among the continuous regressors are summarized in Table 5.

These correlations will be discussed as we analyze the results from the cross-sectional regression results. Table 6 shows the results from the cross-sectional regression on the average annual firm birth rates for all private firms together for Pennsylvania, West Virginia, and Ohio based on the MSAs. In this specification, a normal distribution with a log link function is chosen to model these data. More specifically, $\log\left(\mu_i\right) = x_i^{'}\beta$ so that the $\mu_i = \exp(x_i^{'}\beta)$.

For this model, Fisher's Scoring Algorithm was used to estimate the GLM. This does not tell us much other than the fact that the model did indeed converge and had no difficulty in converging. From the output, deviance is a measure of goodness

Table 5. Pearson Correlation Coefficients (Prob > |r| under H_0: Rho=0)

	Unemployment (Unem)	Share	Establishment Size (EST)	Population Growth (Pop)	Less than High School Education (HS)	Bachelor's Degree and Higher (BA)	Employment (Emp)	Industry Size (Industry)
Unemployment (Unem)	1.00000							
Share	-0.02119 0.8968	1.00000						
Establishment Size (EST)	0.03142 0.8474	-0.4988 0.0011	1.00000					
Population Growth (Pop)	0.06406 0.6945	-0.0023 0.9886	-0.04513 0.7821	1.00000				
Less than High School Education (HS)	0.08105 0.6191	0.02097 0.8978	0.01492 0.9272	-0.04249 0.7946	1.00000			
Bachelor's Degree and Higher (BA)	0.16775 0.3008	-0.1429 0.3788	-0.07941 0.6262	-0.26646 0.0965	0.57289 0.0001	1.00000		
Employment (Emp)	0.31583 0.0471	-0.1462 0.3678	0.13822 0.3950	0.13655 0.4008	-0.06666 0.6828	0.18877 0.2434	1.00000	
Size of Industry (Size)	-0.08843 0.5874	0.02047 0.9002	0.84305 <.0001	-0.06028 0.7118	0.01568 0.9235	-0.16400 0.3119	-0.01380 0.9327	1.00000

Table 6. Results from the fixed effects regression Using GLM

Criteria for Assessing Goodness of Fit[1]			
Criterion	**DF**	**Value**	**Value/DF**
Deviance	30	0.0111	0.0004
Scaled Deviance	30	40.0000	1.3333
Pearson Chi-Square	30	0.0111	0.0004
Scaled Pearson X^2	30	40.0000	1.3333
Log Likelihood		107.0668	
Full Log Likelihood		107.0668	
AIC (smaller is better)		-192.1335	
AICC (smaller is better)		-182.7050	
BIC (smaller is better)		-173.5559	

[1]A careful reader may think of this as overdispersion in GLM models. Overdispersion occurs in GLM models that are modeled with the binomial or Poisson distributions, not normal distributions.

Dependent Variable: Employment

Link Function: Log

of fit of a generalized linear model. In other words, it is a measure of badness of fit – higher numbers indicate a worse fit. The deviance statistic from this model is quite small (0.0111) which indicates this GLM model is a good fit.

Now, the results from this analysis from Table 6 will be explained. The scale parameter under a normal distribution in a GLM is the standard deviation. Based on the estimate, the size of the standard deviation would be small which may be indicative of not a high level of dispersion. From Table 6, the marginal explanatory variable (MEXVAL) of each variable is the percentage by which the standard error of the estimate (SEE) of a regression is affected if the variable is omitted from the regression and is not replaced by another variable. The MEXVAL shows the importance of each variable to the fit of the regression model rather than relying on the p-values to assess statistical significance (Almon, 2014). From these results, for the omission of any of these variables which are not replaced, the standard error of the estimate (SEE) would increase. Thus, we can conclude that most of the regressors with the exception of unemployment and the binary variables of these variables contribute to the explaining of employment in Pennsylvania, Ohio, and West Virginia.

The coefficient for the unemployment rate is negative for all private firms which is consistent with earlier cross-sectional studies (Storey, 1991; Audretsch & Fritsch, 1994). The intuition is that as workers shift from being employed to unemployed, the overall entry rate in the region tends to decrease. We need to interpret with care that there is no evidence that it is necessarily the unemployed who are starting the new firms in Pennsylvania, Ohio, and West Virginia.

The coefficient on the share of proprietors in the region is negative, which is what we would expect because the share of proprietors is negatively correlated with employment. Intuitively, as the average establishment size in a region increases there could be fewer opportunities for establishing new firms, and a smaller proportion of the labor force is comprised of owners.

Table 7.

Parameter	Estimate	Standard Error	Wald 95% Confidence Limits		Wald Chi-Square[4]	Pr > χ^2	MEXVAL
Intercept	-29.3079	9.0019	-46.9513	-11.6645	10.60	0.0011**	846.0462
Unemployment (Unem)	-0.2075	0.1718	-0.5443[1]	0.1292	1.46[2]	0.2271	5.990009
Share	-69.2241	23.3153	-23.5269	114.9212	8.82	0.0030**	1998.328
Establishment Size (EST)	92.5264	30.3329	33.0749	151.9778	9.30	0.0023**	2671.007
Population Growth (Pop)	12.2406	6.3644	-0.2334	24.7145	3.70	0.0544**	353.3557
Less than High School Education (HS)	-4.0651	2.3043	-8.5814	0.4513	3.11	0.0777**	117.3493
Bachelor's Degree or Higher (BA)	6.3587	3.6167	-0.7298	13.4472	3.09	0.0787**	183.5599
Industry Size (Industry)	175.243	63.1356	-298.987	-51.5000	7.70	0.0055**	5058.83
Binary Variable: Ohio (DOH)	0.2651	0.3804	-0.4805	1.0107	0.49	0.4859	7.652778
Binary Variable: West Virginia (DWV)	0.2974	0.3176	-0.3252	0.9199	0.88	0.3492	8.585199
Scale[3]	0.0166	0.0019	0.0134	0.0207			0.479201

Note: * denotes statistical significance at the 5% level; ** denotes statistical significance at the 10% level

[1]For the Wald Confidence intervals, using unemployment as an example, the lower limit is calculated as -0.2075-0.1718*1.96=-0.5443 while the upper limit it is -0.2075+0.1718*1.96=0.1292. 1.96 comes from standard normal Z.

[2]The Wald test statistic is calculated as $\left(\frac{-0.2075}{0.1718}\right)^2 = 1.46$ which a chi is square with 1 degree of freedom.

[3]The scale parameter was estimated via maximum likelihood estimation.

[4]The Wald test statistic is equivalent to the t test statistic.

The coefficient for human capital, as measured by share of college graduates, is positive. Intuitively, a positive coefficient would suggest that MSAs that have higher levels of education will have higher start-up rates. The latter would be consistent with Savage et al. (1988) and Anselin, Varga, and Acs (1997, 2000) because the technologically advanced industry individuals with greater skills, knowledge, and expertise are more likely to start businesses. In our case, the sign of the coefficient was positive.

The negative coefficient for the percentage of the population without a high school degree is not surprising given that the correlation coefficient is -0.066 as shown in Table 5 between those without a high school degree and employment in Pennsylvania, Ohio, and West Virginia, which would be expected. This negative sign on the percentage of those without a high school degree suggests that it would increase in this population and would reduce employment.

As for the regress for industry size, this variable was strongly positive and statistically significant as posited by the theory of regional spillovers or the likelihood of greater spillovers (Krugman, 1991a, 1991b). In other words, entrepreneurs can stimulate employment growth by creating more jobs in a region which can spillover into surrounding areas because of the positive externalities of these entrepreneurial activities.

CONCLUSION AND POLICY IMPLICATIONS

This chapter examined the issue of new firm formation the Quarterly Workforce Indicators (QWI) from the Longitudinal Employer Household Data (LEHD) from the Census Bureau. We constructed annual data on firm births for 2017 for the MSAs in Pennsylvania, Ohio, and West Virginia. From this analysis, we find considerable variation in the new firm formation rate across these MSAs. In fact, these variations in the firm birth rates are substantially explained by regional differences in population growth and other variables that have been espoused by the new economic geography.

Though we find that most of the signs coincide with our expectations with the exception of the human capital variables, each of the regressors was not statistically significant. As a remedy to assess the importance of each of the regressors, we estimated the marginal explanatory variable (MEXVAL) for each of the regressors. From these MEXVALS, the omission of these variables increases the standard error quite significantly, so each of these regressors contributes to the explaining of birth rates of new firms in Pennsylvania, Ohio, and West Virginia. In general, people in these MSAS that have a high percentage of college graduates are much more likely to start businesses than those in MSAs with lower percentages, but we saw the opposite which can be attributed to population shifts or those leaving these

MSAs for other areas. In fact, the population data showed declines in population in these MSAs. Given the results of this analysis, this research could be expanded to include all of the MSAs in the United States using the Quarterly Workforce Indicators (QWI) from the Longitudinal Employer Household Data (LEHD) to determine the outcome of the results.

Finally, the policy implications in this paper are as follows:

1. **Negative Unemployment:** The three states can provide more training, workshops, and free college tuition for workers to go back to school to acquire more training and skills;
2. **Negative Share of Proprietors:** The three states could provide investment tax credit or lower profit tax to starting firms to attract them into the region;
3. **Negative Human Capital as Measured by the Share of College Graduates:** This negatively impacted the hiring of college graduates by new start-up firms. Policy that provides incentive to workers to attend training sessions, workshops, go back to school will increase their skills; thus, this will enhance their productivity while leading to higher start-up rates.
4. The creation of an industrial free tax zone and other economic attractions might lead to reverse migration to these regions. This will increase the population and provide a steady viable labor force to the startup firms. Moreover, there might be greater spillovers from the creation of an industrial zone to higher start up rates of firms.
5. Policy, such as grant, small business loan, and promoting a startup concentration of export-oriented industries, can make the industry very profitable and thus provide a steady viable labor force to the startup firms.
6. The application of the theory of efficiency wage might attract the best and more productive workers who get paid above average wages. Labor productivity is essential in the success of startup firms. In addition, it will require less monitoring of the workers and less shrinking and more effort from them. This might also boost the educational attainability and achievement of the labor force such as higher average years of schooling completed and/or higher adult literacy rate.
7. Policies that promotes startup firms attracting new capital investments are likely to experience higher labor productivity due to higher quality machinery and other capital. This can lead to a higher profitability of the new startup firms and thus to a steady gradual employment growth.

REFERENCES

Acs, Z., & Armington, C. (2000). *The Determinants of Regional Variation in New Firm Formation*. A working paper from the Center of Economic Studies, Bureau of the Census. Retrieved from http://citeseerx.ist.psu.edu/viewdoc/download?doi=10.1.1.199.6358&rep=rep1&type=pdf

Acs, Z. J., & Audretsch, D. B. (2003). Innovation and Technological Change. In Z. J. Acs & D. B. Audretsch (Eds.), *Handbook of Entrepreneurship Research* (pp. 55–79). Kluwer Academic Publishers. doi:10.1007/b105789

Acs, Z. J., Carlsson, B., & Karlsson, C. (1999). *Entrepreneurship, Small & Medium-Sized Enterprises and the Macroeconomy*. Cambridge University Press.

Acs, Z. J., Stam, E., Audretsch, D. B., & O'Connor, A. (2017). The lineages of the entrepreneurial ecosystem approach. *Small Business Economics*, *49*(1), 1–10. doi:10.100711187-017-9864-8

Almon, C. (2014). *The Craft of Econometric Modeling*. Ginn Press. Retrieved from http://inforumweb.umd.edu/papers/publishedwork/books/craft1.pdf

Andersson, M., & Henrekson, M. (2015). Local competitiveness fostered through local institutions for entrepreneurship. In D. B. Audretsch, A. N. Link, & M. L. Walshok (Eds.), *The Oxford Handbook of Local Competitiveness* (pp. 145–190). Oxford University Press.

Andersson, M., & Koster, S. (2011). Sources of persistence in regional start-up rates—Evidence from Sweden. *Journal of Economic Geography*, *11*(1), 179–201. doi:10.1093/jeg/lbp069

Audretsch, D. B., & Fritsch, M. (1994). The Geography of Firm Births in Germany. *Regional Studies*, *28*(4), 359–365. doi:10.1080/00343409412331348326

Audretsch, D. B., & Keilbach, M. (2004). Entrepreneurship Capital and Economic Performance. *Regional Studies*, *38*(8), 949–959. doi:10.1080/0034340042000280956

Carlsson, B. (2016). Industrial dynamics: A review of the literature 1990–2009. *Industry and Innovation*, *23*(1), 1–61. doi:10.1080/13662716.2015.1120658

Carree, M. A., & Thurik, A. R. (2010). The impact of entrepreneurship on economic growth. In *Handbook of Entrepreneurship Research* (pp. 557–594). Springer. doi:10.1007/978-1-4419-1191-9_20

Chinitz, B. (1961). Contrasts in Agglomeration: New York and Pittsburgh. *The American Economic Review*, *51*(2), 279–289.

Ciccone, C., & Hall, R. E. (1996). Productivity and the Density of Economic Activity. *The American Economic Review*, *86*(1), 54–70.

Davidson, P., Lindmark, L., & Olofsson, C. (1994). New firm formation and regional development in Sweden. *Regional Studies*, *38*(4), 395–410. doi:10.1080/0034340 9412331348356

Delgado, M., Porter, M., & Stern, S. (2010). Clusters and Entrepreneurship. *Journal of Economic Geography*, *10*(4), 495–518. doi:10.1093/jeg/lbq010

Feldman, M. P. (2014). The character of innovative places: Entrepreneurial strategy, economic development, and prosperity. *Small Business Economics*, *43*(1), 9–20. doi:10.100711187-014-9574-4

Fritsch, M., & Mueller, P. (2004). Effects of new business formation on regional development over time. *Regional Studies*, *38*(8), 961–975. doi:10.1080/0034340042000280965

Fritsch, M., & Wyrwich, M. (2017). The effect of entrepreneurship on economic development—An empirical analysis using regional entrepreneurship culture. *Journal of Economic Geography*, *17*(1), 157–189. doi:10.1093/jeg/lbv049

Gennaioli, N., La Porta, R., Lopez-de-Silanes, F., & Shleifer, A. (2012). Human capital and regional development. *The Quarterly Journal of Economics*, *128*(1), 105–164. doi:10.1093/qje/qjs050

Geroski, P. A. (1989). Entry, Innovation, and Productivity Growth. *The Review of Economics and Statistics*, *71*(4), 572–578. doi:10.2307/1928098

Glaeser, E., Kerr, W., & Ponzetto, G. (2010). Clusters of Entrepreneurship. *Journal of Urban Economics*, *67*(1), 150–168. doi:10.1016/j.jue.2009.09.008

Guesnier, B. (1994). Regional Variations in New Firm Formation in France. *Regional Studies*, *28*(4), 347–358. doi:10.1080/00343409412331348316

Haltiwanger, J., Jarmin, R. S., & Miranda, J. (2013). Who creates jobs? Small versus large versus young. *The Review of Economics and Statistics*, *95*(2), 347–361. doi:10.1162/REST_a_00288

Huggins, R., & Thompson, P. (2014). Culture, entrepreneurship and uneven development: A spatial analysis. *Entrepreneurship and Regional Development*, *26*(9-10), 726–752. doi:10.1080/08985626.2014.985740

Isenberg, D. (2010). How to start an entrepreneurial revolution. *Harvard Business Review*, *88*(6), 40–50.

Keeble, D., & Walker, S. (1994). New Firms, Small Firms and Dead Firms: Spatial Patterns and Determinants in the United Kingdom. *Regional Studies*, *28*(4), 411–4427. doi:10.1080/00343409412331348366

Krugman, P. (1991a). Increasing returns and economic geography. *Journal of Political Economy*, *99*(3), 483–499. doi:10.1086/261763

Krugman, P. (1991b). History and industry location: The case of the manufacturing belt. *The American Economic Review*, *81*, 80–83.

Malecki, E. J., & Spigel, B. (2017). Innovation and entrepreneurship. In *Elgar companion to innovation and knowledge creation* (pp. 625–637). Edward Elgar. doi:10.4337/9781782548522.00050

Nelder, J. A., & Wedderburn, R. W. M. (1972). Generalized linear models. *Journal of the Royal Statistical Society. Series A (General)*, *135*(3), 370–384. doi:10.2307/2344614

Nickell, S., Nicolitsas, P., & Dryden, N. (1997). What Makes Firms Perform Well? *European Economic Review*, *41*(3-5), 783–796. doi:10.1016/S0014-2921(97)00037-8

Nickell, S. J. (1996). Competition and Corporate Performance. *Journal of Political Economy*, *104*(4), 724–746. doi:10.1086/262040

Pfeiffer, F., & Reize, F. (2000). Business Start-ups by the Unemployed - an Econometric Analysis Based on Firm Data. *Labour Economics*, *7*(5), 629–663. doi:10.1016/S0927-5371(00)00016-6

Samila, S., & Sorenson, O. (2011). Venture capital, entrepreneurship and economic growth. *The Review of Economics and Statistics*, *93*(1), 338–349. doi:10.1162/REST_a_00066

Sauka, A. (2008). *Productive, unproductive and destructive entrepreneurship: A theoretical and empirical exploration*. William Davidson Institute Working Paper Number 917 March 2008. Retrieved from https://econpapers.repec.org/paper/wdipapers/2008-917.htm

Saxenian, A. L. (1994). *Regional Advantage: Culture and Competition in Silicon Valley and Route 128*. Harvard University Press.

Schumpeter, J. A. (1911). The Theory of Economic Development. An Inquiry into Profits, Capital, Credit, Interest, and the Business Cycle (R. Opie, Trans.). Oxford: Oxford University Press. (Original publication 934).

Schumpeter, J. A. (1947). The creative response in economic history. *The Journal of Economic History*, *7*(2), 149–159. doi:10.1017/S0022050700054279

Solow, R. M. (1956). A Contribution to the Theory of Economic Growth. *The Quarterly Journal of Economics*, *70*(1), 65–94. doi:10.2307/1884513

Stel, A. V., Carree, M., & Thurik, R. (2005). The effect of entrepreneurial activity on national economic growth. *Small Business Economics*, *24*(3), 311–321. doi:10.100711187-005-1996-6

Stough, R. R. (2016). Entrepreneurship and regional economic development: Some reflections. *Journal of Regional Research*, *36*, 129–150.

Stough, R. R., Aberman, J., Baycan, K., & Vulto, P. (2013). Knowledge spillovers and commercialization in universities and their regions. In Knowledge Commercialization and Valorization in Regional Economic Development. Cheltenham, UK: Edward Elgar.

Stough, R. R., Welter, F., Block, J., Wennberg, K., & Brasco, R. (2015). Family business and regional science: "Bridging the gap. *Journal of Family Business*, *6*(4), 208–218. doi:10.1016/j.jfbs.2015.11.002

KEY TERMS AND DEFINITIONS

Entrepreneurship: It is the process of designing, launching and running a new business, which often starts as a small business. It can also be described as the capacity and willingness to develop, organize, and manage a venture along with taking risks to earn a profit.

Generalized Linear Models (GLM): It is a flexible generalization of ordinary linear regression (OLS) that allows for the dependent variable to have error distribution models other than a normal distribution.

Metropolitan Statistical Area (MSA): It is a geographical region with a relatively high population density at its core and close economic ties throughout the area. MSAs are defined by the U.S. Office of Management and Budget (OMB), and the MSAs are used by federal government agencies for statistical purposes.

Micropolitan Areas: It is a geographical region in which the labor market and statistical areas in the United States are centered around an urban area with a population of at least 10,000 but fewer than 50,000 people. It is defined by the U.S. Office of Management and Budget (OMB), and they are used by federal government agencies for statistical purposes.

Proprietorship: It is a business model which an individual and his/her company are considered a single entity for tax purposes. A proprietorship is often not registered with the state as a corporation.

Startup Concentrations: It is a very young company founded by one or more entrepreneurs to develop a unique product or service that is introduced to the market. Its initial funding is usually from its own finances or from families and friends.

APPENDIX

Table 8. Population density of the three states

	Population Density (Square Mile)
Pennsylvania	284
Ohio	282.3
West Virginia	77.1

Table 9a. Population repartition of the three states: Pennsylvania

Year	Rural	Rural Growth Rate	Urban	Urban Growth Rate	Total	Population Growth Rate
1980	1,533,365		10,331,355		11,864,720	
1990	1,490,582	-3	10,392,260	1	11,882,842	0
2000	1,519,378	2	10,761,170	4	12,280,548	3
2010	1,510,313	-1	11,192,555	4	12,702,868	3
2019	1,446,887	-4	11,355,102	1	12,801,989	1

Source: 1980, 1990, 2000, 2010 Census of Population, U.S. Census Bureau, U.S. Department of Commerce; Annual Estimates of the Resident Population, April 1, 2010 to July 1, 2019, U.S. Census Bureau, Population Division.

Table 9b. Population repartition of the three states: Ohio

Year	Rural	Rural Growth Rate	Urban	Urban Growth Rate	Total	Population Growth Rate
1980	2,270,083		8,527,520		10,797,603	
1990	2,267,130	0	8,579,985	1	10,847,115	0
2000	2,375,891	5	8,977,445	5	11,353,336	5
2010	2,394,257	1	9,142,494	2	11,536,751	2
2019	2,347,371	-2	9,341,729	2	11,689,100	1

Source: 1980, 1990, 2000, 2010 Census of Population, U.S. Census Bureau, U.S. Department of Commerce; Annual Estimates of the Resident Population, April 1, 2010 to July 1, 2019, U.S. Census Bureau, Population Division.

Table 9c. Population repartition of the three states: West Virginia

Year	Rural	Rural Growth Rate	Urban	Urban Growth Rate	Total	Population Growth Rate
1980	819,286		1,130,900		1,950,186	
1990	737,075	-10	1,056,402	-7	1,793,477	-8
2000	720,506	-2	1,087,687	3	1,808,193	1
2010	720,515	0	1,132,503	4	1,853,018	2
2019	682,651	-5	1,109,496	-2	1,792,147	-3

Source: 1980, 1990, 2000, 2010 Census of Population, U.S. Census Bureau, U.S. Department of Commerce; Annual Estimates of the Resident Population, April 1, 2010 to July 1, 2019, U.S. Census Bureau, Population Division.

Table 10a. Per Capita Income of the three States: Pennsylvania

	Per-capita Income		
	Rural	**Urban**	**Total**
2017	40,225	54,809	53,144
2018	42,463	57,987	56,225
Percent change	5.6	5.8	5.8

Table 10b. Per Capita Income of the three States: Ohio

	Per-capita Income		
	Rural	**Urban**	**Total**
2017	39,898	48,361	46,651
2018	41,806	50,486	48,739
Percent change	4.8	4.4	4.5

Table 10c. Per Capita Income of the three States: West Virginia

	Per-capita Income		
	Rural	**Urban**	**Total**
2017	35,042	40,871	38,644
2018	37,003	43,258	40,873
Percent change	5.6	5.8	5.8

Table 11a. Earnings per job of the three states: Pennsylvania

	Earnings per Job		
2017	47,749	63,118	61,712
2018	49,137	65,023	63,578
Percent change	2.9	3	3

Table 11b. Earnings per job of the three states: Ohio

	Earnings per Job		
2017	48,454	57,319	55,787
2018	50,076	58,826	57,319
Percent change	3.3	2.6	2.7

Table 11c. Earnings per job of the three states: West Virginia

	Earnings per Job		
2017	43,459	51,102	48,532
2018	46,834	53,289	51,099
Percent change	7.8	4.3	5.3

Table 12a. Poverty rates of the three states: Pennsylvania

	Poverty Rate (percent)		
1979	11.5	10.3	10.5
1989	13.6	10.8	11.1
1999	12.1	10.8	11
2018	13.6	12.1	12.2

Source: US Census Bureau, Census poverty measures (1979, 1989, 1999) and 2018 Small Area Income and Poverty Estimates), poverty tables.

Table 12b. Poverty rates of the three states: Ohio

	Poverty Rate (percent)		
1979	10.7	10.2	10.3
1989	13.5	12.3	12.5
1999	10.7	10.6	10.6
2018	13.6	13.9	13.8

Source: US Census Bureau, Census poverty measures (1979, 1989, 1999) and 2018 Small Area Income and Poverty Estimates), poverty tables.

Table 12c. Poverty rates of the three states: West Virginia

	Poverty Rate (percent)		
1979	17.4	13.2	15
1989	23	17.3	19.7
1999	20.3	16.3	17.9
2018	19.3	16.3	17.4

Source: US Census Bureau, Census poverty measures (1979, 1989, 1999) and 2018 Small Area Income and Poverty Estimates), poverty tables.

Table 13a. Education achievement in the three states: Pennsylvania

	Rural	Urban	Total
	Not Completing High School		
1980	38.6	35.3	35.3
1990	28.5	24.9	25.3
2000	20.7	17.7	18.1
2014-2018	11.4	9.6	9.8
	Completing High School Only		
1980	44.3	40.4	40.4
1990	46.7	37.4	38.6
2000	48.2	36.7	38.1
2014-2018	47.1	33.5	35.1
	Completing Some College		
1980	8.5	10.7	10.7
1990	14.3	18.7	18.2
2000	18.2	21.9	21.4
2014-2018	23.6	24.4	24.3
	Completing College		
1980	8.6	13.6	13.6
1990	10.5	19	17.9
2000	12.9	23.7	22.4
2014-2018	17.9	32.5	30.8

Source: U.S. Census Bureau, decennial Census education measures (1980, 1990, 2000) and 2014-18 (5-Year estimates) from the American Community Survey, education tables.

Table 13b. Education achievement in the three states: Ohio

	Rural	Urban	Total
	Not Completing High School		
1980	36.2	33	33
1990	27.6	23.5	24.3
2000	19.5	16.4	17
2014-2018	12.2	9.3	9.9
	Completing High School Only		
1980	44.6	40.5	40.5
1990	43.8	34.4	36.3
2000	45.3	33.7	36.1
2014-2018	43	30.8	33.3
	Completing Some College		
1980	10	12.8	12.8
1990	18.2	23.4	22.4
2000	22.6	26.6	25.8
2014-2018	27.9	29.3	29.1
	Completing College		
1980	9.2	13.7	13.7
1990	10.4	18.7	17
2000	12.6	23.3	21.1
2014-2018	16.9	30.6	27.8

Source: U.S. Census Bureau, decennial Census education measures (1980, 1990, 2000) and 2014-18 (5-Year estimates) from the American Community Survey, education tables.

Table 13c. Education achievement in the three states: West Virginia

	Rural	Urban	Total
	Not Completing High School		
1980	48.7	44	44
1990	38.5	30.9	34
2000	28.7	22.2	24.8
2014-2018	15.9	12	13.5
	Completing High School Only		
1980	34.4	35.6	35.6
1990	37.2	36.2	36.6
2000	41	38.3	39.4
2014-2018	44.3	38.1	40.5
	Completing Some College		
1980	8.5	10	10
1990	14.8	18.6	17
2000	18.8	22.4	21
2014-2018	23.7	27	25.7
	Completing College		
1980	8.4	10.4	10.4
1990	9.5	14.3	12.3
2000	11.5	17.1	14.8
2014-2018	16	22.9	20.3

Source: U.S. Census Bureau, decennial Census education measures (1980, 1990, 2000) and 2014-18 (5-Year estimates) from the American Community Survey, education tables.

Table 14a. Employment and Unemployment in the three States: Pennsylvania

	Rural	Urban	Total
	Employment Change (percent)		
2016-2017	-0.6	0.3	0.2
2017-2018	0.1	0.7	0.6
2018-2019	0.1	1	0.9
	Unemployment Rate (percent)		
2018	4.7	4.2	4.2
2019	5	4.3	4.4

Source: Local Area Personal Income and Employment, Bureau of Economic Analysis, U.S. Department of Commerce; Local Area Personal Income and Employment, Bureau of Economic Analysis, U.S. Department of Commerce.

Table 14b. Employment and Unemployment in the three States: Ohio

	Rural	Urban	Total
	Employment Change (percent)		
2016-2017	0.4	0.7	0.7
2017-2018	-0.1	0.7	0.5
2018-2019	0.6	0.8	0.8
	Unemployment Rate (percent)		
2018	4.7	4.4	4.5
2019	4.4	4	4.1

Source: Local Area Personal Income and Employment, Bureau of Economic Analysis, U.S. Department of Commerce; Local Area Personal Income and Employment, Bureau of Economic Analysis, U.S. Department of Commerce.

Table 14c. Employment and Unemployment in the three States: West Virginia

	Rural	Urban	Total
	Employment Change (percent)		
2016-2017	-0.4	1	0.5
2017-2018	1.4	0.5	0.8
2018-2019	1.2	2.2	1.8
	Unemployment Rate (percent)		
2018	5.7	4.9	5.2
2019	5.7	4.5	4.9

Source: Local Area Personal Income and Employment, Bureau of Economic Analysis, U.S. Department of Commerce; Local Area Personal Income and Employment, Bureau of Economic Analysis, U.S. Department of Commerce.

Related Readings

To continue IGI Global's long-standing tradition of advancing innovation through emerging research, please find below a compiled list of recommended IGI Global book chapters and journal articles in the areas of panel data, economic forecasting, applied economics, econometric analysis, time series, microeconomics, and statistical methods for predicting business and finance. These related readings will provide additional information and guidance to further enrich your knowledge and assist you with your own research.

Abduh, M., & Jamaludin, N. (2020). Baitul Maal wat-Tamwil Services for SMEs: Evidence From Indonesia. In A. Rafay (Ed.), *Handbook of Research on Theory and Practice of Global Islamic Finance* (pp. 259–276). IGI Global. doi:10.4018/978-1-7998-0218-1.ch014

Abubakar, M. (2020). Social Empowerment Through Islamic Finance. In A. Rafay (Ed.), *Handbook of Research on Theory and Practice of Global Islamic Finance* (pp. 115–128). IGI Global. doi:10.4018/978-1-7998-0218-1.ch006

Adžić, S. (2019). Financial Systems Reforms in Western Balkans Countries. In D. Ushakov (Ed.), *Global Trends of Modernization in Budgeting and Finance* (pp. 260–279). IGI Global. doi:10.4018/978-1-5225-7760-7.ch013

Agrawal, G., & Jain, P. (2019). Digital Financial Inclusion in India: A Review. In T. Tripathi, M. Kumar Dash, & G. Agrawal (Eds.), *Behavioral Finance and Decision-Making Models* (pp. 195–203). IGI Global. doi:10.4018/978-1-5225-7399-9.ch011

Agyemang, O. S. (2019). Linking Personal Values to Investment Decisions Among Individual Shareholders in a Developing Economy. In T. Tripathi, M. Kumar Dash, & G. Agrawal (Eds.), *Behavioral Finance and Decision-Making Models* (pp. 24–45). IGI Global. doi:10.4018/978-1-5225-7399-9.ch002

Ahmed, J., Collins, P., & Meera, A. K. (2020). Conditional Currency Convertibility Based on Primary Commodities: The Shari'ah-Compliant Grondona System. In A. Rafay (Ed.), *Handbook of Research on Theory and Practice of Global Islamic Finance* (pp. 61–84). IGI Global. doi:10.4018/978-1-7998-0218-1.ch004

Ahmed, M. U. (2020). Financial Reporting of Islamic Financial Institutions: Comparative Analysis of AAOIFI and IFRS. In A. Rafay (Ed.), *Handbook of Research on Theory and Practice of Global Islamic Finance* (pp. 854–873). IGI Global. doi:10.4018/978-1-7998-0218-1.ch043

Ai, T. H., & Ushakov, D. (2019). Taxation Regime and Macroeconomic Systems' Dynamics. In D. Ushakov (Ed.), *Global Trends of Modernization in Budgeting and Finance* (pp. 225–240). IGI Global. doi:10.4018/978-1-5225-7760-7.ch011

Aksoy, E. E. (2019). Individual Factors Affecting the Participation of Turkish People in the New Individual Pension System. In T. Tripathi, M. Kumar Dash, & G. Agrawal (Eds.), *Behavioral Finance and Decision-Making Models* (pp. 104–116). IGI Global. doi:10.4018/978-1-5225-7399-9.ch006

Al-Malkawi, H. N., Pillai, R., & AlShiab, M. S. (2020). Evaluating Microeconomic Factors, Financial Crisis, and Stock Price Dynamics: Evidence From MENA Region. In L. Farinha, A. B. Cruz, & J. R. Sebastião (Eds.), *Handbook of Research on Accounting and Financial Studies* (pp. 131–153). IGI Global. doi:10.4018/978-1-7998-2136-6.ch007

Ali, B., Terzi, C., Mhadhbi, K., & Fakhri, I. (2019). Theoretical Analysis of the Relationship Between Monopoly's Optimal Tariffs and Consumer Utility. *International Journal of Sustainable Economies Management*, *8*(1), 39–51. doi:10.4018/IJSEM.2019010104

Arora, P. (2012). Financial Performance Measures, Efficiency and Indian Banking: Empirical Evidence. *International Journal of Productivity Management and Assessment Technologies*, *1*(2), 43–56. doi:10.4018/ijpmat.2012040104

Ayhan, F. (2019). The Effects of Political and Economic Risk on FDI: A Theoretical Survey. In D. Ushakov (Ed.), *Global Trends of Modernization in Budgeting and Finance* (pp. 44–63). IGI Global. doi:10.4018/978-1-5225-7760-7.ch003

Ayuk, E. T., Fonta, W. M., & Kouame, E. B. (2014). Application of Quantitative Methods in Natural Resource Management in Africa: A Review. In P. V. Schaeffer & E. Kouassi (Eds.), *Econometric Methods for Analyzing Economic Development* (pp. 205–234). IGI Global. doi:10.4018/978-1-4666-4329-1.ch013

Azevedo, G. M., Oliveira, J. D., Ferreira, A. D., & Dias, S. R. (2019). The Use of Financial Graphics as an Impression Management Tool: Evidence of Portuguese Listed Companies. In J. D. Oliveira, G. M. Azevedo, & A. D. Ferreira (Eds.), *International Financial Reporting Standards and New Directions in Earnings Management* (pp. 239–255). IGI Global. doi:10.4018/978-1-5225-7817-8.ch011

Aziz, S., Md Husin, M., & Ashfaq, M. (2020). Harmonising Microfinance With Islamic Banking. In A. Rafay (Ed.), *Handbook of Research on Theory and Practice of Global Islamic Finance* (pp. 240–258). IGI Global. doi:10.4018/978-1-7998-0218-1.ch013

Baber, H. (2020). Crowdfunding Framework in Islamic Finance. In A. Rafay (Ed.), *Handbook of Research on Theory and Practice of Global Islamic Finance* (pp. 307–320). IGI Global. doi:10.4018/978-1-7998-0218-1.ch017

Berguiga, I., Ben Said, Y., & Adair, P. (2020). Islamic and Conventional Micro-Financing in the MENA Region: A Performance Analysis. In A. Rafay (Ed.), *Handbook of Research on Theory and Practice of Global Islamic Finance* (pp. 216–239). IGI Global. doi:10.4018/978-1-7998-0218-1.ch012

Bieri, D. S. (2014). Regional Structure and Economic Development: Growth Empirics for U.S. Metropolitan Areas. In P. V. Schaeffer & E. Kouassi (Eds.), *Econometric Methods for Analyzing Economic Development* (pp. 153–176). IGI Global. doi:10.4018/978-1-4666-4329-1.ch010

Bozkurt, İ., & Hatipoğlu, M. (2019). Does Parasocial Breakup Affect the Stock Market Returns?: Evidence From an Emerging Market. In T. Tripathi, M. Kumar Dash, & G. Agrawal (Eds.), *Behavioral Finance and Decision-Making Models* (pp. 70–87). IGI Global. doi:10.4018/978-1-5225-7399-9.ch004

Burger, R., & du Plessis, S. (2014). A New Keynesian Phillips Curve for South Africa. In P. V. Schaeffer & E. Kouassi (Eds.), *Econometric Methods for Analyzing Economic Development* (pp. 30–48). IGI Global. doi:10.4018/978-1-4666-4329-1.ch003

Carikci, O., & Ozturk, M. S. (2019). Developments in Earnings Management Practices in the IFRS Perspective: An Application in a Public Company. In J. D. Oliveira, G. M. Azevedo, & A. D. Ferreira (Eds.), *International Financial Reporting Standards and New Directions in Earnings Management* (pp. 274–288). IGI Global. doi:10.4018/978-1-5225-7817-8.ch013

Casciello, R., Caldarelli, A., & Maffei, M. (2019). Earnings Management and Mergers and Acquisitions: Empirical Evidence From Italian-Listed Companies. In J. D. Oliveira, G. M. Azevedo, & A. D. Ferreira (Eds.), *International Financial Reporting Standards and New Directions in Earnings Management* (pp. 77–100). IGI Global. doi:10.4018/978-1-5225-7817-8.ch004

Çelik, S., & Koy, A. (2019). Chicken-Egg Dilemma for the Relationship Between Price and Volume in Borsa Istanbul. In T. Tripathi, M. Kumar Dash, & G. Agrawal (Eds.), *Behavioral Finance and Decision-Making Models* (pp. 46–69). IGI Global. doi:10.4018/978-1-5225-7399-9.ch003

Cerqueira, A. M., & Pereira, C. F. (2019). Earnings Management and Stock Market Reaction. In J. D. Oliveira, G. M. Azevedo, & A. D. Ferreira (Eds.), *International Financial Reporting Standards and New Directions in Earnings Management* (pp. 32–52). IGI Global. doi:10.4018/978-1-5225-7817-8.ch002

Chakraborty, S. (2020). Financial Infrastructure and Economic Growth. In Foreign Direct Investments: Concepts, Methodologies, Tools, and Applications (pp. 329-358). IGI Global. http://doi:10.4018/978-1-7998-2448-0.ch013

Chen, N. (2020). Asset Diversification and Efficiency of Islamic Banks. In A. Rafay (Ed.), *Growth and Emerging Prospects of International Islamic Banking* (pp. 117–140). IGI Global. doi:10.4018/978-1-7998-1611-9.ch007

Chhatoi, B. P., & Sahoo, S. P. (2019). A Review on Role of Macro and Micro Banking Environment on Non-Performing Assets Management. In T. Tripathi, M. Kumar Dash, & G. Agrawal (Eds.), *Behavioral Finance and Decision-Making Models* (pp. 281–294). IGI Global. doi:10.4018/978-1-5225-7399-9.ch016

Choudhury, M. A. (2020). PasarMalam and PasarPaghi: Grassroots Application of Islamic Ontological Methodology. In A. Rafay (Ed.), *Handbook of Research on Theory and Practice of Global Islamic Finance* (pp. 150–160). IGI Global. doi:10.4018/978-1-7998-0218-1.ch008

Čulková, K., Csikósová, A., & Janošková, M. (2019). Financing of International Business Through Private Equity: European Industry Case Study. In D. Ushakov (Ed.), *Global Trends of Modernization in Budgeting and Finance* (pp. 83–109). IGI Global. doi:10.4018/978-1-5225-7760-7.ch005

D'Rosario, M., & Hsieh, C. (2018). Predicting Credit Rating Migration Employing Neural Network Models. *International Journal of Strategic Decision Sciences*, *9*(4), 70–85. doi:10.4018/IJSDS.2018100105

Das, C. P., & Swain, R. K. (2019). Determinants of Market Capitalization in India and Its Impact. In T. Tripathi, M. Kumar Dash, & G. Agrawal (Eds.), *Behavioral Finance and Decision-Making Models* (pp. 163–176). IGI Global. doi:10.4018/978-1-5225-7399-9.ch009

Deji, M. S. O. & Salleh, M. C. (2020). Cash Waqf for Entrepreneurship Development. In Handbook of Research on Theory and Practice of Global Islamic Finance (pp. 290-305). IGI Global. http://doi:10.4018/978-1-7998-0218-1.ch016

Dinç, D. T., Gökmen, A., & Soygür, S. (2018). Fresh Fruit and Vegetable Exportation of Turkey and its Contribution to the Economic Growth. *International Journal of Sustainable Economies Management*, *7*(3), 1–18. doi:10.4018/IJSEM.2018070101

Dokas, I., Giokas, D., & Tsamis, A. (2014). Liquidity Efficiency in the Greek Listed Firms: A Financial Ratio Based on Data Envelopment Analysis. *International Journal of Corporate Finance and Accounting*, *1*(1), 40–59. doi:10.4018/ijcfa.2014010103

Dunn, L., & Dunn, R. (2014). Natural Resources and Welfare: A Study of U.S. States. In P. V. Schaeffer & E. Kouassi (Eds.), *Econometric Methods for Analyzing Economic Development* (pp. 235–261). IGI Global. doi:10.4018/978-1-4666-4329-1.ch014

Erdoğan, S. (2015). The Effect of Capital Structure on Profitability: An Empirical Analysis. In U. Akkucuk (Ed.), *Handbook of Research on Developing Sustainable Value in Economics, Finance, and Marketing* (pp. 307–323). IGI Global. doi:10.4018/978-1-4666-6635-1.ch018

Fauzel, S. (2020). Determinants of Islamic Banking in Africa: An Econometric Analysis. In A. Rafay (Ed.), *Growth and Emerging Prospects of International Islamic Banking* (pp. 174–188). IGI Global. doi:10.4018/978-1-7998-1611-9.ch010

Fiodendji, K., Kamgnia, B. D., & Tanimoune, N. A. (2014). Inflation and Economic Performance in the CFA Franc Zone: Transmission Channels and Threshold Effects. In P. V. Schaeffer & E. Kouassi (Eds.), *Econometric Methods for Analyzing Economic Development* (pp. 10–29). IGI Global. doi:10.4018/978-1-4666-4329-1.ch002

Franc, S., & Hladika, M. (2020). Appropriateness of Standard Accounting Tools in Measuring Social Innovation in the New Global Economy. In U. Akkucuk (Ed.), *Handbook of Research on Creating Sustainable Value in the Global Economy* (pp. 332–348). IGI Global. doi:10.4018/978-1-7998-1196-1.ch019

Gazel, S. (2019). The Effects of Macroprudential Policies on Financial Stability in Developing Countries. In A. Behl & S. Nayak (Eds.), *Maintaining Financial Stability in Times of Risk and Uncertainty* (pp. 92–114). IGI Global. doi:10.4018/978-1-5225-7208-4.ch005

Georgantopoulos, A. G., Filos, I., & Poutos, E. I. (2018). Banks, Stock Markets, and Growth Relationships in the EU28 Countries. In C. Zopounidis, A. G. Christopoulos, & P. Kalantonis (Eds.), *Perspectives, Trends, and Applications in Corporate Finance and Accounting* (pp. 129–161). IGI Global. doi:10.4018/978-1-5225-6114-9.ch006

Ghosh, I., & Chakrabarti, S. (2016). Inward and Outward Foreign Investments of the Asian Economies in Transition and India: Determinants of FDI and India's Prospects in CLMV. In V. Erokhin (Ed.), *Global Perspectives on Trade Integration and Economies in Transition* (pp. 212–237). IGI Global. doi:10.4018/978-1-5225-0451-1.ch011

Güngör, S., Demirel, E., & Küçün, N. T. (2019). Personality and Emotional Biases. In T. Tripathi, M. Kumar Dash, & G. Agrawal (Eds.), *Behavioral Finance and Decision-Making Models* (pp. 139–161). IGI Global. doi:10.4018/978-1-5225-7399-9.ch008

Ha, L., & Forgionne, G. (2006). Econometric Simulation for E-Business Strategy Evaluation. *International Journal of E-Business Research*, *2*(2), 38–53. doi:10.4018/jebr.2006040103

Hailu, Y. G., Adelaja, A., Akaeze, H., & Hanson, S. (2014). Explaining International Land Transactions in Africa. In P. V. Schaeffer & E. Kouassi (Eds.), *Econometric Methods for Analyzing Economic Development* (pp. 111–130). IGI Global. doi:10.4018/978-1-4666-4329-1.ch008

Hasan, Z. (2020). Risk and Islamic Finance: A Misconception Corrected. In A. Rafay (Ed.), *Handbook of Research on Theory and Practice of Global Islamic Finance* (pp. 441–454). IGI Global. doi:10.4018/978-1-7998-0218-1.ch024

Holynskyy, Y., & Onyusheva, I. (2019). The Impact of Budget and Fiscal Policy on Entrepreneurial Activity and Country's Competitiveness: The Case of Ukraine. In D. Ushakov (Ed.), *Global Trends of Modernization in Budgeting and Finance* (pp. 280–298). IGI Global. doi:10.4018/978-1-5225-7760-7.ch014

Ibrahim, A. R., & Ashafa, S. A. (2020). Zakat Distribution in the Context of Shari'ah Corporate Governance: Evidence From South-Western Nigeria. In A. Rafay (Ed.), *Handbook of Research on Theory and Practice of Global Islamic Finance* (pp. 161–178). IGI Global. doi:10.4018/978-1-7998-0218-1.ch009

Ibrahim, B. E. (2020). Interest-Free Micro-Finance Without Any Religious Connotation: An Inclusive Global Model. In A. Rafay (Ed.), *Handbook of Research on Theory and Practice of Global Islamic Finance* (pp. 196–215). IGI Global. doi:10.4018/978-1-7998-0218-1.ch011

Iyengar, V., & Bharathi, S. V. (2018). Bibliometric Analysis of Lean, Agile, and Leagile Supply Chains in Automobile Industry (1990 - 2017). *International Journal of Information Systems and Supply Chain Management, 11*(3), 22–45. doi:10.4018/IJISSCM.2018070102

Jackson, R. W., & Court, C. D. (2014). Embedding New Technologies and Extending Time Horizons in Input-Output Analysis. In P. V. Schaeffer & E. Kouassi (Eds.), *Econometric Methods for Analyzing Economic Development* (pp. 192–204). IGI Global. doi:10.4018/978-1-4666-4329-1.ch012

Katsampoxakis, I., Basdekis, H., & Anathreptakis, K. (2018). How the Greek Crisis Determined Firm Profitability and Optimal Debt Ratio. In C. Zopounidis, A. G. Christopoulos, & P. Kalantonis (Eds.), *Perspectives, Trends, and Applications in Corporate Finance and Accounting* (pp. 1–31). IGI Global. doi:10.4018/978-1-5225-6114-9.ch001

Kazakova, N., & Sivkova, A. (2019). Financial Security of Economic Activity: Analysis, Control, Risk Management. In D. Ushakov (Ed.), *Global Trends of Modernization in Budgeting and Finance* (pp. 110–130). IGI Global. doi:10.4018/978-1-5225-7760-7.ch006

Kazi, R. R. (2020). Dual Legal Framework in Islamic Capital Markets: Issues and Problems. In A. Rafay (Ed.), *Handbook of Research on Theory and Practice of Global Islamic Finance* (pp. 524–546). IGI Global. doi:10.4018/978-1-7998-0218-1.ch028

Kchouri, B., & Lehnert, T. (2020). Islamic Banking and Economic Growth. In A. Rafay (Ed.), *Handbook of Research on Theory and Practice of Global Islamic Finance* (pp. 86–114). IGI Global. doi:10.4018/978-1-7998-0218-1.ch005

Keri, I., Gromova, E., & Sinelschikova, N. (2019). Features of Financial Policy Development by Russian Companies in Today's Conditions. In D. Ushakov (Ed.), *Global Trends of Modernization in Budgeting and Finance* (pp. 64–82). IGI Global. doi:10.4018/978-1-5225-7760-7.ch004

Keswani, S. (2019). Emotional Finance Plays an Important Role in Investment Decisions. In T. Tripathi, M. Kumar Dash, & G. Agrawal (Eds.), *Behavioral Finance and Decision-Making Models* (pp. 89–103). IGI Global. doi:10.4018/978-1-5225-7399-9.ch005

Khairiree, K., & Ushakov, D. (2019). Budgeting Administration and Economic Growth Dynamics in Conditions of National Markets' Integration. In D. Ushakov (Ed.), *Global Trends of Modernization in Budgeting and Finance* (pp. 1–21). IGI Global. doi:10.4018/978-1-5225-7760-7.ch001

Kia, A. (2020). Positive Interest Rate, Stationary Economy, and Inefficiency. In A. Rafay (Ed.), *Handbook of Research on Theory and Practice of Global Islamic Finance* (pp. 1–17). IGI Global. doi:10.4018/978-1-7998-0218-1.ch001

Kollias, I. (2014). Optimal Control Indicators for the Assessment of the Influence of Approximate Optimal Feedback in the Baseline RBC Model. *International Journal of Sustainable Economies Management*, *3*(1), 1–15. doi:10.4018/ijsem.2014010101

Köseoğlu, S. D. (2019). Behavioral Finance vs. Traditional Finance. In Behavioral Finance and Decision-Making Models (pp. 1-23). IGI Global. http://doi:10.4018/978-1-5225-7399-9.ch001

Lipovetsky, S. (2018). MaxDiff Choice Probability Estimations on Aggregate and Individual Level. *International Journal of Business Analytics*, *5*(1), 55–69. doi:10.4018/IJBAN.2018010104

Lipovetsky, S., & Conklin, W. M. (2019). Choice Models Adjusted to Non-Available Items and Network Effects. *International Journal of Business Analytics*, *6*(1), 1–19. doi:10.4018/IJBAN.2019010101

Malikov, A. (2020). Sukuk as an Infrastructure-Financing Tool. In A. Rafay (Ed.), *Handbook of Research on Theory and Practice of Global Islamic Finance* (pp. 770–787). IGI Global. doi:10.4018/978-1-7998-0218-1.ch039

Manzoor, A. (2016). Early Warning System for Financial Crises. In Q. Munir (Ed.), *Handbook of Research on Financial and Banking Crisis Prediction through Early Warning Systems* (pp. 22–45). IGI Global. doi:10.4018/978-1-4666-9484-2.ch002

Mariia, E. (2019). Financing at the Housing Market: Analysis of Best Practices in the Selected Countries. In D. Ushakov (Ed.), *Global Trends of Modernization in Budgeting and Finance* (pp. 131–150). IGI Global. doi:10.4018/978-1-5225-7760-7.ch007

Md Husin, M., & Haron, R. (2020). Financial Sustainability of SMEs Through Islamic Crowdfunding. In A. Rafay (Ed.), *Handbook of Research on Theory and Practice of Global Islamic Finance* (pp. 321–337). IGI Global. doi:10.4018/978-1-7998-0218-1.ch018

Mduma, J. K. (2014). Point Density Estimation of Changes in Income Polarization in Tanzania, 1992–2001. In P. V. Schaeffer & E. Kouassi (Eds.), *Econometric Methods for Analyzing Economic Development* (pp. 50–65). IGI Global. doi:10.4018/978-1-4666-4329-1.ch004

Megaravalli, A. V. (2019). Macroeconomics and Its Impact on Stock Markets of India, China, and Japan: ASIAN Markets. In Behavioral Finance and Decision-Making Models (pp. 177-194). IGI Global. http://doi:10.4018/978-1-5225-7399-9.ch010

Mendes, C. A., Rodrigues, L. L., & Parte, L. (2019). An Overall Perspective of Income Smoothing as a Strategy of Earnings Management. In J. D. Oliveira, G. M. Azevedo, & A. D. Ferreira (Eds.), *International Financial Reporting Standards and New Directions in Earnings Management* (pp. 53–76). IGI Global. doi:10.4018/978-1-5225-7817-8.ch003

Michieka, N. M. (2014). Population Dynamics, Economic Growth, and Energy Consumption in Kenya. In P. V. Schaeffer & E. Kouassi (Eds.), *Econometric Methods for Analyzing Economic Development* (pp. 178–191). IGI Global. doi:10.4018/978-1-4666-4329-1.ch011

Miranda, M. C. (2020). Extremal Index Estimation: Application to Financial Data. In L. Farinha, A. B. Cruz, & J. R. Sebastião (Eds.), *Handbook of Research on Accounting and Financial Studies* (pp. 96–130). IGI Global. doi:10.4018/978-1-7998-2136-6.ch006

Mishra, S., & Bansal, R. (2019). Credit Rating and Its Interaction With Financial Ratios: A Study of BSE 500 Companies. In T. Tripathi, M. Kumar Dash, & G. Agrawal (Eds.), *Behavioral Finance and Decision-Making Models* (pp. 251–268). IGI Global. doi:10.4018/978-1-5225-7399-9.ch014

Mohamed, H. B., & Mat Sari, N. (2020). Artificial Intelligence and Blockchain-Driven Islamic Capital Markets. In A. Rafay (Ed.), *Handbook of Research on Theory and Practice of Global Islamic Finance* (pp. 874–888). IGI Global. doi:10.4018/978-1-7998-0218-1.ch044

Mukherjee, S., & Das, R. C. (2019). Reflections on Microfinance: Poverty Nexus From India – An Empirical Inquest. In R. C. Das (Ed.), *Handbook of Research on Microfinancial Impacts on Women Empowerment, Poverty, and Inequality* (pp. 188–207). IGI Global. doi:10.4018/978-1-5225-5240-6.ch009

Mukherjee, S., & Karmakar, A. K. (2019). A Tri-Variate Nexus of Microfinance-Growth-Inequality: The South-Asian Experience. In R. C. Das (Ed.), *Handbook of Research on Microfinancial Impacts on Women Empowerment, Poverty, and Inequality* (pp. 247–265). IGI Global. doi:10.4018/978-1-5225-5240-6.ch012

Mulatinho, C. E., Pereira, D. M., Monteiro, J. A., Leal, L. A., Pederneiras, M. M., Ribeiro, M. V., & Amaro, R. G. (2019). Convergence of Accounting Standards to International Standards and Earnings Management in Brazilian Companies. In J. D. Oliveira, G. M. Azevedo, & A. D. Ferreira (Eds.), *International Financial Reporting Standards and New Directions in Earnings Management* (pp. 256–273). IGI Global. doi:10.4018/978-1-5225-7817-8.ch012

Muriithi, M. K., & Mwabu, G. (2014). Demand for Health Care in Kenya: The Effects of Information about Quality. In P. V. Schaeffer & E. Kouassi (Eds.), *Econometric Methods for Analyzing Economic Development* (pp. 102–110). IGI Global. doi:10.4018/978-1-4666-4329-1.ch007

N'Guessan, C. F. (2014). Asymmetric Equilibrium Adjustment between Employment and Economic Growth in Côte d'Ivoire: A Consistent Momentum Threshold Autoregressive Model. In P. V. Schaeffer & E. Kouassi (Eds.), *Econometric Methods for Analyzing Economic Development* (pp. 1–9). IGI Global. doi:10.4018/978-1-4666-4329-1.ch001

Nadezhda, K., Elena, D., & Larisa, Z. (2019). Financial Behavior of Russian Population under Crisis Phenomena. In D. Ushakov (Ed.), *Global Trends of Modernization in Budgeting and Finance* (pp. 22–43). IGI Global. doi:10.4018/978-1-5225-7760-7.ch002

Naser, H. (2020). The Economic and Environmental Impact of Large Financial Developments in an Oil-Dependent Economy: The Case of Bahrain. In U. Akkucuk (Ed.), *Handbook of Research on Creating Sustainable Value in the Global Economy* (pp. 221–240). IGI Global. doi:10.4018/978-1-7998-1196-1.ch013

Nasir, M. A. (2020). The Relevance of Maqasid al Shari'ah to Anti-Money Laundering and Terrorism Financing. In A. Rafay (Ed.), *Handbook of Research on Theory and Practice of Global Islamic Finance* (pp. 179–194). IGI Global. doi:10.4018/978-1-7998-0218-1.ch010

Nembua, C. C. (2014). Measuring and Explaining Economic Inequality: An Extension of the Gini Coefficient. In P. V. Schaeffer & E. Kouassi (Eds.), *Econometric Methods for Analyzing Economic Development* (pp. 87–101). IGI Global. doi:10.4018/978-1-4666-4329-1.ch006

Ng, W. L. (2013). Improving Long-Term Financial Risk Forecasts using High-Frequency Data and Scaling Laws. In B. Alexandrova-Kabadjova, S. Martinez-Jaramillo, A. L. Garcia-Almanza, & E. Tsang (Eds.), *Simulation in Computational Finance and Economics: Tools and Emerging Applications* (pp. 255–278). IGI Global. doi:10.4018/978-1-4666-2011-7.ch013

Nkoro, E., & Uko, A. K. (2014). Impact of the Volatility of Macroeconomic Variables on the Volatility of Stock Market Returns: Nigeria's Experience. In H. Dinçer & Ü. Hacioğlu (Eds.), *Global Strategies in Banking and Finance* (pp. 218–230). IGI Global. doi:10.4018/978-1-4666-4635-3.ch014

Nogueira, M. F. (2019). The Relationship Between the Quality of Financial Information in Industrial Companies and Discretionary Inventory Management. In J. D. Oliveira, G. M. Azevedo, & A. D. Ferreira (Eds.), *International Financial Reporting Standards and New Directions in Earnings Management* (pp. 179–198). IGI Global. doi:10.4018/978-1-5225-7817-8.ch008

Nondo, C., Kahsai, M. S., & Schaeffer, P. V. (2014). The Role of Governance in Teledensity and Economic Growth: GMM Estimation. In P. V. Schaeffer & E. Kouassi (Eds.), *Econometric Methods for Analyzing Economic Development* (pp. 262–278). IGI Global. doi:10.4018/978-1-4666-4329-1.ch015

Oliveira, J. D., Azevedo, G. M., Ferreira, A. D., Martins, S. P., & Pinto, C. R. (2019). Determinants of the Readability and Comprehensibility of Risk Disclosures: Evidence From Portuguese Listed Companies. In J. D. Oliveira, G. M. Azevedo, & A. D. Ferreira (Eds.), *International Financial Reporting Standards and New Directions in Earnings Management* (pp. 216–238). IGI Global. doi:10.4018/978-1-5225-7817-8.ch010

Oliveira, J. D., Azevedo, G. M., Pinheiro, S. F., & Borges, M. F. (2019). Impression Management Strategies in the Chairmen's Statements: Evidence From the Portuguese Banking Industry. In J. D. Oliveira, G. M. Azevedo, & A. D. Ferreira (Eds.), *International Financial Reporting Standards and New Directions in Earnings Management* (pp. 199–215). IGI Global. doi:10.4018/978-1-5225-7817-8.ch009

Ostovskaya, A., & Pavlenko, I. (2019). Financial Instruments of Regional Economic Policy Implementation. In D. Ushakov (Ed.), *Global Trends of Modernization in Budgeting and Finance* (pp. 177–206). IGI Global. doi:10.4018/978-1-5225-7760-7.ch009

Oyekale, A. S., Adeoti, A. I., & Oyekale, T. O. (2014). Sources of Income Inequality in Nigeria: Decomposition Approaches. In P. V. Schaeffer & E. Kouassi (Eds.), *Econometric Methods for Analyzing Economic Development* (pp. 66–86). IGI Global. doi:10.4018/978-1-4666-4329-1.ch005

Paiva, I. S., & Dias, P. V. (2019). Earnings Management and Audit in Private Firms: The Effect of Financial Recuperation. In J. D. Oliveira, G. M. Azevedo, & A. D. Ferreira (Eds.), *International Financial Reporting Standards and New Directions in Earnings Management* (pp. 154–178). IGI Global. doi:10.4018/978-1-5225-7817-8.ch007

Pamuncak, M. B., Possumah, B. T., & Halim, Z. A. (2020). Integrating Zakat and Microfinance: A Proposed Framework. In A. Rafay (Ed.), *Handbook of Research on Theory and Practice of Global Islamic Finance* (pp. 277–289). IGI Global. doi:10.4018/978-1-7998-0218-1.ch015

Patlasov, O. Y., & Mzhelskaya, O. K. (2019). Scoring Modeling in Estimating the Financial Condition of Russian Agro-Industrial Companies. In D. Ushakov (Ed.), *Global Trends of Modernization in Budgeting and Finance* (pp. 151–175). IGI Global. doi:10.4018/978-1-5225-7760-7.ch008

Patra, S. (2018). Determinants of Participation and Impact of Microfinance: An Econometric Analysis. In R. C. Das (Ed.), *Microfinance and Its Impact on Entrepreneurial Development, Sustainability, and Inclusive Growth* (pp. 156–184). IGI Global. doi:10.4018/978-1-5225-5213-0.ch009

Pimentel, L. M., & Jorge, S. M. (2019). Earnings Quality and Firm Valuation: A "New" Perspective Deriving From the Literature. In J. D. Oliveira, G. M. Azevedo, & A. D. Ferreira (Eds.), *International Financial Reporting Standards and New Directions in Earnings Management* (pp. 1–31). IGI Global. doi:10.4018/978-1-5225-7817-8.ch001

Plaku, D., & Hysa, E. (2019). The Impact of Tax Policies on Behavior of Albanian Taxpayers. In T. Tripathi, M. Kumar Dash, & G. Agrawal (Eds.), *Behavioral Finance and Decision-Making Models* (pp. 219–250). IGI Global. doi:10.4018/978-1-5225-7399-9.ch013

Rab, H. (2020). Money and Monetary Issues in Islamic Finance. In A. Rafay (Ed.), *Handbook of Research on Theory and Practice of Global Islamic Finance* (pp. 38–60). IGI Global. doi:10.4018/978-1-7998-0218-1.ch003

Rabatinová, M., Válek, J., & Kušnírová, J. (2019). Taxation System in Slovakia: National Featues and Prospects of Integration. In D. Ushakov (Ed.), *Global Trends of Modernization in Budgeting and Finance* (pp. 207–224). IGI Global. doi:10.4018/978-1-5225-7760-7.ch010

Rassool, N. H. (2020). Innovation in Takaful: The Musharakataan Business Model. In A. Rafay (Ed.), *Handbook of Research on Theory and Practice of Global Islamic Finance* (pp. 623–641). IGI Global. doi:10.4018/978-1-7998-0218-1.ch032

Rodríguez-Gulías, M. J., Fernández-López, S., Rodeiro-Pazos, D., Faria, A. P., & Barbosa, N. (2020). Effect of Venture Capital on the Growth of Information and Communication Technology University Spin-Offs: Venture Capital Effect on the Growth of ICT-USOs. In B. Álvarez-García & J. Abeal-Vázquez (Eds.), *Emerging Tools and Strategies for Financial Management* (pp. 82–105). IGI Global. doi:10.4018/978-1-7998-2440-4.ch004

Sengupta, A., & Glavin, S. E. (2013). Predicting Volatile Consumer Markets using Multi-Agent Methods: Theory and Validation. In B. Alexandrova-Kabadjova, S. Martinez-Jaramillo, A. L. Garcia-Almanza, & E. Tsang (Eds.), *Simpulation in Computational Finance and Economics: Tools and Emerging Applications* (pp. 339–358). IGI Global. doi:10.4018/978-1-4666-2011-7.ch016

Shaikh, I. M., & Noordin, K. (2020). An Analysis of Determinants to Choose Family Takaful. In A. Rafay (Ed.), *Handbook of Research on Theory and Practice of Global Islamic Finance* (pp. 642–662). IGI Global. doi:10.4018/978-1-7998-0218-1.ch033

Sharmiladevi, J. C. (2020). Cointegration and Causality Study Among Inward FDI, Economic Growth and Exports: An Indian Perspective. *International Journal of Asian Business and Information Management*, *11*(1), 63–77. doi:10.4018/IJABIM.2020010104

Singh, R. (2014). *A Survey of Economic Growth*. IGI Global. doi:10.4018/978-1-4666-5848-6.ch004

Singh, R. (2014). *Analysis of Trade-Growth Nexus*. IGI Global. doi:10.4018/978-1-4666-5848-6.ch009

Singh, R. (2014). *Comparative Analysis and Robustness Tests*. IGI Global. doi:10.4018/978-1-4666-5848-6.ch008

Singh, R. (2014). *East Asian Growth Controversy*. IGI Global. doi:10.4018/978-1-4666-5848-6.ch003

Singh, R. (2014). *Growth Accounts of the Asian Economies*. IGI Global. doi:10.4018/978-1-4666-5848-6.ch006

Singh, R. (2014). *Growth Experiences of the Asian Economies*. IGI Global. doi:10.4018/978-1-4666-5848-6.ch002

Singh, R. (2014). *New Method New Estimates*. IGI Global. doi:10.4018/978-1-4666-5848-6.ch007

Singh, R. (2014). *Overview of Global Development Patterns*. IGI Global. doi:10.4018/978-1-4666-5848-6.ch001

Singh, R. (2014). *The Empirical Growth Literature*. IGI Global. doi:10.4018/978-1-4666-5848-6.ch005

Singh, V. V., Pandey, M., & Vashisht, A. (2019). Employees Perception Regarding CSR Initiatives of the Companies in India. In T. Tripathi, M. Kumar Dash, & G. Agrawal (Eds.), *Behavioral Finance and Decision-Making Models* (pp. 204–217). IGI Global. doi:10.4018/978-1-5225-7399-9.ch012

Sinha, M., & Sengupta, P. P. (2017). FDI and Trade in Services Towards Sustainable Economic Growth: An Empirical Evidence from India. *International Journal of Sustainable Economies Management*, *6*(1), 22–33. doi:10.4018/ijsem.2017010102

Sohail, H., & Arshed, N. (2020). Cost-Efficiency Analysis of Mudarabah Companies. In A. Rafay (Ed.), *Handbook of Research on Theory and Practice of Global Islamic Finance* (pp. 568–592). IGI Global. doi:10.4018/978-1-7998-0218-1.ch030

Sousa, A., Góis, C. G., & Viseu, C. (2019). Earnings Management in SMEs: Evidence From Portugal and Spain. In J. D. Oliveira, G. M. Azevedo, & A. D. Ferreira (Eds.), *International Financial Reporting Standards and New Directions in Earnings Management* (pp. 101–126). IGI Global. doi:10.4018/978-1-5225-7817-8.ch005

Spaseski, N. (2018). *Fractal and Wavelet Market Analysis in Pattern Recognition*. IGI Global. doi:10.4018/978-1-5225-3259-0.ch007

Spulbar, C., & Birau, R. (2019). *Estimating Long-Term Volatility on National Stock Exchange of India*. IGI Global. doi:10.4018/978-1-5225-9269-3.ch011

Spulbar, C., & Birau, R. (2019). *Financial Nexus: Efficiency and Soundness in Banking and Capital Markets*. IGI Global. doi:10.4018/978-1-5225-9269-3.ch004

Spulbar, C., & Birau, R. (2019). *Investigating Long-Term Behavior of Milan Stock Exchange*. IGI Global. doi:10.4018/978-1-5225-9269-3.ch017

Suprijanto, T. (2020). The Role of Profit Rate in Islamic Monetary Policy. In A. Rafay (Ed.), *Handbook of Research on Theory and Practice of Global Islamic Finance* (pp. 18–37). IGI Global. doi:10.4018/978-1-7998-0218-1.ch002

Szczerbicki, E., & Waszczyk, M. (2006). Modelling of Complex Economic Systems: Toward Conceptual Platform. *International Journal of Enterprise Information Systems*, *2*(1), 67–78. doi:10.4018/jeis.2006010105

Tomar, D. S., & Tomar, R. S. (2019). Comparative Analysis of Service Quality Perception Between Public Sector and Private Sector Banks of India. In T. Tripathi, M. Kumar Dash, & G. Agrawal (Eds.), *Behavioral Finance and Decision-Making Models* (pp. 117–138). IGI Global. doi:10.4018/978-1-5225-7399-9.ch007

Triantafyllou, A. (2020). Investing in Commodities in Times of Uncertainty and Lax Monetary Policy. In C. Zopounidis, D. Kenourgios, & G. Dotsis (Eds.), *Recent Advances and Applications in Alternative Investments* (pp. 1–36). IGI Global. doi:10.4018/978-1-7998-2436-7.ch001

Tripathi, T., & Dash, M. K. (2019). An Impact Assessment of Goods and Services Tax in India Through Strategic Analysis Approach (SAA). In T. Tripathi, M. Kumar Dash, & G. Agrawal (Eds.), *Behavioral Finance and Decision-Making Models* (pp. 269–280). IGI Global. doi:10.4018/978-1-5225-7399-9.ch015

Vieira, E., & Madaleno, M. (2019). Earnings Management and Corporate Governance in Family Firms: Evidence From a Small Market. In J. D. Oliveira, G. M. Azevedo, & A. D. Ferreira (Eds.), *International Financial Reporting Standards and New Directions in Earnings Management* (pp. 127–153). IGI Global. doi:10.4018/978-1-5225-7817-8.ch006

Wajeetongratana, P. (2019). Environmental Accounting Implementation and Stimulation of National Business Global Competitiveness: The Case of Thailand. In D. Ushakov (Ed.), *Global Trends of Modernization in Budgeting and Finance* (pp. 299–324). IGI Global. doi:10.4018/978-1-5225-7760-7.ch015

Wan Jusoh, W. N. (2020). Corporate Social Responsibility: Conventional and Islamic Perspectives. In A. Rafay (Ed.), *Handbook of Research on Theory and Practice of Global Islamic Finance* (pp. 129–149). IGI Global. doi:10.4018/978-1-7998-0218-1.ch007

West, G. R., & Jackson, R. W. (2014). Simulating Impacts on Regional Economies: A Modeling Alternative. In P. V. Schaeffer & E. Kouassi (Eds.), *Econometric Methods for Analyzing Economic Development* (pp. 132–152). IGI Global. doi:10.4018/978-1-4666-4329-1.ch009

Zeldner, A., Osipov, V., & Skryl, T. (2019). Model of Socioeconomic Development Based on Market Economy and Public-Private Partnership (PPP) Mechanism: Key Approaches and Terms for Implementation. In D. Ushakov (Ed.), *Global Trends of Modernization in Budgeting and Finance* (pp. 241–259). IGI Global. doi:10.4018/978-1-5225-7760-7.ch012

About the Contributors

Oluwasogo Adediran is article editor for SAGE Publications and reviewer for International Business Information Management Association (IBIMA) conferences which are indexed in Web of Science and Scopus. Currently in a series of research which has resulted in publications in high impact and world-class Journals locally and internationally and has participated in seminars, conferences, workshops and short courses. Astute in research in the area of International Economics, Macroeconomics, Applied Econometrics, Financial Economics, Development Economics and Sustainable Development Goals (SDGs).He is visible on ResearchGate, Google Scholar and Scopus Page. In addition, he is a member of Nigeria Institute of Management and a student-member of Chartered Institute of Stockbrokers. Presently a member of Faculty at Covenant University in the Department of Economics and Development Studies, where he involves in community service, research, teaching and mentoring both undergraduate and postgraduate students.

Philip O. Alege is a Professor of Economics and currently serving as the Dean of College of Business and Social Sciences, Covenant University, Ota-Nigeria. He has Teaching and Supervision experiences both at Covenant University and at Obafemi Awolowo University, Ile-Ife spanning over two decades. He is a Visiting Professor to CPEEL, University of Ibadan, Ibadan. He has published papers in International and Local Journals in the areas of Dynamic Macroeconomic Modelling, Econometrics, International Trade, Renewable Energy and Economic Growth. He has experience in the private sector of the economy as a management consultant. Prof. Alege is well travelled across the world attending Workshops/Training progammes and Conferences. He is visible on ResearchGate, Scival, Google and Scopus Page. He is bilingual with fluency in English and French.

Abdul-Wakeel Alhassan is a postgraduate researcher at the School of Economics, University of Cape Coast, Ghana. He started researching when he served as a Research Assistant for Educational Network for West And Central Africa (ENWACA), in May – June 2009. He had his first degree in Economics, MSc. Economics of

Technology and Development as well as Master of Philosophy in Economics all from the University of Cape Coast, Ghana. Alhassan A. Karakara has published some articles in peer review journals with other several articles co-authored with Prof. Evans Osabuohien which are under peer review in various Journals. He has served as a discussant and presenter in international conferences across the African Continent. He was a panel in the African Innovation Summit II, in Kigali Rwanda in June 2018. His research interests include poverty, economics of innovation and technology, development economics, and international trade with emphasis on developing economies.

Özcan Ceylan obtained his B.A. in Economics from Galatasaray University (Istanbul) in 2005. He then earned his M.A. in Economics in 2006 and Ph.D. in Economics in 2011, both from Université Paris Ouest Nanterre La Défense. He is currently a faculty member in the School of Applied Sciences in Özyeğin University. His research focuses on behavioral finance and financial asset pricing.

Patrick Edwards, a 2017 graduate of Indiana University of Pennsylvania, with a dual degree in Economics and Political Science, Patrick has worked for former Congressman Dennis Kucinich. While working as a political activist and volunteer, Patrick is also working toward his Bachelor in Psychology from the University of Dayton with the ultimate goal of obtaining a Ph.D.

Kayla Good holds Bachelor of Arts degrees in both Economics and Spanish from the Indiana University of Pennsylvania. She completed her undergraduate studies in 2018 and is pursuing a Master of Public Policy at the University of Maryland, College Park.

Olivia Habacivch has earned her B.A. in Economics and in Criminology from Indiana University of Pennsylvania. She has also earned her Master of Urban Education degree from Union University and is currently a history educator in Memphis City Schools in Tennessee. She has used econometrics to help explain the unemployment-crime relationship and discover crime rate convergence.

James J. Jozefowicz is a professor in the Department of Economics at Indiana University of Pennsylvania (IUP), where he has taught since 1999. Dr. Jozefowicz received the IUP University Senate Distinguished Faculty Award for Teaching in 2005 and the IUP Award of Excellence in Volunteer Leadership for Advancement Support in 2020. In 2012, Dr. Jozefowicz was one of fourteen economics professors selected for inclusion in the Princeton Review's "Best 300 Professors", a guide recognizing top professors in the nation. Dr. Jozefowicz teaches Introduction to

Econometrics and Advanced Econometrics as part of the honors track in economics, and he has supervised in excess of 70 honors theses. Dr. Jozefowicz's research interests include economics of crime, economics of religion, economic education, and movie economics. He has published nearly twenty articles in refereed journals such as Applied Economics, Atlantic Economic Journal, Economics Bulletin, Journal of Economic Education, and Journal for the Scientific Study of Religion. The majority of these journal articles have been co-authored with IUP undergraduate students. Dr. Jozefowicz is an Ex-Officio member of the Pennsylvania Economic Association (PEA) Board of Directors, and he previously served two terms as the president of the PEA.

Kasım Kiracı completed his undergraduate education in Aviation Management at Kocaeli University and Economics at Anadolu University. He completed his master's degree in Anadolu University Aviation Management. He completed his second master's degree in Economics at Gebze Institute of Technology. He received his doctorate in Anadolu University's Aviation Management field in 2017. He has been working as a faculty member at the Department of Aviation Management at İskenderun Technical University since 2018. Kasım Kiracı has many articles published in international scientific refereed journals on aviation economy and airline financing. In addition, there are many book chapters published on different topics of aviation.

Anthony Maticic is a 2019 graduate of the Indiana University of Pennsylvania holding a Bachelor of Science in accounting and a Bachelor of Arts in economics.

Hannah Mercer, a 2017 graduate of Indiana University of Pennsylvania, with a dual degree in Economics and Marketing, now works full-time as a data analyst for Thermo Fisher Scientific. While working in the scientific industry, Hannah is also working towards her MS in Economics from Purdue University with a specialization in business/data analytics. During her time at Indiana University of Pennsylvania, Hannah was a four year starter on the NCAA intercollegiate softball team where her passion to study gender inequality in the world of sports began.

Evans Osabuohien is a Professor of Economics at Covenant University, Ota, Nigeria. He has executed funded research projects as an individual, team leader, and team member. He is astute in research, which has resulted in the publication of over 110 scholarly articles and has participation in conferences/workshops/short courses across the world. He was appointed as the Head of Department (HOD) in 2016, emerging as the Youngest HOD in the University. He received a Double Promotion to the Rank of a Full Professor of Economics in December 2017, which made him the Youngest Professor in the University. In May 2020, he was recognised as 'One of the 6 Youngest Professors Nigeria Ever Had'. He is the Pioneer Chair, Centre for Economic Policy and Development Research (CEPDeR) as well as the Pioneer Chair, Regional Centre of Expertise, Ogun State (RCE Ogun). He is an Alexander von Humboldt Visiting Professor at Witten/Herdecke University, Germany, and also a Visiting Scholar at University of Economics Ho Chi Minh City, Vietnam. He is the Editor of 'Handbook of Research on In-Country Determinants and Implications of Foreign Land Acquisitions' (2015) and 'The Palgrave Handbook of Agricultural and Rural Development in Africa' (2020) as well as the Guest Editing for African Journal of Economic and Management Studies (AJEMS) on 'Labour Issues in Africa's Agricultural and Rural Transformation' (2020). He was a research fellow at the German Development Institute, Bonn with a fellowship from Alexander von Humboldt Foundation (October 2013–December 2014). He held the same fellowship at German Institute for Global and Area Studies (GIGA), Hamburg (January–September 2013). His other international awards: Swedish Institute's Guest Doctoral Fellowship (as guest PhD Candidate at Lund University 2009/2010); Council for the Development of Social Science Research in Africa (CODESRIA)'s grant for PhD Thesis in 2009; First Prize for FLACSO-WTO Chair Award in 2012, to mention a few. He is a member of numerous International Learned Societies/Professional Associations as well as a reviewer and editorial board member for many journals.

Ryan Redilla attended Ligonier Valley High School and Indiana University of Pennsylvania. Graduated with a Bachelor of Arts in Economics and a Master's Degree in Business Administration. Former Broadcast Journalist for the United States Army and plans to become a Foreign Service Officer for the Department of State.

Index

F

G

H

I

J

L

M

N

O

P

R

www.ingramcontent.com/pod-product-compliance
Lightning Source LLC
LaVergne TN
LVHW081327300926
849161LV00008B/1894
* 9 7 8 1 7 9 9 8 1 0 9 3 3 *